# CATALOGUE OF SADDLERY
## TRAVELWARE & GRINDERY

ISBN 0 947338 77 2

Copyright © Axiom Publishers, 1996.
This book is copyright. Apart from any fair dealing for the purpose of
private study, research, criticism or review, as permitted under the
Copyright act, no part may be reproduced by any process without
written permission. Enquiries should be made to the publisher.

**Axiom
Australia**

# INTRODUCTION

## The Leather House

WE have much pleasure in presenting this Illustrated Catalogue of Saddlery and Grindery, Sole and Harness Leather, Travelling Bags, Fitted and Empty Suit Cases, Trunks, and other Leather and Canvas Goods, and take the opportunity of pointing out that as we manufacture all these articles in our own factory, we are therefore in a position to guarantee the best of materials and workmanship.

All goods illustrated herein, are made by skilled workmen under expert supervision, thus enabling us to offer the very latest and best designs of all kinds of Saddlery and Travelling Requisites, together with the highest class of handwork, at very moderate prices.

As it is only possible to illustrate a small selection of our very large stock, we would suggest the advantage of a visit to our showrooms.

Special attention is given to postal orders and enquiries.

※　※　※

## HARRIS, SCARFE, LIMITED,

1938

# Index to Saddlery (HF) Department

## A

| | Page |
|---|---|
| Adjustoe Plates | 117 |
| Air Cushions | 92 |
| Airway Luggage | 104 |
| American Breast Collar Harness | 8 |
| Anvils or Lasts, Boot | 113 |
| Aprons, Leather | 40 |
| Attache Cases, Fibre | 107 |
| Leather | 98 |
| School Cases, Fitted | 107 |
| Awl Blades | 74, 114 |
| Hafts | 74, 114 |
| Peg | 114 |
| Awls, Shoemakers' | 114 |
| Awls | 114 |
| Axle Washers | 93 |

## B

| | Page |
|---|---|
| Backband Hooks | 64 |
| Back Chains | 62 |
| Bag Leather | 40 |
| Bags, Betting | 101 |
| Brief | 99 |
| Bulge | 99 |
| Bullion | 99 |
| Courier | 100 |
| Hot Water | 92 |
| Kit | 99 |
| Pack | 22 |
| Saddle | 24 |
| School | 100 |
| Soiled Linen | 103 |
| Water | 23, 24 |
| Ball, Heel | 116 |
| Bandages | 82 |
| Barrels, Lamp | 70 |
| Basils | 40 |
| Beaded Nails | 60 |
| Bar and Chain, Leading | 32 |
| Beaters, Fire | 94 |
| Bell Boots | 34 |
| Straps | 38 |
| Bells, Bullock | 88 |
| Cow or Cattle | 88 |
| Horse | 88 |
| Sheep | 88 |
| Bellybands, Leading | 15 |
| Roller Hooks | 64 |
| Belly Stuffers | 77 |
| Belt Web | 46 |
| Belts, Waist | 93 |
| Berg Oil | 85 |
| Betting Bags | 101 |
| Bicycle Gaiters | 89 |
| Bifurcated Rivets | 93 |
| Bike or Gig, Trotting | 34 |
| Billets | 67 |
| Bills, Cut | 119 |
| Binder, Crop and Thong | 72 |
| Bit Burnishers | 68 |
| Straps | 38 |
| Bits, Drenching | 78 |
| Riding | 49 |
| Driving | 48 |
| Bits and Rings | 61 |
| Black Dye Powder | 87 |
| Fat | 87 |
| Quick | 116 |
| Wax | 45 |
| Blades, Awl | 74 |
| Blind Straps | 39 |
| Blister, Horse | 84 |
| Bloomers, Trotting | 34 |
| Blouse Cases, Leather | 98 |
| Body Brushes | 73 |
| Chains | 62 |
| Bolts, Cab | 60 |
| Pole Ring | 60 |
| Bone Radiol | 84 |
| Bones, Hollow | 77 |
| Boot Laces | 118 |
| Pegs | 119 |
| Protectors | 117 |
| Rivets | 119 |
| Boots, Bell | 34 |
| Elastic Side | 90 |
| Horse | 35, 36 |
| Jackeroo, I.R. | 90 |
| Knee, I.R. | 90 |
| Polo or Pull-on | 90 |
| Thigh, I.R. | 90 |
| Transport | 90 |
| Trotters | 37 |
| Bosco Dye | 87 |

| | Page |
|---|---|
| Bowls Cases | 101 |
| Grip | 101 |
| Box, Hat | 104 |
| Hide | 40 |
| Boxes, Hat | 102 |
| Hat, Fibre | 103 |
| Lunch, Fibre | 107 |
| Brace Webbing | 46 |
| Bradoons | 50 |
| Brands, Fire | 82 |
| Breast Chains | 61 |
| Breast Plates | 31 |
| Breast Plate Fork Parts | 31 |
| Breeching Dees | 55 |
| Chains | 61 |
| Rings | 56 |
| Breechen Fittings | 58 |
| Bridle Leather | 40 |
| Bridles, Cart | 16 |
| Riding | 27-28 |
| Brief Bags | 99 |
| Brushes, Body | 73 |
| Compo | 73 |
| Dandy | 73 |
| Buckles | 51-52-53-54, 61 |
| Dog Collar | 54 |
| Inlet | 55 |
| Gaiter | 55 |
| Gear | 61 |
| Girth | 54 |
| Harness | 51-53 |
| Hobble | 61 |
| Stirrup Leather | 55 |
| Tug | 52 |
| Buggy Colars | 17 |
| Harness, Camel | 19 |
| Saddles | 8 |
| Whips | 72 |
| Bull Lead Snaps | 82 |
| Rings | 80 |
| Nose Pliers | 82 |
| Bulge Bags | 99 |
| Bullion Bags | 99 |
| Bullock Bells | 88 |
| Thongs | 72 |
| Burdizzo Pliers | 81 |
| Burnishers | 68 |
| Bush Mirrors | 93 |
| Burnishing Ink | 116 |
| Business Case, Fibre | 108 |
| Butchers' Pouches | 93 |
| Button Fasteners | 117 |
| Buttons, Tufting | 47 |
| Buttonhole Pliers | 115 |

## C

| | Page |
|---|---|
| Cab Bolts | 60 |
| Cantles | 60 |
| Saddles | 8 |
| Cabin Case, Fibre | 108 |
| Trunk, Fibre | 108 |
| Trunks | 102, 104 |
| Calf Weaners | 81 |
| Camel Buggy Harness and Parts | 19 |
| Harness and Parts | 20 |
| Leading Harness and Parts | 21 |
| Pack Saddle | 20 |
| Riding Saddle | 20 |
| Candles | 70 |
| Canes | 71 |
| Canteens, Pack | 23 |
| Motor | 23 |
| Water | 23 |
| Cantles, Cab | 60 |
| Carbox | 86 |
| Carriage Harness, Pair Horse | 11 |
| Cart Bridles | 16 |
| Collars | 17 |
| Crops | 71 |
| Cart, Waggon, Plow and Leading Harness | 14 |
| Case, Blouse or Suit, Lady's | 104 |
| Business, Fibre | 108 |
| Cabin, Fibre | 108 |
| Tennis, Leather | 99 |
| Tennis, Fibre | 108 |
| Wardrobe | 104 |
| Cases, Bowls | 101 |
| Dressing, Fitted | 97 |
| Fibre, Attache | 107 |
| Fitted School Attache | 107 |
| Leather, Attache | 98 |
| Leather, Blouse | 98 |
| Music, Fibre | 108 |

| | Page |
|---|---|
| Music, Leather | 101 |
| Regalia | 101 |
| Suit, Fibre | 106 |
| Suit Leather | 95 |
| Writing, Leather | 101 |
| Cattle Drenchers, etc. | 83 |
| Syringes | 80 |
| Catups, Camel | 20 |
| Cement or Solution | 116 |
| Chafe, Hopple | 85 |
| Chains, Back | 62 |
| Body | 62 |
| Breast | 61 |
| Breeching | 61 |
| Curb | 68 |
| Front | 60 |
| Hobble | 61-62 |
| Leading | 62 |
| Plough | 62 |
| Spring Cart | 63 |
| Spur | 68 |
| Trace End | 62 |
| Trolly | 63 |
| Tug | 64 |
| Wheel | 64 |
| Chains, Stallion, Leading | 32 |
| Chamois Leathers | 91 |
| Circles and Knobs | 57 |
| Circlets | 117 |
| Circular Web | 46 |
| Clambs | 77 |
| Claw, Nail | 75 |
| Clicker's Knife | 115 |
| Clippers, Horse | 82 |
| Clogs | 69 |
| Cloth, Goat Hair | 20 |
| Clothing, Horse | 41 |
| Cloths, Polishing | 91 |
| Saddle | 41 |
| Sponge | 91 |
| Coacholine | 87 |
| Cobblers' Kits | 113 |
| Collar Check | 45 |
| Collar Laces | 45 |
| Mallet | 74 |
| Needles | 74 |
| Rod | 74 |
| Twine | 45 |
| Collars, Head | 29 |
| Buggy | 17 |
| Farm | 17 |
| Head | 29 |
| Spring Cart | 17 |
| Stage | 17 |
| Sweat | 17 |
| Comb, Mane | 73 |
| Combs, Curry | 73 |
| Compass | 77 |
| Race | 74 |
| Screw | 75 |
| Compo Brushes | 73 |
| Harness | 87 |
| Compound, Stock | 83 |
| Concertina Leggings | 89 |
| Cord, Whip | 72 |
| Couplings | 15 |
| Courier Bags | 100 |
| Covers for Hot Water Bags | 92 |
| Covert Snaps | 67 |
| Cow or Cattle Bells | 88 |
| Rugs | 42 |
| Crocketts Duck | 46 |
| Crop and Thong Binder | 72 |
| Stock | 71 |
| Crops, Cart | 71 |
| Cruppers, Ridding | 30 |
| Curb Chain | 68 |
| Cure for Sand in Horses | 85 |
| Gall | 85 |
| Foot Rot | 83 |
| Curry Combs | 73 |
| Cushions, Air | 92 |
| Suede | 103 |
| Cut Bills | 119 |
| Soles | 110 |
| Cut Tip Nails | 119 |
| Cutters, Molar | 78 |
| Washer | 77 |
| Cutting Nippers | 75 |

## D

| | Page |
|---|---|
| Dandy Brushes | 73 |
| Dee Straps | 38 |
| Dees | 61 |
| Breeching | 55 |
| Dog Collar | 56 |
| Saddle | 55 |

| | Page |
|---|---|
| Dehorners | 81 |
| Die, Loop | 74 |
| Dilators, Teat | 80 |
| Doe Hair | 45 |
| Dog Collar Buckles | 54 |
| Collar Dees | 56 |
| Collar Plates | 57 |
| Lead Swivels | 67 |
| Rugs | 41 |
| Donkey Harness and Parts | 18 |
| Drag Knives | 115 |
| Drench, Stock | 83 |
| Drenching Bits | 78 |
| Guns | 79 |
| Dressing Cases, Fitted | 97 |
| Hood | 87 |
| Leather Coat | 87 |
| Size | 116 |
| Dubbin | 87 |
| Duck, Crocketts | 47 |
| Dust Rugs | 103 |
| Duster, Dustless | 91 |
| Dye |  |
| Bosco | 87 |
| Leather Coat | 87 |
| Powder, Black | 87 |

## E

| | Page |
|---|---|
| Edge Planes | 114 |
| Tools | 75 |
| Elastic Side Boots | 90 |
| Surgical | 46 |
| Emasculators | 81 |
| Embrocation | 86 |
| Entire Tackle | 32 |
| Esyway | 110 |
| Eurythmic Hopple Chafe | 85 |
| Expanders, Teat | 80 |
| Express Cart Lamps | 70 |
| Extras for Light Buggy Harness | 10 |
| Eyelet Hole Pliers | 115 |
| Eyes, Winker | 24 |

## F

| | Page |
|---|---|
| Facepiece Studs | 58 |
| Facepieces | 58 |
| Farm Collars | 17 |
| Leggings | 89 |
| Saddles | 5 |
| Fasteners, Button | 117 |
| Fat Black | 87 |
| Felt, Saddle | 45 |
| Fibre Business Case | 108 |
| Cases, Attache | 107 |
| Lunch Boxes | 107 |
| Music Cases | 108 |
| Suit Cases | 106 |
| Field Glass Case Straps | 39 |
| Field Glass Straps | 39 |
| Finishing Ink, Wax | 116 |
| Finishes, Dyes, Etc. | 116 |
| Finger Stalls | 93 |
| Fire Beaters | 94 |
| Brands | 82 |
| Lighters | 94 |
| Fittings, Breechen | 58 |
| Fitted Cases | 97 |
| Spider | 65-66 |
| Flags | 92 |
| Flap Loops | 56 |
| Fly Fronts | 16 |
| Foot Rot Cure | 83 |
| Fore-part Irons | 114 |
| Foreparts, Plow | 15 |
| Fork Parts, Breast Plate | 31 |
| Frame and Wheel, Overstitch | 75 |
| Front Chains | 60 |
| Fronts, Bridle | 28 |
| Fly | 16 |
| Fudge Wheels | 114 |
| Full Soles and Heels, Kromhyd | 111 |

## G

| | Page |
|---|---|
| Gaiter Buckles | 55 |
| Gaiters, Bicycle | 89 |
| Gall Cure | 85 |
| Gauges, Plow | 75 |
| Gear Buckles | 61 |
| Dees | 61 |
| Rings | 61 |

## HARRIS, SCARFE, LIMITED.

## Saddlery Index (continued)

| | Page |
|---|---|
| Giffwell Stock Compound | 83 |
| Teat Salve | 83 |
| Girth Buckles | 54 |
| Webbing | 46 |
| Girths | 22, 30 |
| Gladstone Bag Straps | 39 |
| Glazing Irons | 114 |
| Glover's Needles | 74 |
| Goat Hair Cloth | 20 |
| Grip Cases | 101 |
| Music, Leather | 101 |
| Grips, Heel | 112 |
| Rubber Rein | 28 |
| Guns, Drenching, Sayers' Pistolet | 79 |

### H

| | |
|---|---|
| Hafts, Awl | 74, 114 |
| Peg Awl | 114 |
| Hagley's Hopple Chafe | 85 |
| Hair, Doe | 45 |
| Horse | 45 |
| Halters, Rope | 29 |
| Hame Hooks | 25 |
| Hames | 25, 26 |
| Hammers | 75, 113 |
| Handles, Rug Strap | 98 |
| Harness, American, Breast Collar | 8 |
| Buggy | 10 |
| Camel | 19-20 |
| Cart and Waggon | 14 |
| Composition | 87 |
| Donkey | 18 |
| Leather | 40 |
| Light Buggy | 10 |
| Liquid | 87 |
| Needles | 74 |
| Oil | 87 |
| Orchard | 24 |
| Pair Horse Carriage | 11 |
| Skeleton Buggy and Parts | 13 |
| Spring Cart and Parts | 13 |
| Special Station | 12 |
| Trolly and Parts | 12 |
| Harness, Skeleton Buggy | 9 |
| Extras for above | 9 |
| Spring Cart | 13 |
| Station Buggy | 11 |
| Trolley | 12 |
| Trotting | 34 |
| Wagonette | 9 |
| Harvester Traces | 16 |
| Hat Boxes | 102-104 |
| Hat Boxes, Fibre | 108 |
| Head Collars | 29 |
| Headstall Squares | 59 |
| Heel and Toe Plates | 117 |
| Heel and Toe Tips | 118 |
| Heel Ball | 116 |
| Grips | 112 |
| Pads | 112 |
| Plates | 117 |
| Shaves | 115 |
| Heels, Leather and Kromhyd | 110 |
| I.R., Shaped | 112 |
| Kromhyd, Sports | 111 |
| Hemp | 45 |
| Hobble Buckles | 61 |
| Chains | 61-62 |
| Straps | 38 |
| Holdalls | 103 |
| Hollow Bones | 77 |
| Hood Dressing | 87 |
| Material | 47 |
| Hoof Ointment, Dunning's | 86 |
| Hooks, Backband | 64 |
| Bellyband | 64 |
| Hame | 25 |
| Pad | 59 |
| Hoplemuroma Hoof Dressing | 86 |
| Hopple Chafe | 85 |
| Hopples, Trotting | 34 |
| Serving | 34 |
| Horse and Cattle Ties | 29 |
| Horse and Cow Rugs | 42-43 |
| Horse Bells | 88 |
| Blister | 84 |
| Boots | 35-36-37 |
| Clippers | 82 |
| Clothing | 41 |
| Hair | 45 |
| Muzzles | 24 |
| Rugs | 41-42-43 |
| Thongs | 72 |
| Tooth Rasps | 80 |

| | Page |
|---|---|
| Hot Water Bags and Covers | 92 |
| Hungarian Nails | 119 |

### I

| | |
|---|---|
| Ink, Burnishing | 116 |
| Finishing, Wax | 116 |
| Inlet Buckles | 55 |
| Insoles, Cork and Rubber | 112 |
| Instep Supports | 112 |
| Irons, Fore-Part | 114 |
| Glazing | 114 |
| Palm | 77 |
| Pinking | 77 |

### J

| | |
|---|---|
| Jackeroo Boots | 90 |
| Jockey Whips | 71 |
| Joint Stretchers | 115 |

### K

| | |
|---|---|
| Kangaroo Plaited Flogger Whips | 71 |
| Kangaroo Skins | 40 |
| Kersey | 45 |
| Kip Leather | 40 |
| Kit Bags | 99 |
| Kits, Cobblers' | 113 |
| Knee Rugs, Wool | 103 |
| Knee Boots | 90 |
| Knives, Clickers' | 115 |
| Drag | 115 |
| Saddlers' | 76 |
| Shoe | 115 |
| Kromhyd, in Sheets | 110 |
| Cut Soles | 110 |
| Outfits | 110 |

### L

| | |
|---|---|
| Labers, Luggage | 92 |
| Sheep, Ear | 80 |
| Laces, Boot | 118 |
| Collar | 45 |
| Shoe | 118 |
| Lamp Barrels | 70 |
| Candles | 70 |
| Springs | 70 |
| Lamps, Buggy | 70 |
| Cart, Express | 70 |
| Laryngine | 85 |
| Lasts or Anvils, Boot | 113 |
| Leading Harness, Camel | 21 |
| Leading Harness, Cart, Waggon, Plow, and Leading | 14 |
| Chains | 62 |
| Leather | 110 |
| Aprons | 40 |
| Attache Cases | 98 |
| Bag | 40 |
| Basils | 40 |
| Blouse Cases | 98 |
| Box Hide | 40 |
| Bridle | 40 |
| Coat Dressing | 87 |
| Coat Dye | 87 |
| Cut Soles | 110 |
| Goat Skin | 40 |
| Harness | 40 |
| Kangaroo | 40 |
| Kip | 40 |
| Music Grip | 101 |
| Satchells | 101 |
| Sole | 110 |
| Strap | 40 |
| Suit Cases | 95 |
| Writing Cases | 101 |
| Leathemet Nails | 47 |
| Leathers, Chamois | 91 |
| Stirrup | 30 |
| Leg Ropes | 29 |
| Leggings | 89 |
| Lieut. James' Blistering Ointment | 84 |
| Light Buggy Harness | 10 |
| Lighters, Fire | 94 |
| Linen Thread | 44 |
| Lines, Plough | 29 |
| Links, Patent | 66 |
| Split | 64 |
| Liquid, Harness | 87 |
| Loop Die | 74 |
| Loops, Flap | 56 |
| Tug | 56 |
| Luggage, Airway | 104 |
| Labels | 92 |
| Lunch Boxes, Fibre | 107 |
| Lustre Twist | 44 |

| | Page |
|---|---|
| **M** | |
| Machine Silk | 44 |
| Thread | 44 |
| Mallet, Collar | 74 |
| Punching | 74 |
| Mane Comb | 73 |
| Martingale Rings | 56 |
| Martingales | 31 |
| Material, Hood | 47 |
| Medicated Oil | 85 |
| Milk Fever Tubes | 80 |
| Mirrors, Bush | 93 |
| Molar Cutters | 78 |
| Motor Canteens | 23 |
| Straps | 39 |
| Music Cases, Fibre | 108 |
| Cases, Leather | 101 |
| Grip Leather | 101 |
| Roll | 101 |
| Muzzles, Horse | 24 |

### N

| | |
|---|---|
| Nail Claw | 75 |
| Nails, Beaded, Harness | 60 |
| Cut Tip | 119 |
| Hungarian | 119 |
| Leathermet | 47 |
| Saddle | 60 |
| National Roller Snaps | 67 |
| Neck Straps | 38 |
| Swivels | 64 |
| Needles | 114 |
| Collar | 74 |
| Glovers | 74 |
| Harness | 74 |
| Panel | 74 |
| Quilting | 74 |
| Saddlers' Sharp | 74 |
| Shoemakers' | 114 |
| Speying | 80 |
| Nippers, Cutting | 75 |
| Nosebands, Pulling | 31 |
| Nosepieces | 58 |

### O

| | |
|---|---|
| Oil, Berg | 85 |
| Harness | 87 |
| Medicated | 85 |
| Ointment, Blistering, Lieut. James' | 84 |
| Hoof | 86 |
| Orchard Harness | 24 |
| Outfits, Kromhyd | 110 |
| Tattoo | 81 |
| Veterinary, Rega | 80 |
| Ovals | 57 |
| Overstitch Frame and Wheel | 75 |

### P

| | |
|---|---|
| Pack Bags | 22 |
| Saddles | 22 |
| Pad Hooks | 59 |
| Pads, Heel | 112 |
| Palm Irons | 77 |
| Panel Needles | 74 |
| Park and Exercise Saddles | 5-6 |
| Parts for Light Buggy Harness | 10 |
| For Spring Cart Harness | 13 |
| Patent Links | 66 |
| Peg Awl Hafts | 114 |
| Pegs, Boot | 119 |
| Penetrene | 84 |
| Peram Spring Straps | 39 |
| Straps | 39 |
| Perfect Stitchers | 75 |
| Pig Ring Pliers | 78 |
| Pig Rings | 78 |
| Pincers, Shoe | 115 |
| Pinking Irons | 77 |
| Plaited Pitched Thread | 44 |
| Planes, Edge | 114 |
| Plates, Adjustoe | 117 |
| Dog Collar | 57 |
| Heel | 117 |
| Heel and Toe | 117 |
| Staple | 57 |
| Toe | 117 |
| Pliers, Blucher | 74 |
| Bulldog | 74 |
| Bull Ring | 82 |
| Burdizzo | 81 |
| Buttonhole | — |
| Ear, Sheep and Cattle | 80 |
| Eyelet Hole | 115 |
| Pig Ring | 78 |

| | Page |
|---|---|
| Saddlers' | 74 |
| Sheep Ear and Eyeletting | 80 |
| Shoe Punch | 115 |
| Plow Chains | 62 |
| Foreparts | 15 |
| Gauges | 75 |
| Lines | 29 |
| Pole Ring Bolts | 60 |
| Pole Straps | 16 |
| Polishing Cloths | 91 |
| Polo or Pull-on-Boots | 90 |
| Whips | 71 |
| Pouches, Butchers' | 93 |
| Watch | 92 |
| Powder Black Dye | 87 |
| Powders, Leg Wash | 84 |
| Sand and Colic | 85 |
| Worm | 85 |
| Pricking Wheel | 75 |
| Pulling Noseband | 31 |
| Protectors, Boot | 117 |
| Punches, Crews | 76 |
| On Cards | 76 |
| Oval | 76 |
| Revolving | 77 |
| Round | 76 |
| Wad | 76 |
| Punching Mallet | 74 |
| Puttee Leggings | 89 |

### Q

| | |
|---|---|
| Quarter Tips | 117 |
| Quick Black | 116 |
| Russetts | 116 |
| Quilting Needles | 74 |

### R

| | |
|---|---|
| Race, Compass | 74 |
| Racing Saddles | 6 |
| Radiol | 84 |
| Bone | 84 |
| Rasps, Horse Tooth | 80 |
| Shoe | 113 |
| Reducene | 84 |
| Regalia Cases | 101 |
| Rein Grips, Rubber | 28 |
| Reins, Waggon | 14-15 |
| Riding, Bridle | 28 |
| Spliceless | 15 |
| Remedies, Veterinary | 84 |
| Re Nu | 110 |
| Reviver, Upholstery | 87 |
| Revolving Punches | 77 |
| Riding Bits | 49 |
| Bridles | 27-28 |
| Bridle Reins | 28 |
| Rings, Gear | 61 |
| Breeching | 56 |
| Bull | 80 |
| Martingale | 56 |
| Pig | 78 |
| Rivet Sets | 77 |
| Rivets, Bifurcated | 93 |
| Boot | 119 |
| Rod, Collar | 74 |
| Roll, Music | 101 |
| Roller Web | 46 |
| Rope Halters | 29 |
| Thimbles | 67 |
| Ropes, Leg | 29 |
| Rosettes | 57 |
| Rowels, Spur | 68 |
| Rubber Rein Grips | 28 |
| Rug Strap Handles | 93 |
| Rugs, Dog | 41 |
| Dust | 103 |
| Horse | 41 |
| Horse and Cow | 42-43 |
| Knee, Wool | 103 |
| Sheep | 42 |
| Trap | 103 |
| Travelling, Wool | 103 |
| Russetts, Quick | 116 |

### S

| | |
|---|---|
| Saddle Bags | 24 |
| Cloths | 41 |
| Dees | 55 |
| Felt | 45 |
| Nails | 60 |
| Serge | 45 |
| Soap | 87 |
| Staples | 57 |
| Straps | 39 |
| Saddles, Buggy | 8 |
| Camel, Pack | 20 |
| Camel, Riding | 20 |

## HARRIS, SCARFE, LIMITED.

## Saddlery Index (continued)

| Item | Page |
|---|---|
| Cab | 8 |
| Farm | 5 |
| Light Station | 4 |
| Pack | 22 |
| Park and Exercise | 5-6 |
| Racing | 6 |
| Steeplechasers' | 6 |
| Stock or Breaking | 1-4 |
| Trotting | 8 |
| Saddlers' Sharp Needles | 74 |
| Tools | 74-75-76-77 |
| Salve, Teat | 83 |
| Salvitus | 86 |
| Sand and Colic Powders | 85 |
| Cure | 85 |
| Satchells, Leather | 101 |
| Sayer's Pistolet Drenching Guns | 79 |
| School Bags | 100 |
| Screw Compass | 75 |
| Seat Steels | 74 |
| Serge, Saddle | 45 |
| Serving Hopples | 34 |
| Sets, Rivet | 77 |
| Shaped Heels, I.R. | 112 |
| Shave, Skirt | 75 |
| Shaves, Heel | 115 |
| Spoke | 75 |
| Sheep and Cattle Ear Pliers | 80 |
| Bells | 88 |
| Ear and Eyeletting Pliers | 80 |
| Ear Labels | 80 |
| Rugs | 42 |
| Tallies | 78 |
| Shoe Knives | 115 |
| Laces | 118 |
| Rasps | 113 |
| Shoemakers' Requisites | 113-114-115-116 |
| Awls | 114 |
| Needles | 114 |
| Shoe Pincers | 115 |
| Punch Pliers | 115 |
| Rasps | 113 |
| Tingles | 119 |
| Size Dressing | 116 |
| Skins, Kangaroo | 40 |
| Skirt Shave | 75 |
| Smasher | 74 |
| Snaffles, Loose Ring | 50 |
| Wilson's | 48 |
| Snaps, Bull Lead | 82 |
| Covert | 67 |
| National, Roller | 67 |
| Soap, Saddle | 87 |
| Soiled Linen Bags | 103 |
| Sole Sewing Thread | 114 |
| Leather | 110 |
| Soles and Heels, Full, Kromhyd | 111 |
| Heels and Tacks | 110 |
| Kromhyd, Cut | 110 |
| Leather, Cut | 110 |
| Solomon Solution | 84 |
| Solution or Cement | 116 |
| Solution, Solomon | 84 |
| Spavin Treatment, Kendall's | 84 |
| Special Station Harness | 12 |

| Item | Page |
|---|---|
| Speculum | 78 |
| Speying Needles | 80 |
| Spider Fittings | 65-66 |
| Spiders and Bellyband | 15 |
| Split Links | 64 |
| Spoke Shaves | 75 |
| Sponge Cloths | 91 |
| Sponges | 91 |
| Spring Cart Harness | 13 |
| Chains | 63 |
| Springs, Lamp | 70 |
| Spur Chains | 68 |
| Rowels | 68 |
| Straps | 68 |
| Spurs | 68 |
| Squares, Headstall | 59 |
| Stallion Leading Chain | 32 |
| Leading Bar and Chain | 32 |
| Stalls, Finger | 93 |
| Staple Plates | 58 |
| Staples, Saddle | 57 |
| Station Buggy Harness | 11 |
| Steel Trunks | 109 |
| Trunks, Trays for | 109 |
| Steels, Seat | 74 |
| Steeplechasers' Saddles | 6 |
| Stiffener, Toe | 116 |
| Stirrup Leather Buckles | 55 |
| Leathers | 30 |
| Stirrups | 69 |
| Stitchers, Perfect | 75 |
| Stock Compound, Giffwell | 83 |
| Drench | 83 |
| Crops | 71 |
| Or Breaking Saddles | 1-4 |
| Thongs | 72 |
| Straining Web | 46 |
| Strap Leather | 40 |
| Straps, Bell | 38 |
| Bit | 38 |
| Blind | 39 |
| Breastplate | 31 |
| Dee | 38 |
| Field Glass | 39 |
| Field Glass Case | 39 |
| Gladstone Bag | 39 |
| Hobble | 38 |
| Motor | 39 |
| Neck | 38 |
| Peram | 39 |
| Peram Spring | 39 |
| Pole | 16 |
| Saddle | 39 |
| Spur | 68 |
| Throat | 28 |
| Wrist | 93 |
| Stretchers, Joint | 115 |
| Stubbs | 119 |
| Studs, Facepiece | 58 |
| Stuffers, Belly | 77 |
| Suede Cushions | 103 |
| Suit Cases, Fibre | 106 |
| Cases, Leather | 95-96 |
| Cases, Solid Leather | 96 |
| Sundries | 91 |
| Travelware | 103 |

| Item | Page |
|---|---|
| Supports, Instep | 112 |
| Surcingles | 22, 30-31 |
| Sweat Collars | 17 |
| Surgical Elastic | 46 |
| Swivels, Dog Lead | 67 |
| Neck Strap | 64 |
| Sword Belt | 67 |
| Syringes, Cattle | 80 |

### T

| Item | Page |
|---|---|
| Tackle, Entire | 32 |
| Tallies, Sheep | 78 |
| Tattoo Outfits | 80 |
| Tandem Thongs | 72 |
| Teat Dilators | 80 |
| Expanders | 80 |
| Salve, Giffwell | 83 |
| Tennis Cases, Leather | 99 |
| Tennis Case, Fibre | 108 |
| Terrets | 58-59 |
| Thigh Boots | 90 |
| Thimbles, Rope | 67 |
| Thongs, Bullock | 72 |
| Horse | 72 |
| Stock | 72 |
| Tandem | 72 |
| Thread, Linen | 44 |
| Lustre Twist | 44 |
| Machine | 44 |
| Machine Silk | 44 |
| Plaited, Pitched | 44 |
| Sole Sewing | 44 |
| Wax, on Cards | 44 |
| Throat Straps | 28 |
| Ties, Horse and Cattle | 29 |
| Tingles, Shoe | 119 |
| Tips, Heel and Toe | 118 |
| Quarter | 117 |
| Toe Plates | 117 |
| Stiffener | 166 |
| Tools, Edge | 75 |
| Saddlers' | 74 |
| Tourobe Trunk | 104 |
| Trace End Chains | 63 |
| Traces, Harvester | 16 |
| Transport Boots | 90 |
| Trap Rugs | 103 |
| Travelling Rugs, Wool | 103 |
| Travelware Sundries | 103 |
| Trays for Steel Trunks | 109 |
| Treatment Spavin, Kendall's | 84 |
| Trees | 20-22-23 |
| Trimmers, Welt | 114 |
| Trocars | 82 |
| Trolley Chains | 63 |
| Harness | 12 |
| Pole Straps | 16 |
| Trotters' Boots | 37 |
| Tourobe | 104 |
| Wardrobe | 104-105 |
| Trotting Bike or Gig | 34 |
| Harness | 34 |
| Saddles | 8 |
| Whips | 71 |
| Trunk, Cabin, Fibre | 108 |
| Trunks, Cabin | 102, 104 |
| Steel | 109 |

| Item | Page |
|---|---|
| Tubes, Milk Fever | 80 |
| Tufting Buttons | 47 |
| Tug Chains | 64 |
| Loops | 56 |
| Twine, Collar | 45 |

### U

| Item | Page |
|---|---|
| Upholstery Reviver | 87 |

### V

| Item | Page |
|---|---|
| Veterinary Instruments and Sundries | 78 |
| Outfits, Rega | 80 |
| Remedies | 84 |

### W

| Item | Page |
|---|---|
| Waders | 90 |
| Waggon Harness | 14 |
| Wagonette Harness | 9 |
| Wagstaff's Stock Drench | 83 |
| Waist Belts | 93 |
| Wardrobe Case | 104 |
| Trunk | 104-105 |
| Washer Cutters | 77 |
| Washers | 93 |
| Watch Pouches | 92 |
| Water Bags | 23-24 |
| Wax, Black | 45 |
| Finishing Ink | 116 |
| Thread, on Cards | 44 |
| Weaners, Calf | 81 |
| Web, Straining | 46 |
| Webbing, Belt Web | 46 |
| Brace | 46 |
| Circular White | 46 |
| Girth | 46 |
| Race Girth | 46 |
| Roller Web | 46 |
| Welt Trimmers | 114 |
| Wheel Chains | 64 |
| Pricking | 75 |
| Wheels, Fudge | 114 |
| Whip Cord | 72 |
| Whips and Thongs | 72 |
| Whips, Buggy | 72 |
| Jockey | 71 |
| Kangaroo Plaited Floggers | 71 |
| Polo | 71 |
| Trotting | 71 |
| Wilson's Snaffles | 48 |
| Winker Eyes | 24 |
| Worm Powders | 85 |
| Wrist Straps | 93 |
| Writing Cases, Leather | 101 |

HARRIS, SCARFE, LIMITED.                                   HF 1

# RIDING SADDLES

## INTRODUCTORY

For more than sixty years the Holdfast series of saddles have been extensively used throughout Australasia. They have also been used for many years in India and the East.

We issue this illustrative descriptive catalogue with full confidence that the saddlery trade will appreciate the completeness of our range and the thorough grasp of saddle manufacture that is evidenced throughout the whole series.

The average weight of each saddle is given in the descriptions, but it should be understood that the weights vary according to size of saddle ordered.

Any make of saddle can be varied to suit the rider. For instance, if a Winnecke saddle is ordered it can be made in either rough flesh-out leather (for stock work) or in stained and polished hide; or self-colour with grain out. Long or short panel can be supplied, and the shape, sweep, length of flaps, or pattern of knee pads can all be made to specification.

Short panels and leather linings are much the best for saddles that are to be used in hot climates. They are cool to the rider, do not heat the horse's sides, prevent scalding, and are absolutely vermin **proof.**

## STOCK OR BREAKING SADDLES

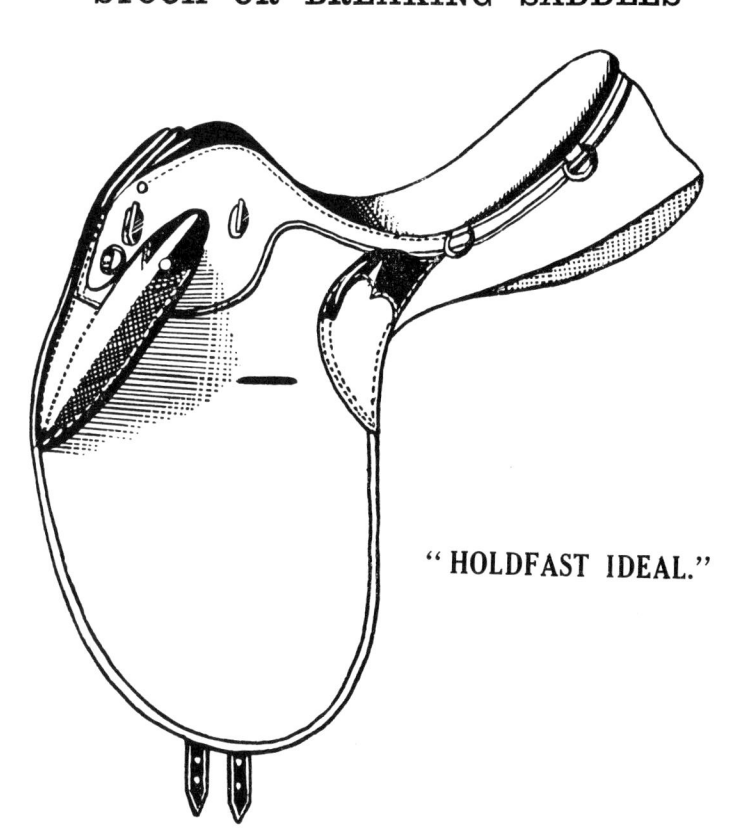

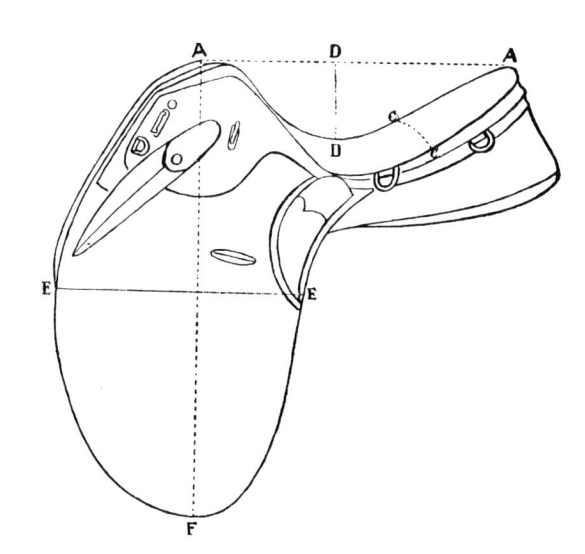

"HOLDFAST IDEAL."

## INSTRUCTIONS WHEN ORDERING.

When ordering a saddle it is well to mention for what purpose it will be used, and also furnish the following measurements as indicated on diagram above.

| | |
|---|---|
| Length of seat | A to A |
| Length of sweep | D to D |
| Length of flap | A to F |
| Width of seat | C to C |
| Width of flap | E to E |

If measurements are not available give height and weight of rider, and state whether long or short stirrups are wanted

"HOLDFAST IDEAL." Best steel bar plated tree with extra heavy gullets. Selected leather throughout 5 in., full-capped, hand-riveted knee pads. Deep leather faced Queensland panel, giving a big bearing on horse's back. Furniture consisting of 3 bar nickel-plated irons, 1⅜ in. stirrup leathers, folded, leather balance end girth. Approximate weight of saddle 22 lbs., furniture 4 lbs.

The "Holdfast Ideal" Saddle is the best, strongest, and most comfortable saddle made. It is, in truth, perfect in every detail and is regarded by experts as such.

HF 2            HARRIS, SCARFE, LIMITED.

# RIDING SADDLES

## STOCK OR BREAKING

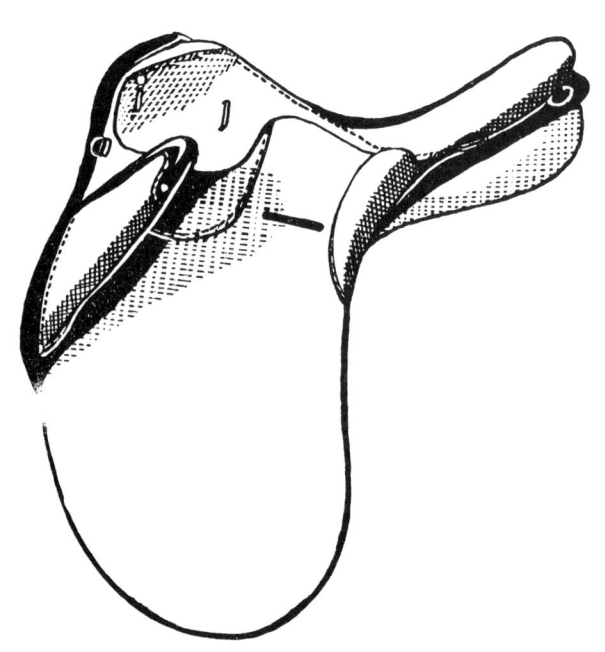

**IMPROVED WINNECKE.** No. 2 Pattern (as illustrated). Best steel bar plated tree. Superior bag leather. 5 in. solid leather, full capped, hand riveted knee pads. Full Queensland pattern panel. Furniture consisting of 3 bar nickel-plated irons, $1\frac{1}{4}$ in. stirrup leather and folded split end girth. Approximate weight of saddle, 20 lbs.; furniture, 4 lbs.

**IMPROVED WINNECKE.** No. 1 Pattern. Saddles have the following improvements on the old style Winnecke saddle, viz.: lengthened flap, extra strength in head of tree (which is aluminium painted to prevent rust, roll cantle, floating seat, etc. The saddle can be made with short or long panel as desired.

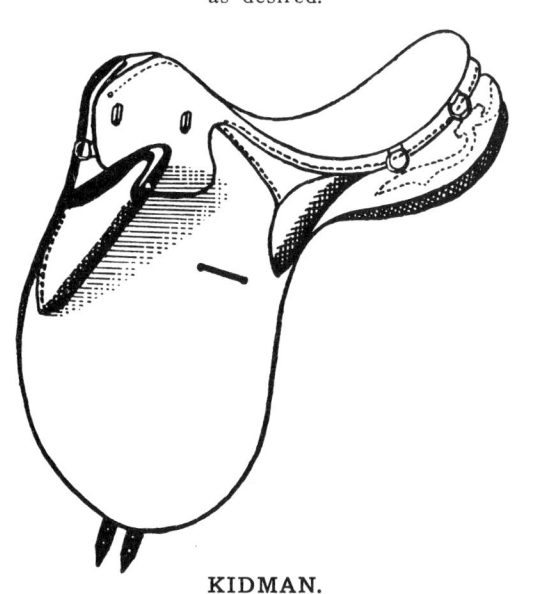

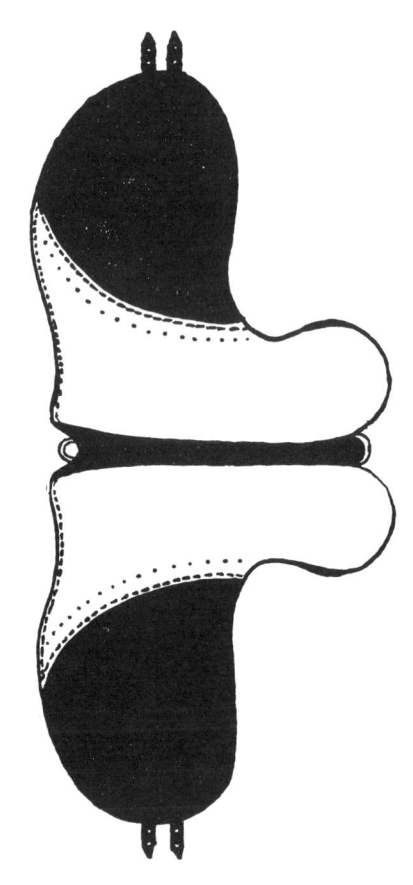

The above illustration shows the type of short Queensland panel with leather continuations used on Winnecke pattern saddles.

**KIDMAN.**

**KIDMAN PATTERN.** Extra quality, steel bar plated tree. Bag leather seat and pads. 5 in. solid leather, full capped hand riveted knee pads. Short Queensland pattern panel with leather continuations. Furniture as No. 2 Winnecke. Approximate weight of saddle, 18 lbs.; furniture, 4 lbs This saddle is made especially for the late Sir Sidney Kidman's stations. It has large rakish flaps, skirt all round and surcingle holes. Usually made all flesh out.

HARRIS, SCARFE, LIMITED. HF 3

# RIDING SADDLES
## STOCK OR BREAKING

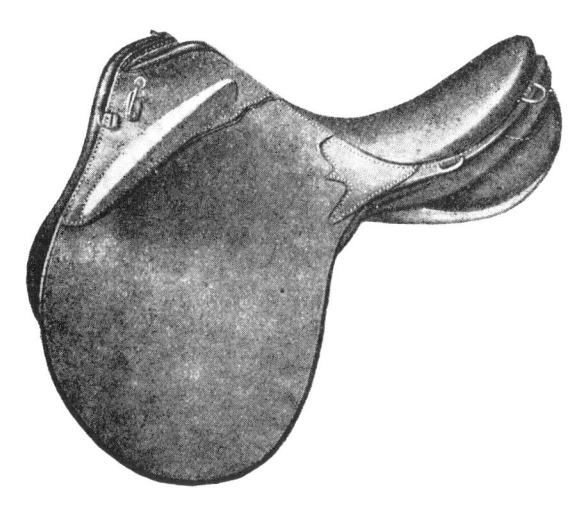

"BEAUFORT." No. 1. Best steel bar plated tree. Superior bag leather. 4 in. solid leather, riveted knee pads. Short Queensland pattern, Queensland facing, open channel, panel. Furniture: 3 bar nickel plated irons, 1¾ in. stirrup leathers, folded leather "Beaufort" girth. Approximate weight of saddle, 19 lbs.; furniture, 7 lbs. Skirt and flap are in one piece.

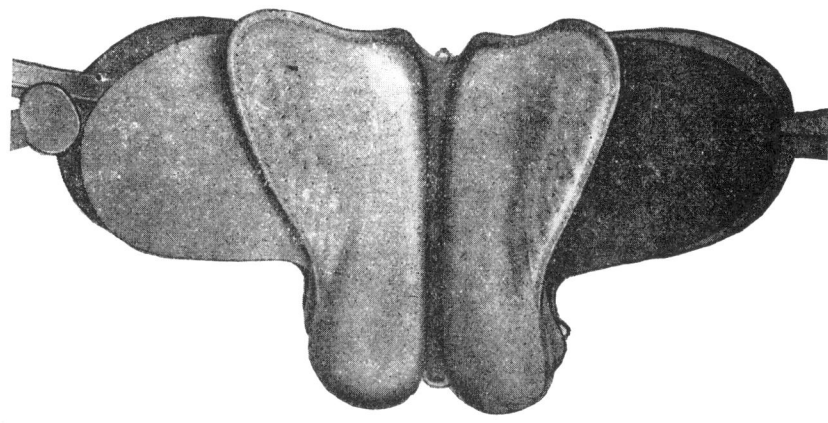

"Beaufort" Saddles are made in various weights for stockmen, polo, and hunting. They are light and cool to the horse, and give the rider a splendid "hold," with nothing to cut or chafe.

Showing Girth to Lace and Short Panel with Open Channel.

"BEAUFORT" No. 2. Similar to No. 1, but plain panel. Approximate weight of saddle, 17 lbs.
"BEAUFORT" No. 3. Similar to No. 2, but made with cheaper materials. Approximate weight of saddle, 17 lbs.
"BEAUFORT" PARK OR HUNTING PATTERN. Nos. 1 and 2. Constructed on the same lines as the No. 1. Approximate weights of saddles: No. 1, 14 lbs.; No. 2, 13 lbs.

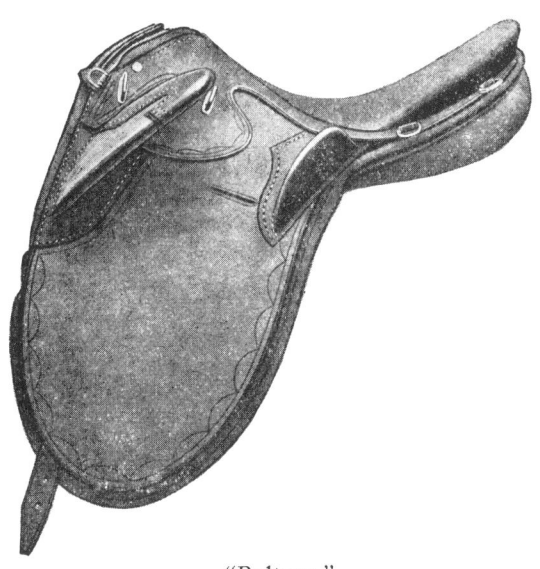

"Beltana."

"BELTANA." Extra quality steel bar plated tree. Bag leather seat and pads. 5½ in. solid leather, hand riveted, full capped, knee pads. Short Queensland pattern panel with leather continuations. 3 bar nickel plated irons, 1¾ in. stirrup leathers, folded leather balance end girths. Approximate weight of saddle, 19 lbs.; furniture, 4 lbs.

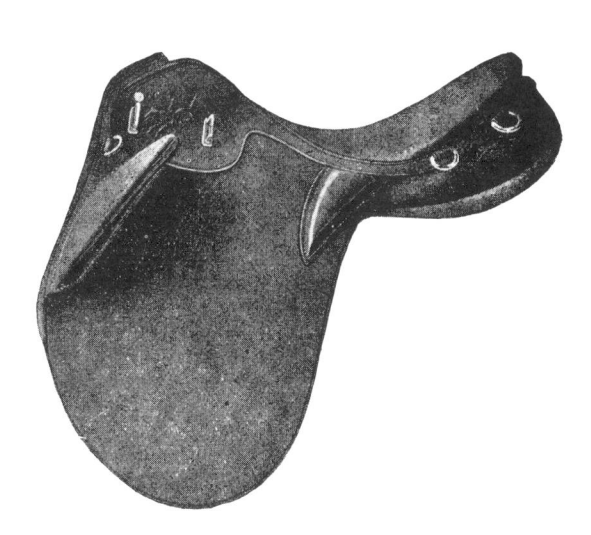

"VICTORIA." Good quality, steel bar plated tree. Bag leather seat and pads. 3½ in. solid leather riveted, knee pads. Queensland pattern panel with Queensland facings. 1¼ in. stirrup leathers, polished irons, split leather girth. Approximate weight of saddle, 16 lbs.; furniture, 4 lbs. A good useful saddle, light in weight and serviceable. Has skirt all round, and Mudgee pattern thigh pads.

HF 4           HARRIS, SCARFE, LIMITED.

# RIDING SADDLES
## LIGHT STATION.

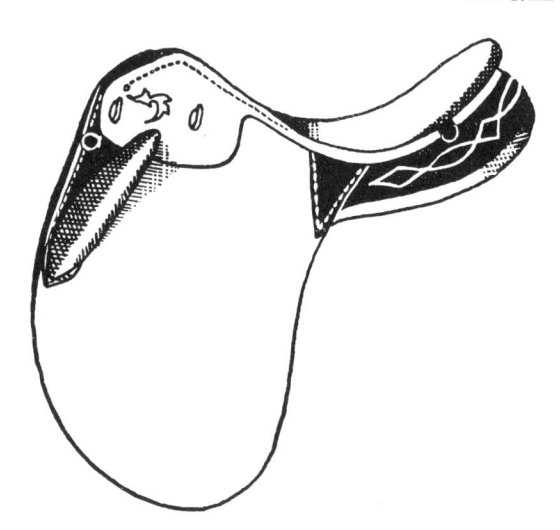

**Nos. 1 and 2.**

No. **400Q.** Good quality, steel bar plated tree. Bag leather seat and pads. 3½ in. solid leather, riveted, knee pads. Queensland pattern panel, leather faced. Furniture similar to that of No. 500Q. Approximate weight of saddle, 16 lbs.; furniture, 4 lbs. Can be supplied with short or long panel, extra half-capped pads, or with higher knee pads. A low priced saddle with many pleasing features

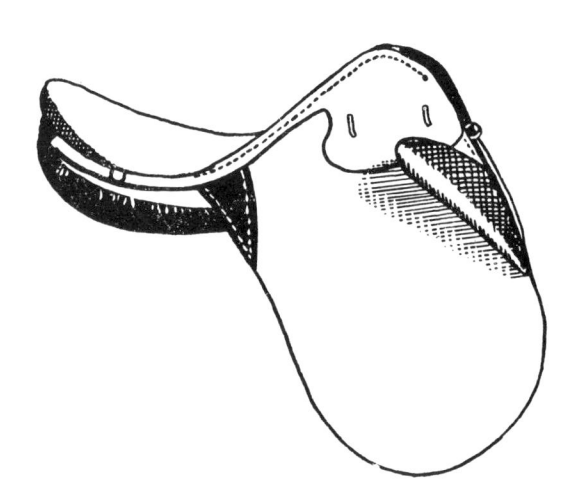

**No. 1.**

No. 350. Farm quality, steel bar plated tree. Bag leather seat and pads. 3 in. stuffed knee pads. Panel without Queensland facing. 1⅛ in. stirrup leathers, polished irons, split leather girth. Approximate weight of saddle, 14 lbs.; furniture, 4 lbs.

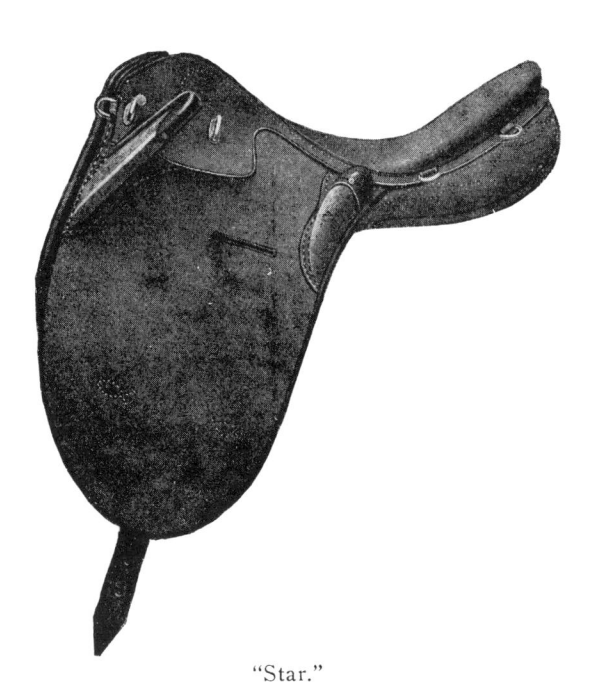

**"Star."**

**"STAR."** Best quality steel bar plated tree. Bag leather seat and pads. 5 in. solid leather, riveted, full capped knee pads. Queensland pattern panel with leather continuations. Nickel plated irons, 1¼ in. stirrup leathers, folded leather girth. Approximate weight of saddle, 18 lbs.; furniture, 4 lbs.

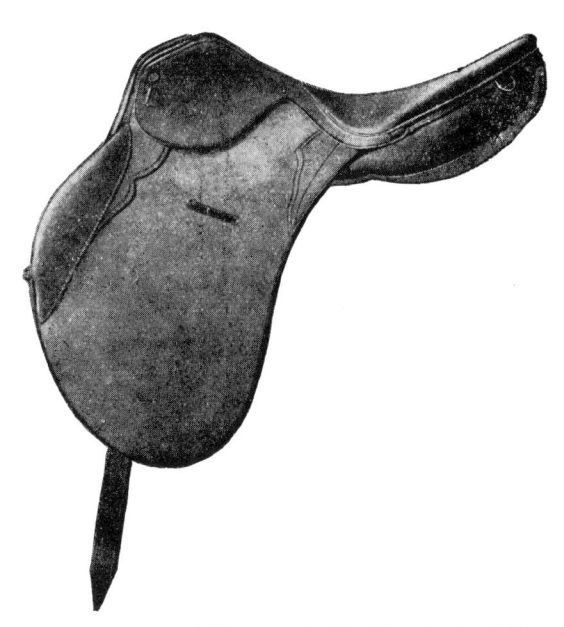

**"Broken Hill" Pattern Light Station Saddle.**

**"BROKEN HILL."** Strong steel bar plated tree. Superior quality, flesh out leather. English pattern knee pads, **large** size. Queensland pattern panel with leather continuations. Nickel plated irons, 1¼ in. leather stirrup leathers, folded leather girths. Approximate weight of saddle, 13 lbs.; furniture, 7 lbs. Forward girth strap riveted to point of tree, thereby bringing it well forward. Second girth strap is extra long so that the rider can tighten up easily. A popular saddle with station managers.

HARRIS, SCARFE, LIMITED.  HF 5

# RIDING SADDLES

## FARM

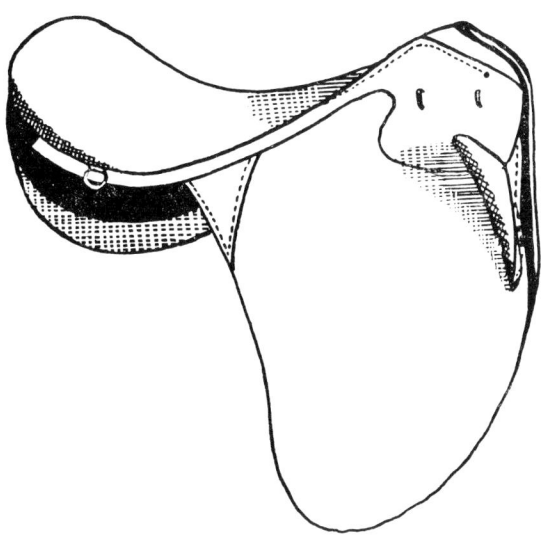

**No. 320Q.** Farm quality, steel bar plated Tree, bag leather seat and pads. 3 in. solid leather knee pads. Panel with Queensland facing. 1⅛ in. stirrup leathers, polished irons, split kip girth. Approximate weight of saddle, 14 lbs.; furniture, 4 lbs.

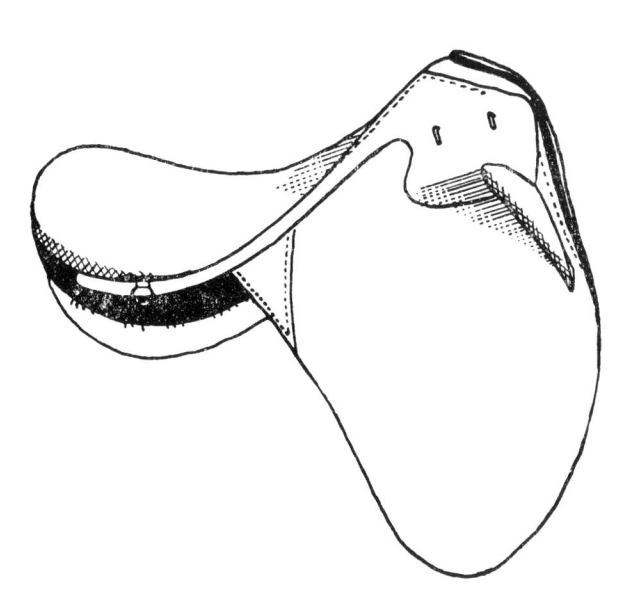

**No. 320S.** Farm quality, steel bar plated tree. Bag leather seat and pads. 3 in. solid leather knee pads. Panel without Queensland facing. 1⅛ in. stirrup leathers, polished irons, split leather girth. Approximate weight of saddle, 14 lbs.; furniture, 4 lbs. This is the cheapest saddle we make, and is specially suitable for farm use where a saddle is expected to undergo rough usage.

## PARK AND EXERCISE.

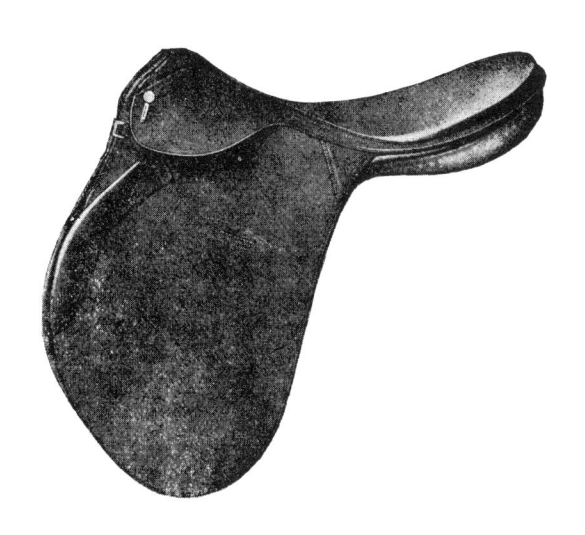

**No. 800.** Extra quality, steel bar plated tree. Special finish leather for seat and pads, bridle leather flaps and skirt. English pattern knee pads, large size. Nickel plated irons, 1¼ in. stirrup leathers, web girth and surcingle. Approximate weight of saddle, 14 lbs.; furniture, 4 lbs. A splendidly finished saddle. Skirt all round. Built on the flat English pattern. Self colour leather, smooth face out. Made in park and exercise weights.

## PARK OR POLO.

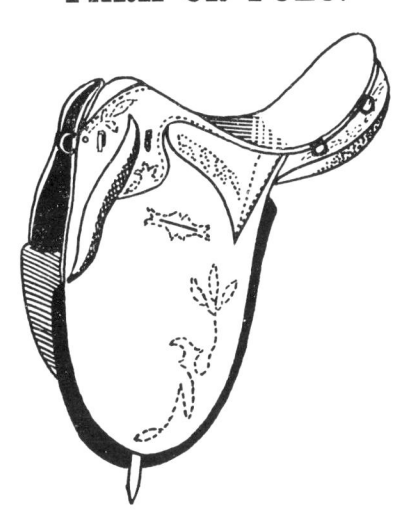

**PARK OR POLO.** Best quality throughout, steel plated tree, skirt all round. All hand sewn. Nickel plated stirrups, leather girth and surcingle, best stirrup leathers. Weight, approximately 14 lbs. mounted.

# RIDING SADDLES

## PARK AND EXERCISE SADDLES

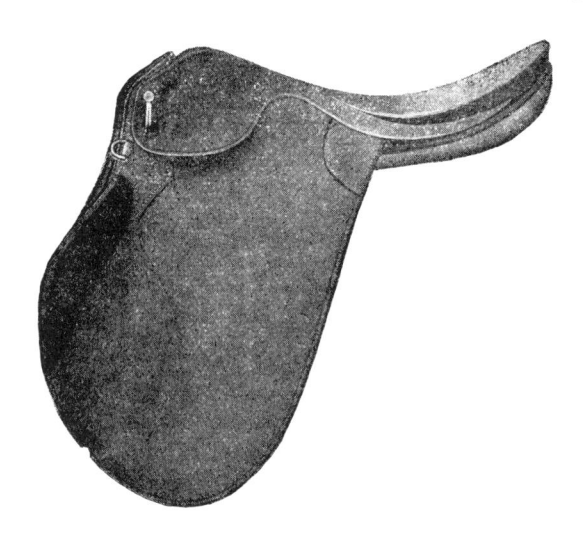

No. 400. Good quality, steel bar plated tree. Bag leather seat and pads. English pattern knee pads. 1¼ in. stirrup leathers, polished irons, split leather girth. Approximate weight of saddle, 9 lbs.; furniture, 4 lbs. Useful for town riding or light work upon farm or station. An excellent saddle for town riding, and one that will give good service. When made for exercise work it is lighter and flatter than the park style.

No. 350. Medium quality, steel bar plated tree. Bag leather seat and pads. English pattern knee pads. Polished irons, 1⅜ in. stirrup leathers, split leather girth. Approximate weight of saddle, 8 lbs.; furniture, 3½ lbs. A saddle for much the same purpose as No. 400. Being lighter, it may be used to advantage for almost any kind of work where a light saddle is essential. Made up in park and exercise weights.

No. 320. As above. Cheaper quality.

## STEEPLECHASE SADDLES

"TOD SLOAN." An exceptionally strong and safe saddle. Made of the finest leather on best quality steel bar plated tree. It has soft roll pattern knee pads ensuring a firm and comfortable grip. We consider that this style of jumper's saddle is the best of its kind made. Skilled workmen are engaged solely in the preparation of racing and steeplechase saddles, and can be relied on to produce a first class article.

Average weight of steeplechase saddles is 4 lbs.

No. 320.    As above, cheaper quality, with knee pads.
No. 320    As above, cheaper quality, without knee pads.

## RACING SADDLES

No. 350. "TOD SLOAN." These saddles are made of finest standard selected leather, and in weight ranging from 1¼ lbs. upwards. The illustration given is that of a 2 lb. saddle and shows how, from the cantle to the extreme front point of flap, the jockey's knee is protected from chafing when riding with short stirrups. We supply all the saddles to many well known stables, and can give every guarantee of **quality, weight, and finish.**

HARRIS, SCARFE, LIMITED.  HF 7

## SHOWING COMPONENT PARTS OF HARNESS.

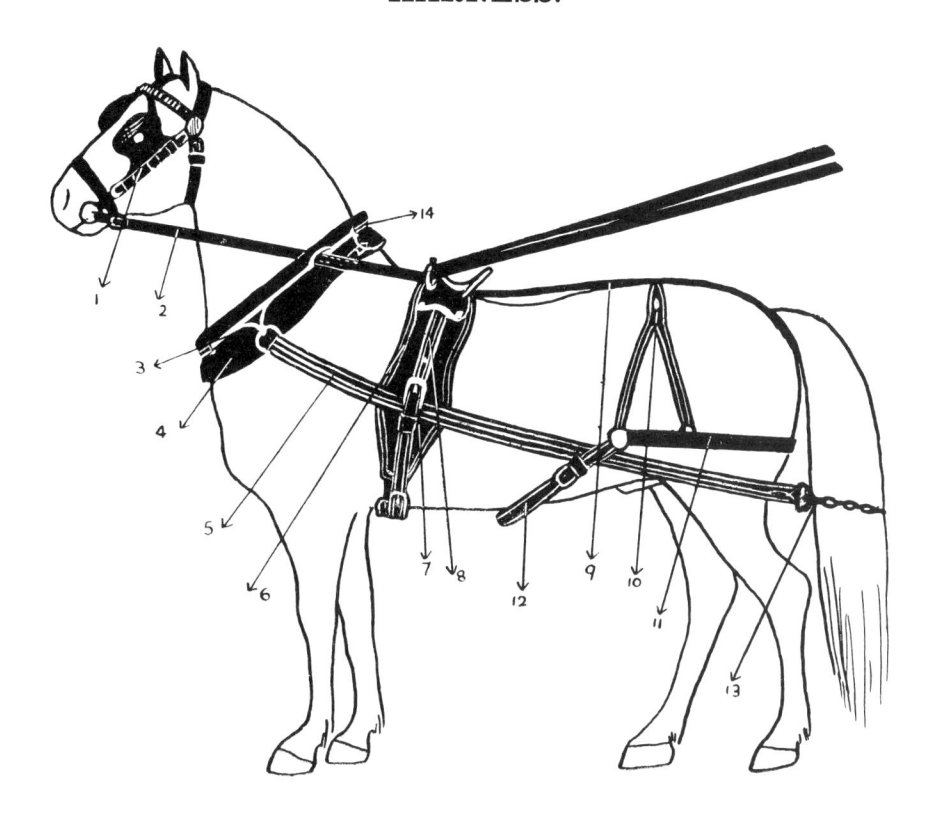

No. 1. **BRIDLE.** Complete with Bit. Buggy, ⅝ and ¾ in.; Spring Cart, ⅞ and 1 in.

No. 2. **REINS.** Single or pair horses. Buggy and Spring Cart, ⅞ and 1 in.

No. 3. **HAMES.** Buggy, with trace tugs; Spring Cart with traces attached.

No. 4. **COLLAR.** Buggy or Spring Cart, round or piped throat, can be substituted with breast collar.

No. 5. **TRACES.** Buggy, fitted to tugs on hames; Spring Cart, stitched to hames, no tugs.

No. 6. **SADDLE.** With or without girth. Buggy, flap saddle (as illustrated); Spring Cart, flap saddle or square saddle for heavy work. When ordering flap (Buggy or Cab) saddle, always state whether girth is required, if not stated girth will not be supplied.

No. 7. **SHAFT TUGS.** Buggy, 1¼, 1⅜, and 1½ in.; Spring Cart, 1½ and 1¾ in.

No. 8. **BACK BAND.** Buggy, 1¼, 1⅜, and 1½ in.; Spring Cart, 1½ and 1¾ in.

No. 9. **CRUPPER.**

No. 10. **LOIN STRAPS.** Split or single.

No. 11. **BREECHING SEAT.**

No. 12. **BREECHING STRAPS.**
Nos. 9, 10, 11, 12 comprise complete Breeching. Buggy, 1¼ and 1¾ in.; Spring Cart, 1½ and 1¾ in. Measurement obtained by measuring width of seat.

No. 13. **TRACE END CHAINS.** Spring Cart only.

No. 14. **HAME STRAPS.** Buggy, ⅝ and ¾ in.; Spring Cart, ⅞ and 1 in.

NOTE.—These parts can be supplied in two or four-row stitching. When ordering parts state parts required, size, and quality; also if saddle, girth, backband, and tugs are required, order as such, not just one saddle.

# HARNESS AND SADDLES

### LIGHT AMERICAN BREAST COLLAR HARNESS.

A Set of American Pattern Breastplate Harness, photographed on Mr. L. M. Darby's celebrated buggy horse, "The General."

Traces, backband and tugs, two or four rows stitching. Made in black or brown leather, N.S. or brass mountings. Single loin strap, flat or rounded. Overhead check and running martingale. Yankee saddle with girth point each side. Short folded bellyband, short backband. Tail tugs.

1⅛ in. Traces, backband and breeching seat.

⅞ in. Reins and breeching straps, ¾ in. crupper body.

⅝ in. Bridle and single loin strap.

1¼ in. Traces, backband, tugs, and breeching seat.

⅝ in. Bridle, ¾ in. single loin strap.

⅞ in. Reins, breeching straps and crupper body.

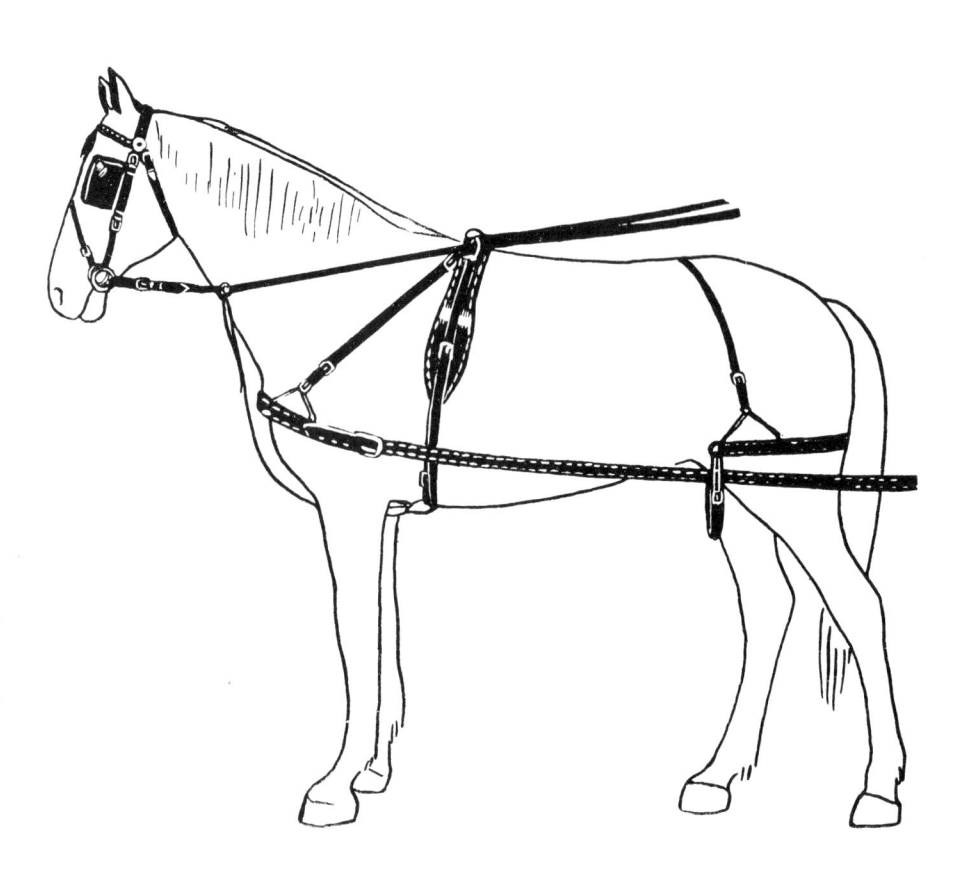

## BUGGY SADDLES.

**BEST QUALITY.** Patent leather skirts and flaps; nickel mounted; three-row stitching; serge lining; patent leather facings.

Sizes: 4 in. to take 1¼ in. backband; 4½ in. to take 1⅜ in. backband; 5 in. to take 1½ in. backband.

**SECOND QUALITY.** As Best Quality, with duck facings.
Sizes: 4 in. to take 1¼ in. backband; 4½ in. to take 1⅜ in. backband; 5 in. to take 1½ in. backband.

**UNION.** Patent leather flaps; no skirts; nickel mounted; duck facings; three-row stitching; serge lining.

Sizes: 4 in. to take 1¼ in. backband; 4½ in. to take 1⅜ in. backband; 5 in. to take 1½ in. backband.

## CAB SADDLES.

**BEST QUALITY.** Patent leather flaps and skirts with London plates; nickel or brass mounted; three-row stitching; serge lining; patent leather facings.

Sizes: 5 in. to take 1½ in backband; 5½ in. to take 1½ in. backband; 6 in. to take 1¾ in. backband; 6½ in. to take 1¾ in. backband.

**UNION.** As Best Quality. Nickel or brass mounted; no skirts.

Sizes: 5 in. to take 1½ in. backband; 5½ in. to take 1½ in. backband; 6 in. to take 1¾ in. backband; 6½ in. to take 1¾ in. backband.

If girth is wanted fitted to Buggy or Cab Saddle, it must be ordered, otherwise saddle only will be sent.

## TROTTING SADDLE.

A light, flexible saddle, especially made for trotting harness. Leather lined.

# HARNESS

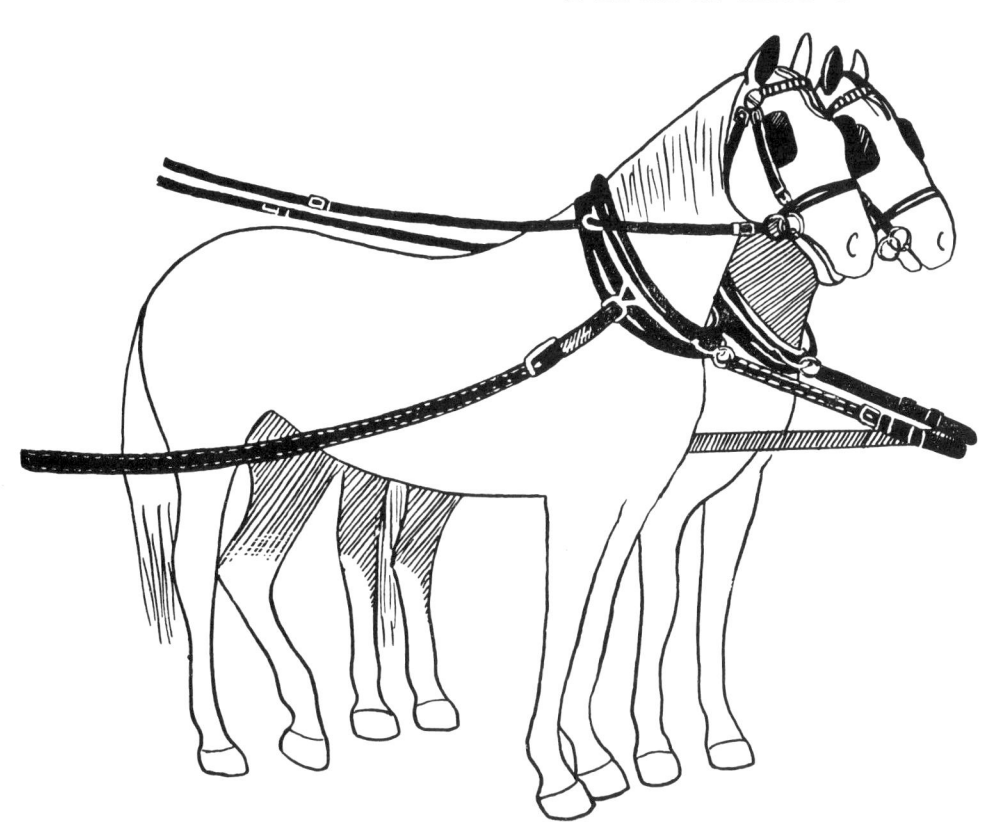

### PAIR HORSE SKELETON BUGGY HARNESS.

Traces, two or four rows stitching, with hame tugs as illustrated, or traces stitched into hames. Made in black or brown leather, N.S. or brass mountings.

1¼ in. Traces and pole straps.

⅝ in. Bridles, ⅞ in. reins.

1⅜ in. Traces and pole straps.

¾ in. Bridles, 1 in. reins.

1½ in. Traces and pole straps.

¾ in. Bridles, 1 in. reins.

### PAIR HORSE WAGGONETTE HARNESS.

Traces, two or four rows stitching, made in black or brown leather, N.S. or brass mountings, with pads, crupper, trace bearers and breastplates.

1⅜ in. Traces and pole straps.

¾ in. Bridles, ⅞ in. reins.

⅞ in. Tracebearers and breastplate with leather ornaments.

1½ in. Traces and pole straps.

¾ in. Bridles, 1 in. reins.

1 in. Tracebearers and breastplate with leather ornaments.

# HARNESS

## LIGHT BUGGY HARNESS.

Traces, backband and tugs, two or four rows stitching. Made in black and brown leather with N.S. or brass mountings. Single loin strap, flat or rounded.

1⅛ in. Traces, backband, tugs, and breeching seat.

⅝ in. Bridle and single loin strap.

⅞ in. Reins and breeching straps, ¾ in. crupper body.

1¼ in. Traces, backband, tugs, and breeching seat.

⅝ in. Bridle, ¾ in. single loin strap.

⅞ in. Reins, breeching straps, and crupper body.

1⅜ in. Traces, backband, tugs, and breeching seat.

¾ in. Bridle, ⅞ in. single loin strap.

⅞ in. Reins, 1 in. breeching straps and crupper body.

## SOUTH EAST BUGGY HARNESS.

Complete with collar. 1¼ and 1⅜.

## No. 5 BUGGY HARNESS.

Complete with collar. 1¼, 1⅜, 1½.

## BUGGY AND SULKY HARNESS.

Traces, backband, and tugs, two or four rows stitching. Made in black or brown leather with N.S. or brass mountings.

1¼ in. Traces, backband, tugs, and breeching seat.

⅝ in. Bridle and split loin straps.

⅞ in. Reins, breeching straps, and crupper body.

## EXPRESS HARNESS.

1⅜ in. Traces, backband, tugs, and breeching seat.

¾ in. Bridle and split loin straps.

⅞ in. Reins, 1 in. breeching straps and crupper body.

## GIG OR SINGLE HORSE WAGGONETTE HARNESS.

1½ in. Traces, backband, tugs, and breeching seat.

¾ in. Bridle and split loin straps.

1 in. Reins, 1⅛ in. breeching straps and crupper body.

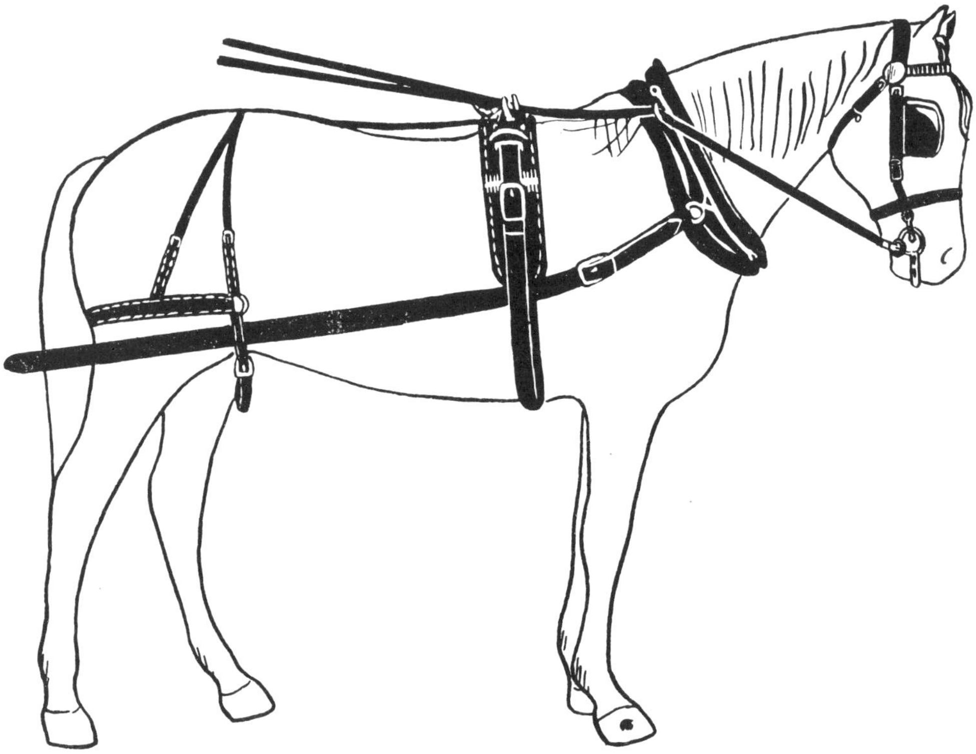

# HARNESS

**PAIR HORSE CARRIAGE HARNESS.**

Best quality leather and workmanship.

Short carriage pads with pad cloths.

1½ in. x 4 row traces and long hame tugs with looped buckles.

1½ in. lined pole straps, 1 in. reins with folded handparts.

¾ in. Bridles with rounded stays and patent leather face pieces.

1 in. Crupper bodies, 1 in. trace bearers and breastplates with patent leather ornaments.

Best patent leather collars.

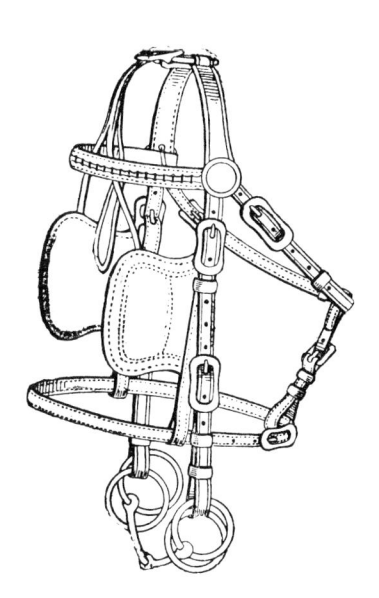

**STATION BUGGY HARNESS, PAIR HORSE (SKELETON).**

Made in black or brown leather, with N.S. or brass mountings. ¾ in. bridles with sensible pattern eyes. Yankee collars, 1½ in. pole straps. 1¼ in breast straps, 1 in. reins. 2¼ in. single leather traces, stitched into hames as illustrated, or with **hame tugs**, and 2¼ in. single leather or 1½ in. stitched traces.

**HOLDFAST IDEAL STATION BRIDLE.**

With loose cheek and simple pattern eyes.

These bridles can be supplied to suit any harness if required.

HF 12   HARRIS, SCARFE, LIMITED.

# HARNESS

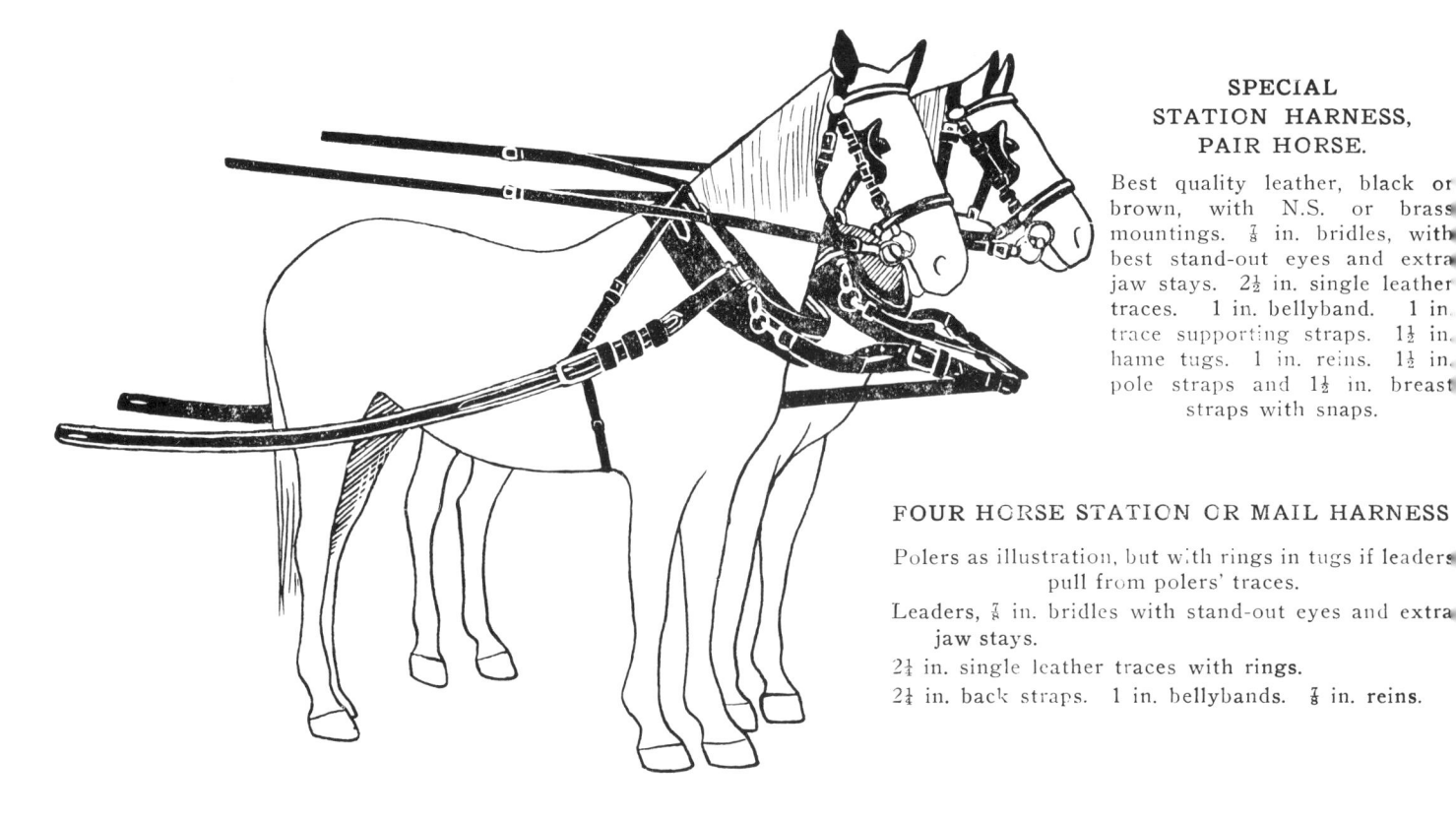

### SPECIAL STATION HARNESS, PAIR HORSE.

Best quality leather, black or brown, with N.S. or brass mountings. ⅞ in. bridles, with best stand-out eyes and extra jaw stays. 2½ in. single leather traces. 1 in. bellyband. 1 in. trace supporting straps. 1½ in. hame tugs. 1 in. reins. 1½ in. pole straps and 1½ in. breast straps with snaps.

### FOUR HORSE STATION OR MAIL HARNESS

Polers as illustration, but with rings in tugs if leaders pull from polers' traces.

Leaders, ⅞ in. bridles with stand-out eyes and extra jaw stays.

2¼ in. single leather traces with rings.

2¼ in. back straps. 1 in. bellybands. ⅞ in. reins.

### TROLLY OR VAN HARNESS, PAIR HORSE.

Made in black or brown leather.

Best quality, as illustrated.
2 in. Traces with chain ends, 2¼ in. shoulder tugs.
1¾ in. Spiders, 2¼ in. breeching seat, 1¼ in. breast straps.
1½ in. Bellybands, 1 in. bridles and reins.
Pipe collars.

Second quality.
1¾ in. Traces with chain ends, 2 in. shoulder tugs.
1½ in. Spiders, 2¼ in. breeching straps, 1½ in. breast straps.
1¼ in. Bellybands, ⅞ in. bridles and reins.
Pipe collars.

Strong, plain.
With chain traces, covered three feet, 2¼ in. shoulder tugs.
1¼ in. Cart bridles, pipe cart collars.
2½ in. Back straps, 1¼ in. bellybands, 1 in. reins.
Iron hames and jap buckles.

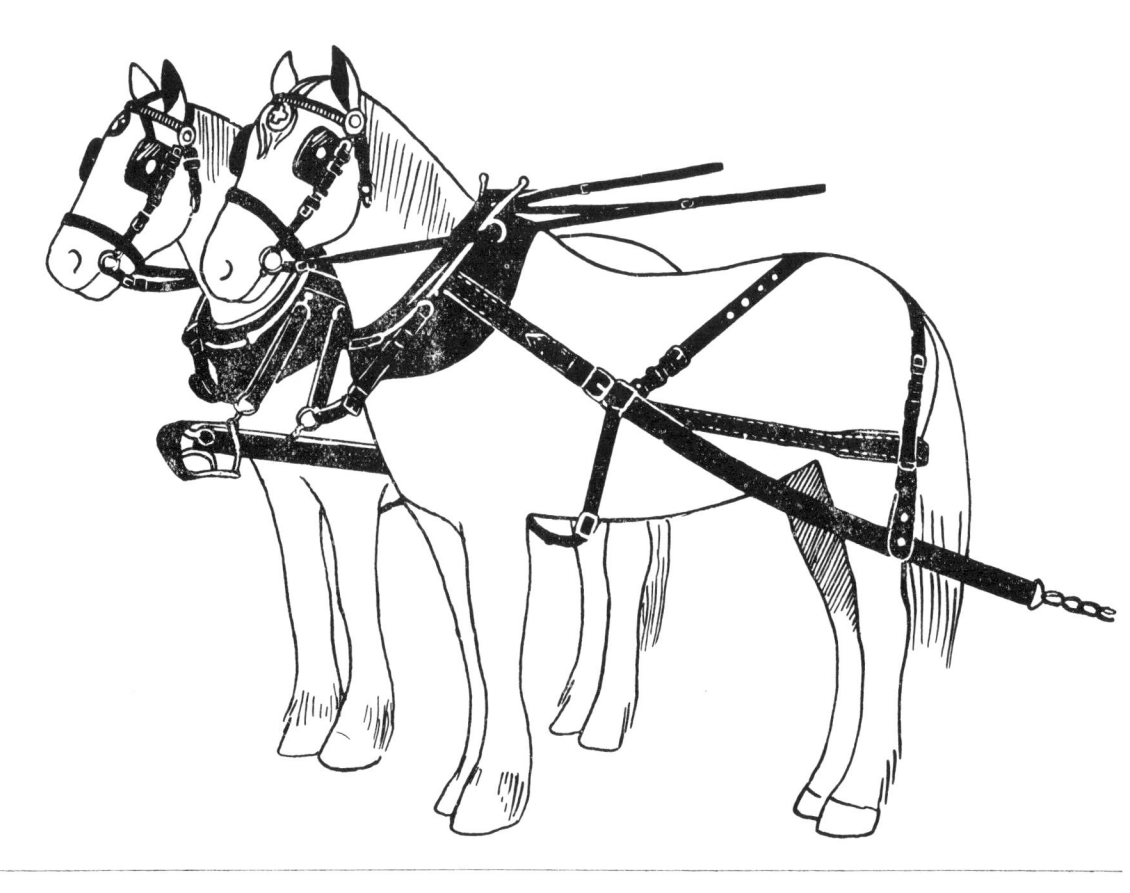

# HARNESS

## SPRING CART OR SINGLE TROLLY HARNESS WITH CAB SADDLE.

Traces, backband and tugs, two or four rows stitching. Made in black or brown leather, brass or N.S. mountings. Double loin straps, traces with chain ends.

$1\frac{1}{2}$ in. Traces, backband, tugs, and breeching seat.
$\frac{3}{4}$ in. Bridle and double loin straps.
$\frac{7}{8}$ in. Reins, $1\frac{1}{8}$ in. breeching straps and crupper body.

$1\frac{3}{4}$ in. Traces, backband, tugs, and breeching seat.
$\frac{7}{8}$ in. Bridle and double loin straps.
1 in. Reins, $1\frac{1}{4}$ in. breeching straps and crupper body.

2 in. Traces, backbands, tugs, and breeching seat.
1 in. Bridle and double loin straps.
1 in. Reins, $1\frac{1}{2}$ in. breeching straps $1\frac{1}{4}$ in. crupper body.

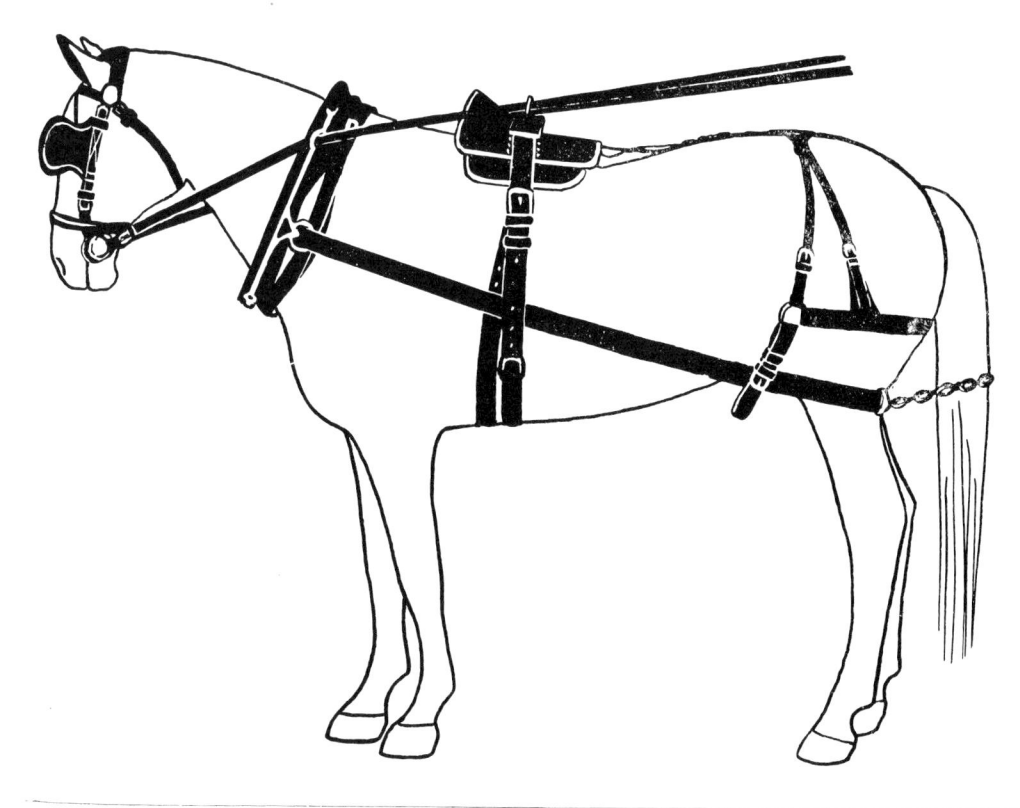

## SPRING CART OR SINGLE TROLLY HARNESS WITH SQUARE SADDLE.

Traces, backband, and tugs, two or four rows stitching. Made in black or brown leather, brass mounted. Double loin straps, traces with chain ends.

$1\frac{1}{2}$ in. Traces, backband, tugs, and breeching seat.
$\frac{3}{4}$ in. Bridle and double loin straps.
$\frac{7}{8}$ in. Reins, $1\frac{1}{8}$ in. breeching straps and crupper body.

$1\frac{3}{4}$ in. Traces, backband, tugs, and breeching seat.
$\frac{7}{8}$ in. Bridle and double loin straps.
1 in. Reins, $1\frac{1}{4}$ in. breeching straps and crupper body.

2 in. Traces, backband, tugs, and breeching seat.
1 in. Bridle and double loin straps.
1 in. Reins, $1\frac{1}{2}$ in. breeching straps, $1\frac{1}{4}$ in. crupper body.

HF 14                     HARRIS, SCARFE, LIMITED.

# HARNESS

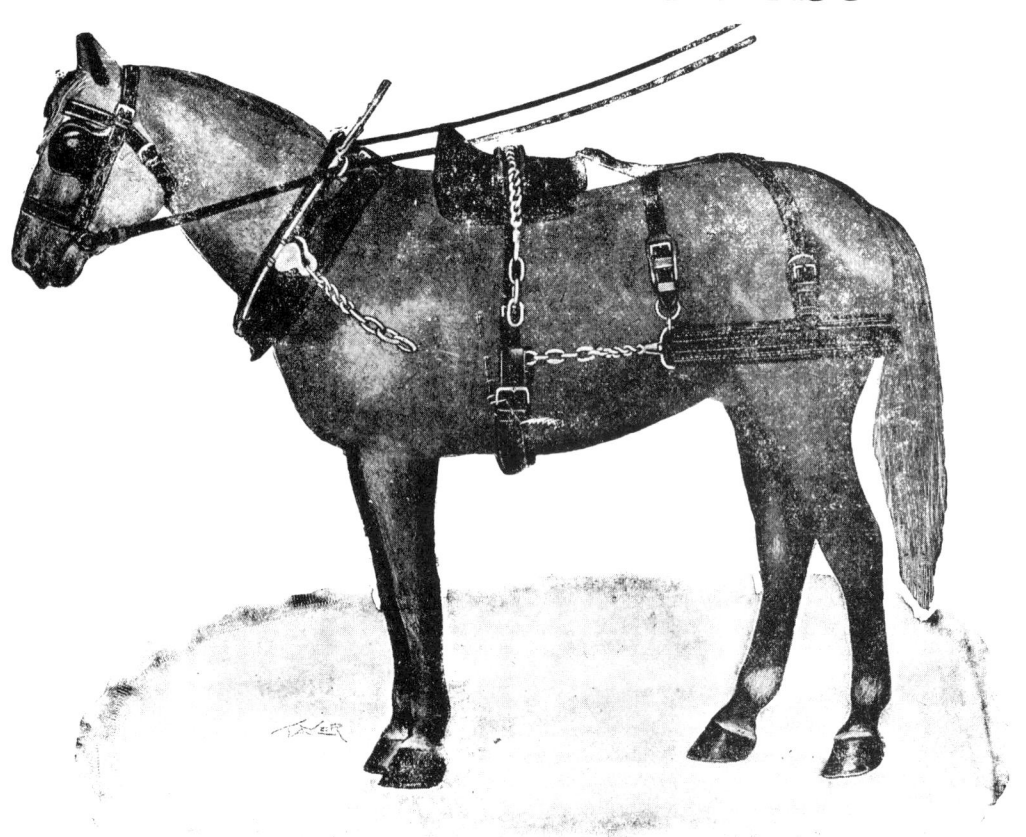

### CART AND WAGGON HARNESS.

Black or brown leather.

**Best.**
- 3½ in. Breeching with 1¾ in. loin straps.
- Double-end tree saddle.
- 1½ in. Bridle, 1 in. reins, pipe collar.
- Bolt and nut hames with 1¼ in. hame straps.
- 3 in. Shaft bellyband, tug chains and back chain.

**Second.**
- 3 in. Breeching with 1½ in. loin straps.
- Single-end tree saddle.
- 1¼ in. Bridle, ⅞ in. reins, pipe collar.
- Bolt and nut hames with 1¼ in. hame straps.

**Third.**
- 2½ in. Breeching with 1½ in. loin straps.
- Single-end tree saddle.
- 1¼ in. Bridle, ⅞ in. reins, pipe collar.
- Bolt and nut hames with hame straps.
- 2½ in. Shaft bellyband, tug chains and back chain.

### LEADING HARNESS.

Black or brown leather.

**Best.**
- 1¾ in. Spider and bellyband, stitched.
- 1¼ in. Bridle, 1 in. reins, pipe collar.
- Bolt and nut hames with 1¼ in. hame straps and leading chains.

**Second.**
- 1½ in. Spider and bellyband, stitched.
- 1¼ in. Bridle, ⅞ in. reins, pipe collar.
- Bolt and nut hames with 1¼ in. hame straps and leading chains.

**Third.**
- 1½ in. Spider and bellyband, riveted.
- 1¼ in. Bridle, ⅞ in. reins, pipe collar.
- Bolt and nut hames with 1¼ in. hame straps and leading chains.

# HARNESS PARTS AND SUNDRIES

### SPIDERS AND BELLYBANDS.

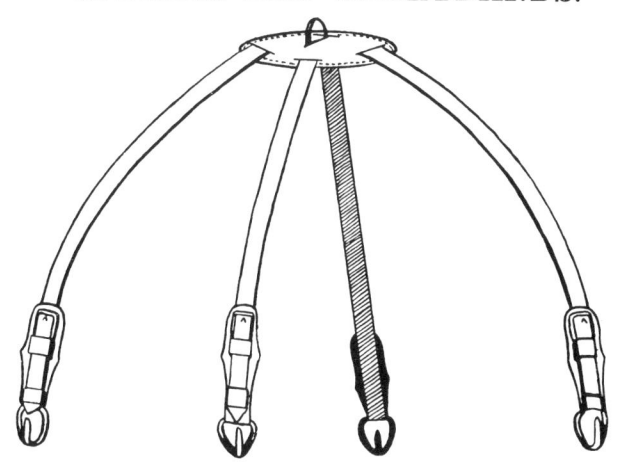

**SPIDERS AND BELLYBAND.** With or without tugs. With tugs, best stitched, 1½ and 1¾ in. Com. Riveted, with tugs, 1½ and 1¾ in.; without tugs, 1½ in. Bellybands only, leading, 1½ and 1¾ in. Best and common riveted.

### COUPLINGS.

**SHORT COUPLINGS.** ⅞ and 1 in. Hand and machine sewn.

### PLOW FORE PARTS.

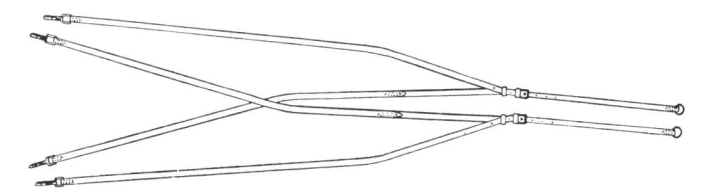

**PAIR HORSE PLOW FOREPARTS.** ⅞ and 1 in. Hand and machine sewn. For using with Rope Plow Reins.

### REINS, WAGGON.

Hand and machine sewn. 5 horse lead, with cross couplings, ⅞ and 1 in.; 6 horse lead, single, 35 ft., ⅞ and 1 in.; 6 horse lead, with cross couplings, ⅞ and 1 in.; 8 horse lead, with cross couplings, 35 or 45 ft., ⅞ and 1 in.

### REINS, SPLICELESS.

⅝ x 50 ft.; ⅝ x 60 ft.; ⅝ x 70 ft.; ¾ x 50 ft.; ¾ x 60 ft.; ¾ x 70 ft. ⅞ x 70 ft.

# HARNESS PARTS AND SUNDRIES

## FARM BRIDLES.

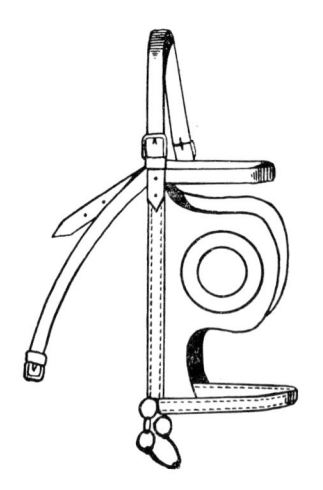

### CART BRIDLES.

No. 1. Ordinary special farm, with eye and corner piece in one. 1¼ and 1½ in.

No. 2. Common special farm. .. 1¼ in. only.

No. 3. Common farm. .. Eye and corner piece separate.

Nos. 1 and 3 can have Queensland heads fitted at extra cost. No. 2 cannot have Queensland head fitted.

### HARVESTER TRACES.

3 in. and 2½ in., with curled hoop.

### POLE STRAPS.

Drill, 1½, 1¾, 2 in., with japanned gear buckles.

**TROLLY.** With brass pole-piece buckles, 1¾ in. With japanned pole-piece buckles, 1¾ in.

### FLY FRONTS.

Cord, light and heavy; Leather, Basil, and Kip. Used on bridle when flies are troublesome.

## HARRIS. SCARFE, LIMITED.

HF **17**

Patent Lea Gig.

Close Top Buggy.

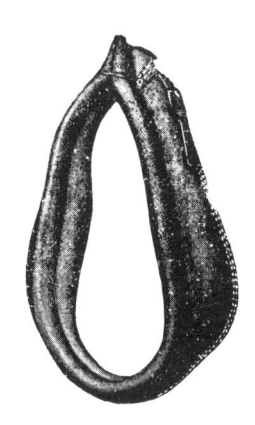

Brown Leather Gig.

**Black** Leather Gig.

Welted Kip Yankee.

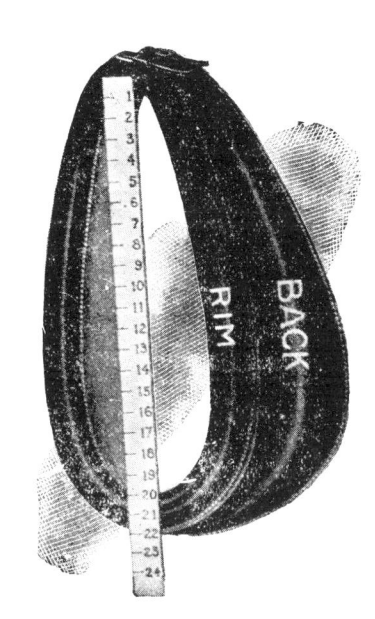

How to Measure a Collar.
This Collar measures 20 in.

Laced **Yankee.**

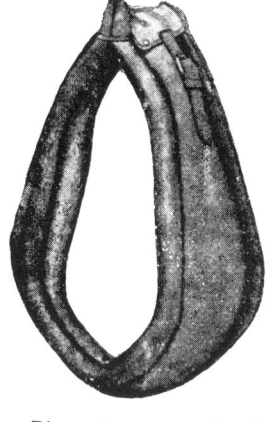

Piper Stage or Coach.

Spring Cart.

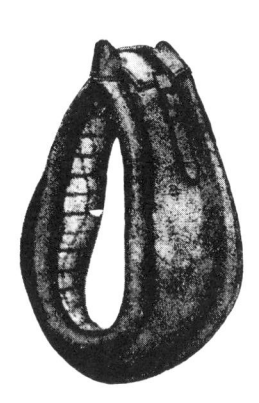

No. 2 Cart.

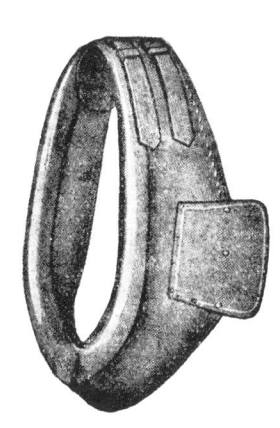

Reliance Cart Collar, with double strap, solid leather lining, reinforced throat piece and extra draft flap.

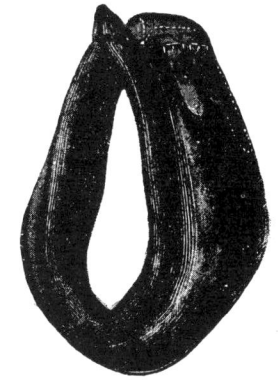

No. 1 Piped, Double Strap.

# DONKEY HARNESS

### BRIDLES, DONKEY.

Scotch Pattern. Single leather, flat eyes, with Bits. Complete sewn.
As above, riveted.

Beltana Pattern. Single leather, flat eyes, but with Noseband, less Bit.

### BACKBANDS.

Leading, with Sweat Guards, 2½ in. and 3 in. Leading, without Sweat Guards, 2½ in. and 3 in.

### BELLYBANDS.

1½ in.

### BREECHINGS.

Lined. Single Riveted.

### COLLARS.

Check lined. Leather lined.

### HAMES.

Iron.

### HAME STRAPS.

1 in.

### SADDLES.

Single Top.    Lined Top

HARRIS, SCARFE, LIMITED.                                                          HF **19**

# HARNESS

## CAMEL TANDEM, OR FOUR-CAMEL BUGGY HARNESS.

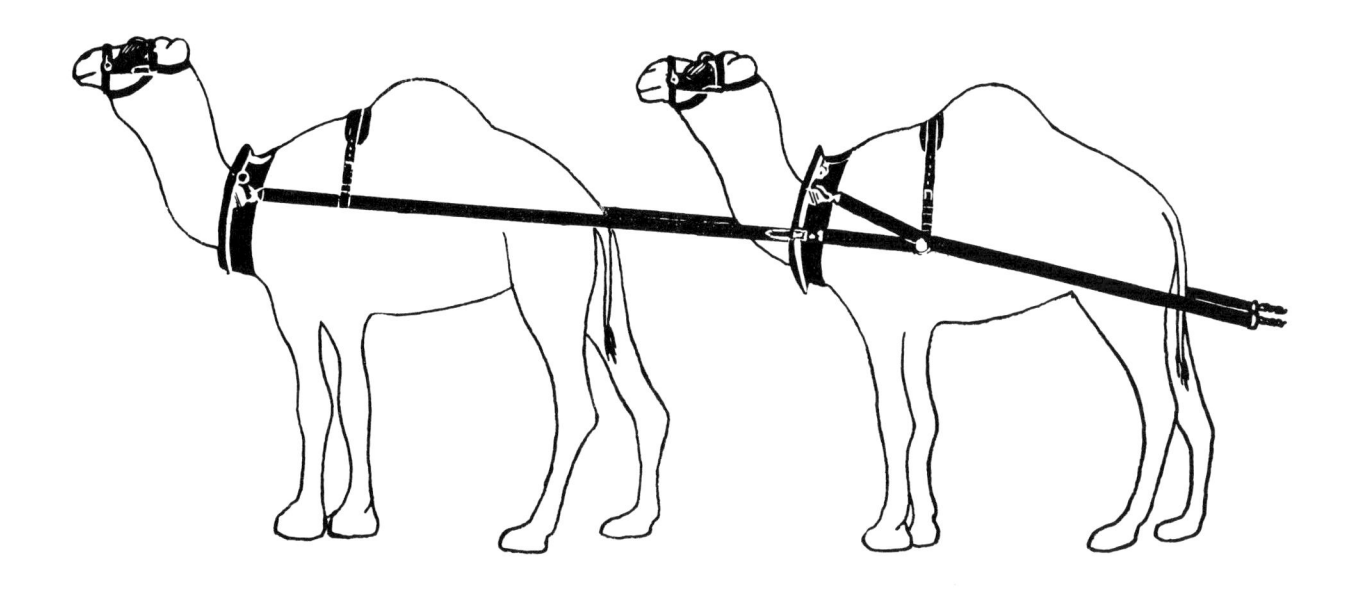

**CAMEL SULKY HARNESS FOR ONE CAMEL,** comprising bridle with iron noseband, collar, hames, traces, spider and tugs to hold shafts, breeching, and reins. Also cheaper line, chain traces.

**CAMEL BUGGY HARNESS FOR PAIR, SINGLE.** Best, with spiders and leather traces and reins. Also, as shown above, in lead, single leather traces and cotton rope reins.

**CAMEL BUGGY HARNESS, TANDEM.** Best, with spiders and single leather traces and reins. Also, as illustrated, single leather traces and cotton rope reins.

**CAMEL BUGGY HARNESS, FOUR-IN-HAND.** Best, with spiders and single leather traces and reins. Also, as illustrated, single leather traces and cotton rope reins.

# HARNESS

## IMPROVED CAMEL RIDING SADDLE.

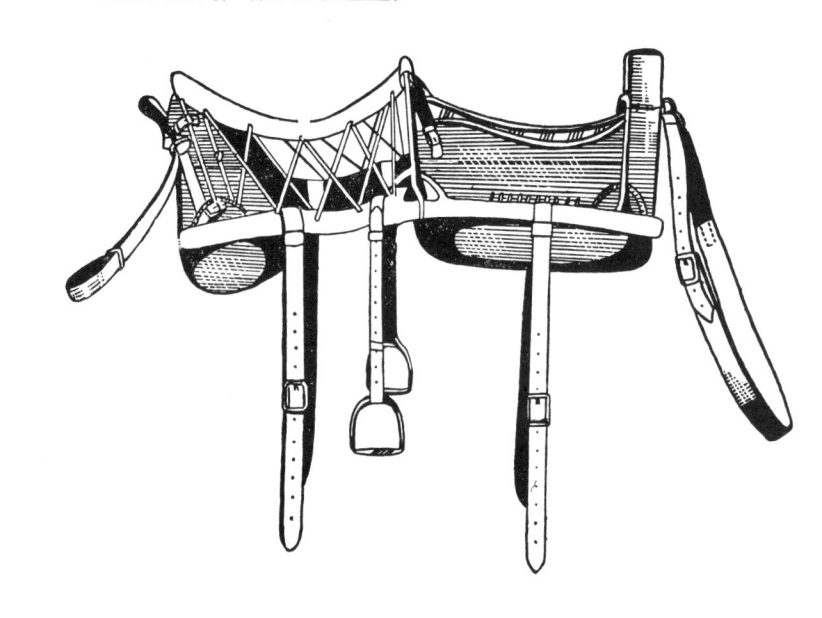

**IMPROVED CAMEL RIDING SADDLE.**

Steel Bridges, all leather covered, complete (as illustration).

Also Steel Tree, enamelled, complete, as supplied to the Government.

Improvement—Bars narrowed at point "a" by curving in, so that the rider's legs are not spread out so wide.

## CAMEL PACK SADDLES.

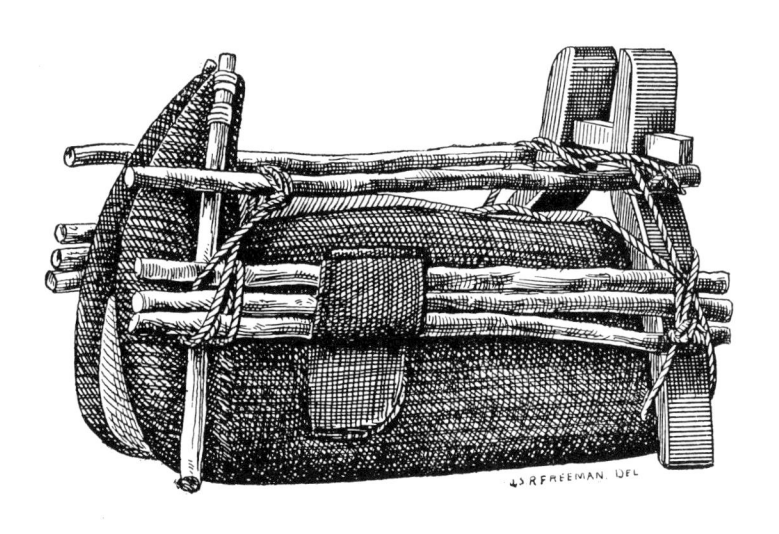

**CAMEL PACK SADDLES.**

Made of goat hair cloth, with wool bale lining (as illustrated), leather crupper, **girth, and breastplate.**
Also made of wool bale throughout, rope crupper, etc.

**CAMEL SUNDRIES ALWAYS KEPT IN STOCK.**

**HOBBLE STRAPS.** Single, 1¼ in., 2 in.; Double, 1¾ in., 2 in.
**HOBBLE CHAINS.** 2 in. x 5 in. ring x 5⁄16 swivel; 2¼ x 6 x ⅜ swivel.
**GOAT HAIR CLOTH.**
**WOOL BALE CLOTH.**
**RYE STRAW** (in 2-cwt bales).
**STOCKHOLM TAR** (5-gallon drums).
**CATUPS FOR PACK SADDLES.** Kauri, 4½ in. and 5 in., Cow; 5½ in. and 6 in., Bull.
**MALLEE STICKS.**
**ROPE, New Zealand.** Up to ⅞ in., 1 in. and upwards.
**ROPE, Manilla.** Up to ⅞ in., 1 in. and upwards.
**BELLS.** Nos. 0 and 1.
**BELL STRAPS.** 1¼ in. and 1½ in.
**WATER CASKS.** 10, 15, and 20 **gallon.**

HARRIS, SCARFE, LIMITED.                                    HF 21

# HARNESS
## CAMEL LEADING HARNESS.

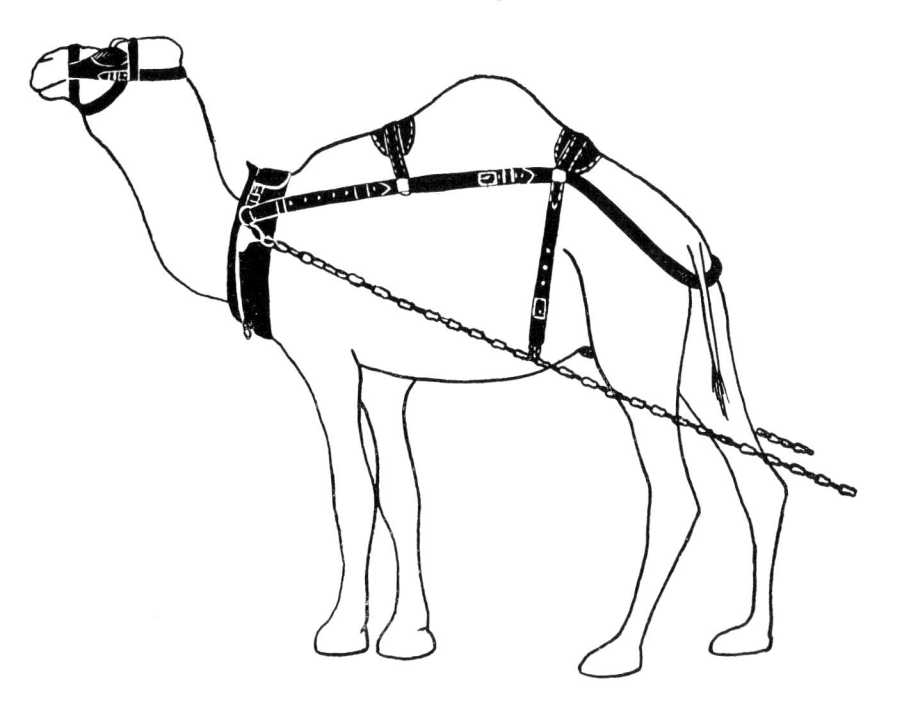

### CAMEL LEADING HARNESS.

#### Kerr's Pattern.

Various ideas are illustrated, and the complete harness has been brought right up-to-date.

It can be supplied as a whole or in parts as required. The breeching is sometimes used as a flank girth.

1¾ in. is the usual line. 1½ in., medium.

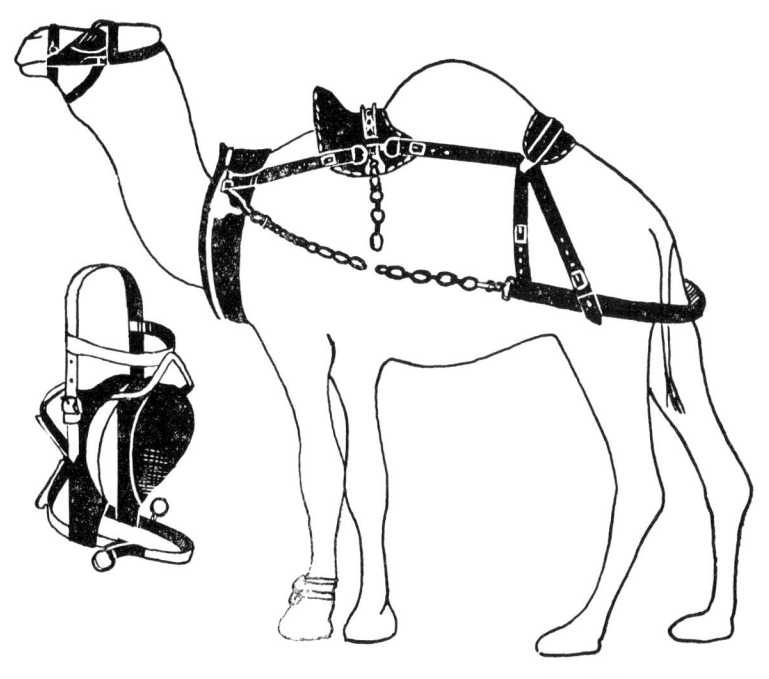

### WAGGON SHAFT HARNESS.

#### Kerr's Pattern.

Please Note—The bridle more fully illustrated as in the inset. The steel noseband and rings enable the camels to be driven perfectly with reins similar to horses.

The latest Gourlay Patent Collar supplied with all harness.

### CAMEL WAGGON SADDLE TREE AND BOARDS.

Tree only. Boards only.

# PACK SADDLES AND BAGS

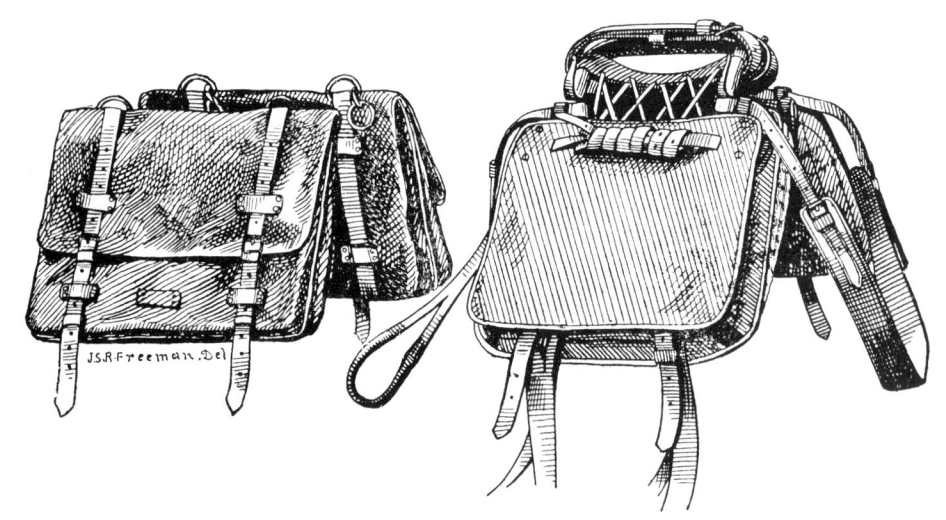

No. 1—Panel 18 x 20, crupper and breastplate, No. 1 bags, 1¼ surcingle, panel bound.

No. 2—Panel 18 x 22, small safes, No. 2 tree, breastplate and crupper, surcingle 1¾, No. 2 bags, panel bound.

No. 3—Panel 20 x 22, large safe, any kind breeching and breastplate, No. 3 tree, No. 3 bags, extra strong surcingle, 2 in., panel bound.

Holden's Patent Tree, with moveable boards, to fit any conditioned horse, extra.

A Cheaper Line can be supplied than the No. 1 for light or temporary use, but they cannot be recommended for permanent station work.

### BAGS ONLY.

No. 1. Kip, light, size 18 x 20, round corner pattern, 5 in. gusset, 1 in. strapping, riveted loops.
No. 2. Kip, medium weight, size 18 x 25, 5½ in. square gusset, round corner pattern, 1⅛ in. strapping, riveted and sewn loops.
No. 3. Good stout kip, size 20 x 22, 6 in. gusset square, round corner pattern, 1¼ in. strapping, riveted and sewn loops, any shape.
No. 4. Canvas.

**PACK TREES.** Common, Medium, Strong, Holden's Patent.

### TREW'S HORSE PACK SADDLE. PATENTED.

**Trew's Pack Saddles**—made only by Harris, Scarfe, Limited—have been deservedly popular throughout Australia for years. We have supplied them from Carnarvon to Brisbane.

They had just one fault in that the irons worked loose on the boards, which sometimes would split (a fault common to all pack saddles).

This fault is entirely remedied by our New Patented Tree, which we illustrate, along with the regular Trew pattern saddle.

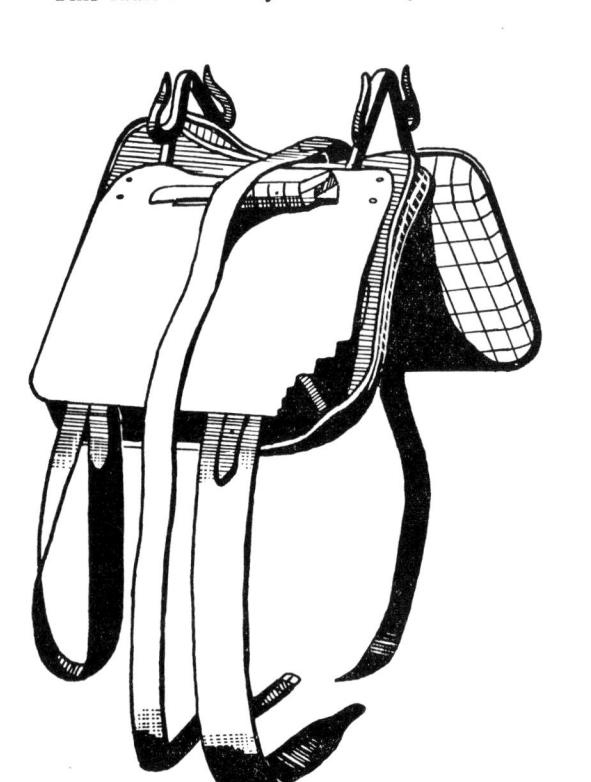

**Description of New Patent Tree.**

This New Tree, with the split ends to the irons, is held by four bolts instead of two to each end of the iron, and the position of the bolts is such that no two come into line with the grain of the wood, thus preventing a split. Also the wooden boards are not cut out for the strapping, but have a special bolted loop for this purpose. The tree and the boards thus become everlasting.

New Patent Tree.
Patent applied for No. 10767.—15-4-19.

**TREW PATTERN PACK SADDLE AND BAGS.**
We will guarantee that each Tree and Saddle will give complete satisfaction.

# WATER CANTEENS

The old plan of riveting the carrying straps to the bag has been dispensed with, as it caused leakage, and the improved cradle, as above, substituted. This buckles on, and carries the weight of the bag evenly.

We guarantee every pair, and will replace, free of cost, any bags not to our customer's satisfaction. We cannot give a better guarantee than this.

### SPECIAL QUALITY PACK WATER BAGS.
"A man's life sometimes depends upon his Water Bags."

This Bag is riveted so closely that it is not only water-tight, but air-tight. The nozzles are of gunmetal, and have a large mouth so that they can be readily filled.

Made in three sizes, 3, 4, and 5 gallons. Leather specially made for the purpose.

### PACK CANTEENS.

No. 1970A. OVERLAND PATTERN. Heavy galvanised iron, strongly banded, with hanging loops. Bands overhanging each end $\frac{3}{8}$ in. as protection against trees, etc. Brass screw cap attached by chain and swivel. Capacity, 4 and 5 gall. Can be supplied in pairs.

### MOTOR WATER CANTEENS.

MOTOR WATER CANTEENS. A strong flax bag with 2 bands, brass screw nozzle, strong harness leather straps, with or without leather safe or back. Capacity, 4 gall.

# HARNESS SUNDRIES, ETC.

## NECK WATER BAGS.

Horse Neck Water Bag, with leather safe and strapping.
Canvas Refills for Horse Neck Water Bag, with leather stopper.
Horse Neck Water Bag, with collar shaped safe; hand and machine sewn.

## HORSE MUZZLES.

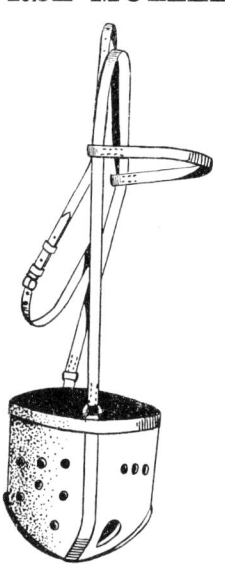

Horse Muzzles. Solid leather; riveted; wire strapped.

## SADDLE BAGS.

A strap leather bag with straps to fasten to saddle. Small and large.

## WINKER EYES.

CART. Stitched and finished. Eye and corner piece in one. Eyes only, and checked up, 1¼ in., 1½ in.
BUGGY .. Plain or Patent, sensible. Dolly Vardon.
SPRING CART .. .. Plain or sensible.

## ORCHARD HARNESS.

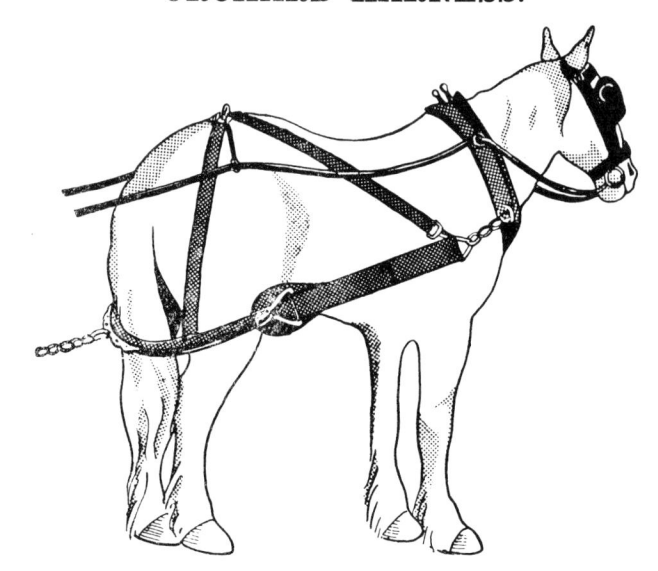

**NO MORE BARKED TREES OR BROKEN BRANCHES.**
Improved patented Orchard Harness, with movable draught, showing chains quite free of trees or vines, and cultivator quite close to trellis.

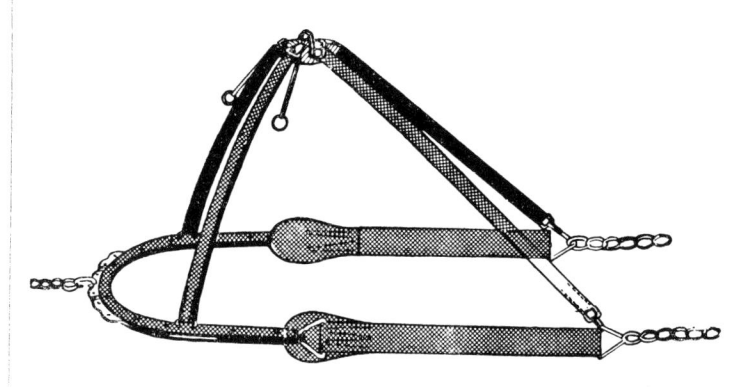

The above illustration shows clearly the Steel Breeching Drawbar, from which the single draw chain it attached (in the case of two horses) to small swingle tree, or in case of one horse, direct to Planet or other Cultivator used. The illustration hardly needs explanation. There are no swingle trees and chains projecting beyond the horse or machine to catch in low branches, or to bark stems of trees. There are no loose trace chains to become entangled in the horses' legs when turning. The harness eliminates swingle trees and brings the horses closer to the plow.

# HAMES

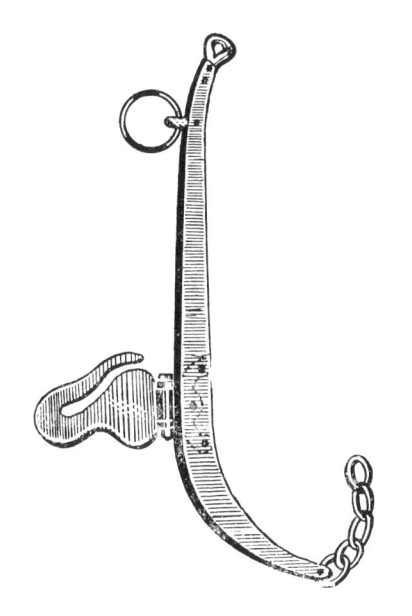

**DOWNEE CHANNEL STEEL VAN HAMES, LOOP TOP.**

**DOWNEE.** As above, with short knob top.

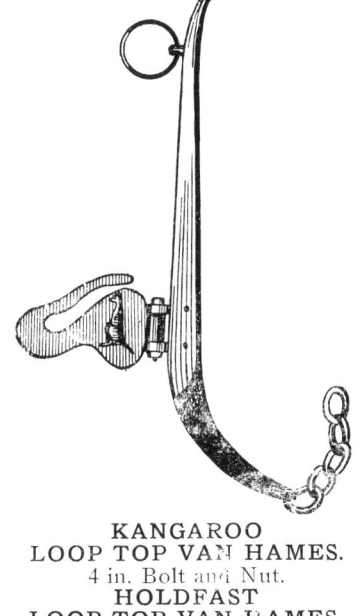

**KANGAROO LOOP TOP VAN HAMES.**
4 in. Bolt and Nut.
**HOLDFAST LOOP TOP VAN HAMES.**
Bolt and Nut, 4 in. and 4¼ in.

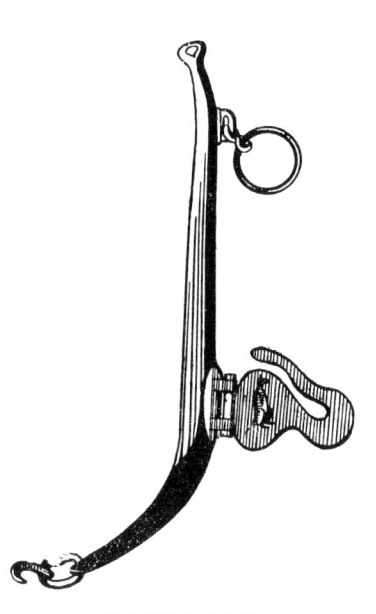

**KANGAROO LOOP TOP VAN HAMES**
Unbreakable. 4 in.

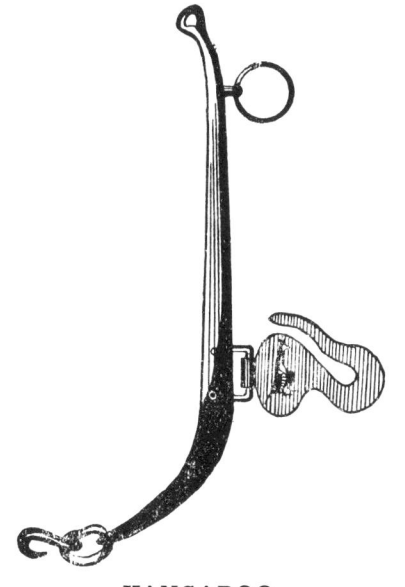

**KANGAROO LOOP TOP VAN HAMES.**
Bolt and Nut. Staple Joint.

**HOOKS, HAME.**
Colonial, 1½ in.; English, 1½ in., 1¾ in.; Downee Forged Steel.

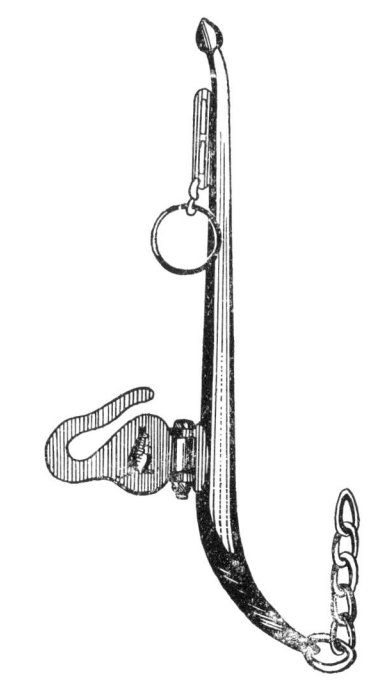

**KANGAROO SHORT KNOB TOP UNBREAKABLE LEAD HAMES.**
4, 4¼, 4½, 5 in.

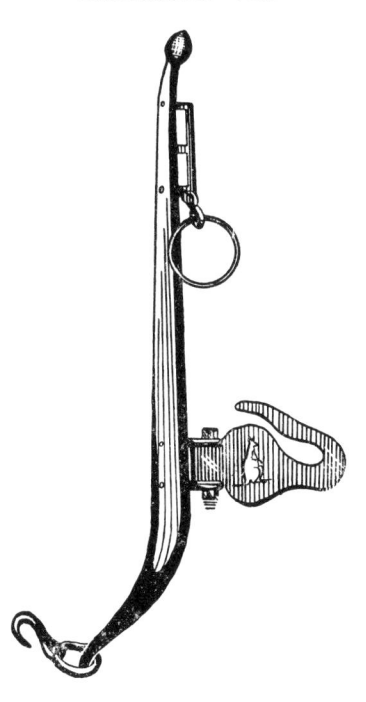

**KANGAROO SHORT KNOB TOP BOLT AND NUT LEAD HAMES.**
4, 4¼, 4½ in.

**HOLDFAST SHORT KNOB TOP BOLT AND NUT LEAD HAMES.**
4, 4¼, 4½ in.

TO MEASURE HAMES—MEASURE AROUND DRAUGHT AS NEAR TO TOP OF HOOK AS POSSIBLE.

# HAMES

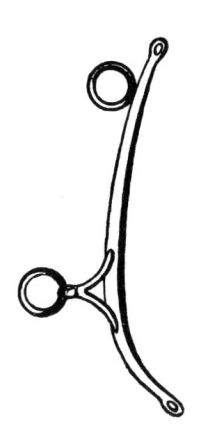

**HAMES.** All over Nickel.
⅞ in. Scroll, Loose Ring, Cab.
19½, 20, 20½, 21.

**HAMES.** All over Brass.
⅞ in. Scroll, Ring, Cab.
18, 18½, 19.

**HAMES.** All over Brass.
1 in. Scroll, Ring, Cab.
19, 19½, 20½, 21, 21½.

**HAMES.** All over Nickel.
¾ in. Scroll, Fast Ring, Plain Wire Dees.
17, 17½, 18, 18½, 19, 19½, 20, 20½, 21.

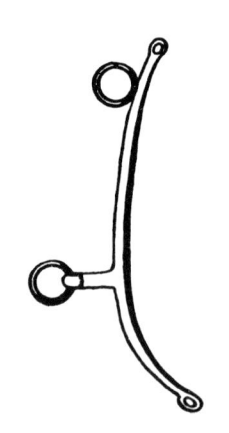

**HAMES.** All over Nickel.
⅞ in. Single Ring, Cab.
19, 19½, 20, 20½, 21.

**HAMES.** All over Brass.
⅞ in. Single Ring, Cab.
19½, 20.

HARRIS, SCARFE, LIMITED, HF 27

# RIDING BRIDLES

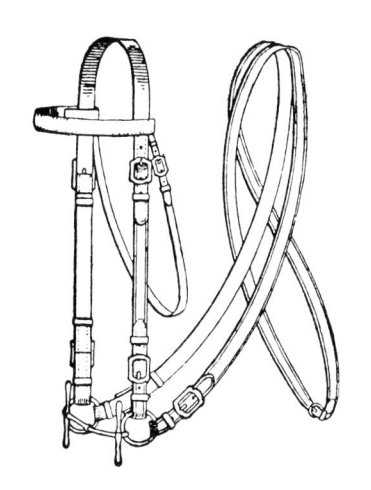

**No. 6. SNAFFLE HEAD AND REINS.** Harness leather, whole tinned bridle buckles. Bit, extra. ¾, ⅞, and 1 in.

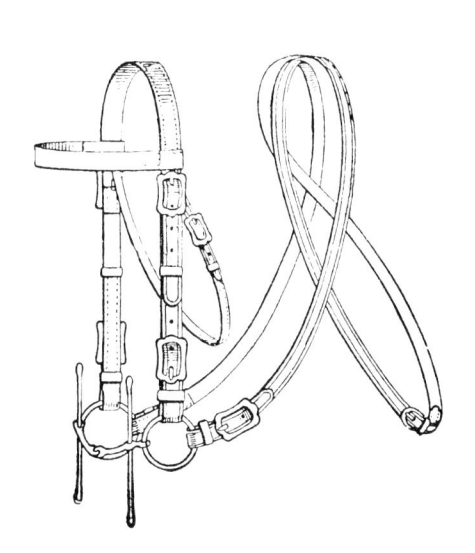

**No. 7. SNAFFLE HEAD AND REINS.** Stained leather, nickel whole bridle buckles, lined head. Bit, extra. ¾, ⅞, 1 in.

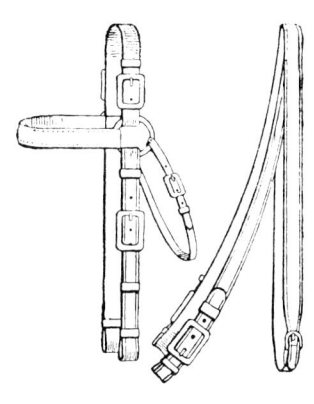

**No. 8. QUEENSLAND HEAD AND REINS.** Harness leather, whole tinned bridle buckles. Bit, extra. ⅞, 1 in.

**No. 9. QUEENSLAND HEAD AND REINS.** Stained leather, whole nickel buckles. Bit, extra. ⅞, 1 in.

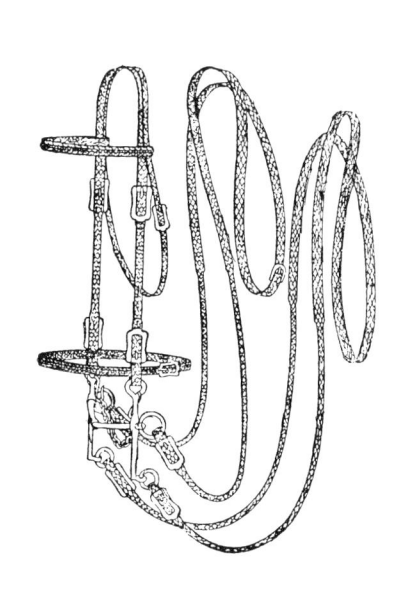

**No. 19. GENT'S PELHAM BRIDLE.** Kangaroo plaited, with double reins, nickel whole buckles and noseband. Bit, extra.

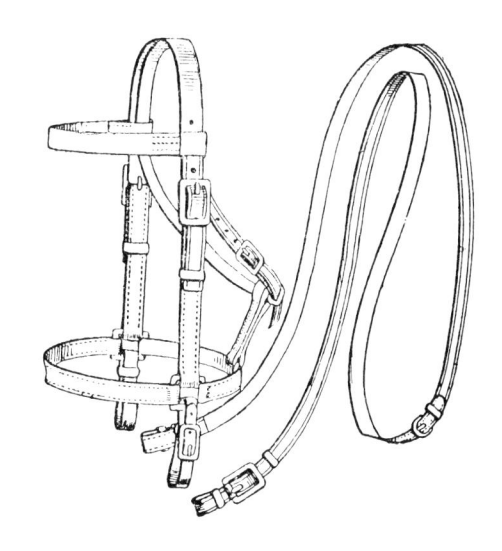

**No. 21. HEADSTALL BRIDLE** and Single Rein. Harness Leather and tinned whole bridle buckles. ⅞–1 in. Bit, extra.

**No. 22. HEADSTALL BRIDLE** and Single Rein. Unstained bridle leather, nickel whole bridle buckles. ⅞–1 in. Bit, extra.

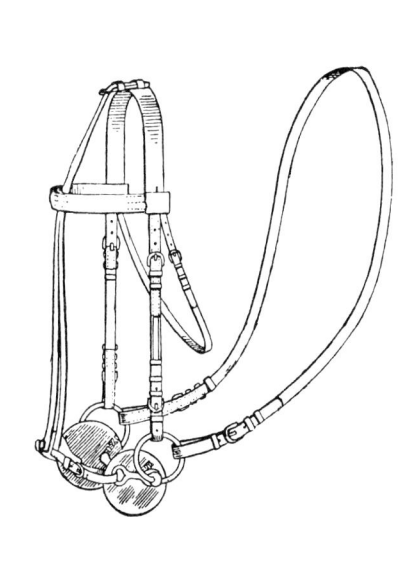

**No. 13. POLO NOSEBAND.** Bridle unstained bridle leather, N.P. inlet buckles. Complete with Bit, as Illustrated.

**No. 14. NELSON'S GAG BRIDLE.**

HF 28　　　　　　　　HARRIS, SCARFE, LIMITED.

# BRIDLES AND SUNDRIES

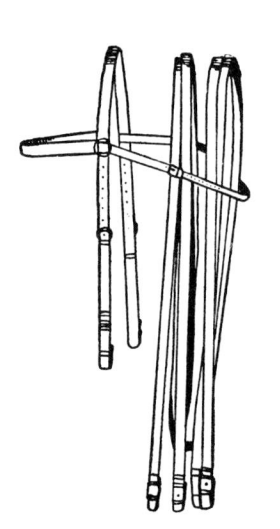

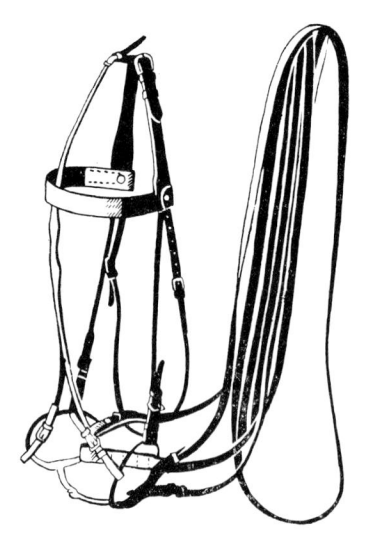

**No. 12. RACE PELHAMS,** with double reins. Round cheeks, throat, and facepiece. Sam Brown leather, nickel inlet buckles.

**No. 11.** As No. 12. except with white bridle leather.

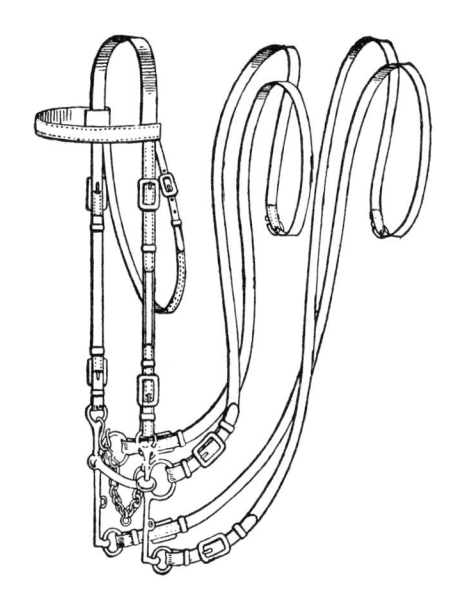

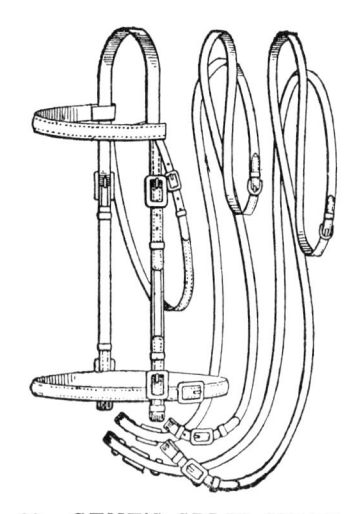

**No. 23. GENT'S SPLIT HEAD PELHAM,** with Double Reins. Nickel whole bridle buckles. Unstained bridle leather and plain lined noseband. Bit, extra.

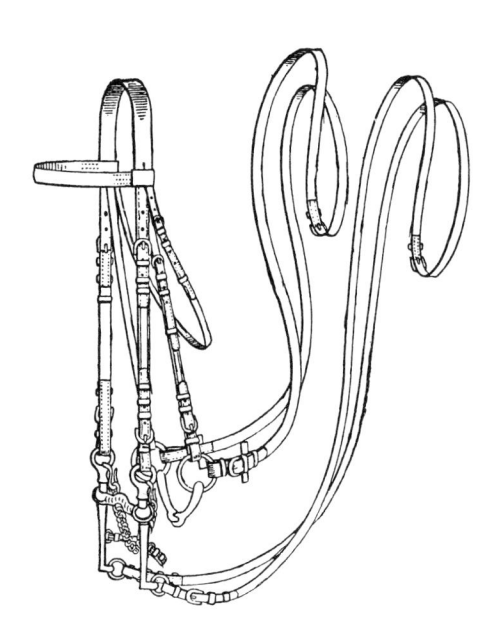

**No. 15. SINGLE QUEENSLAND HEAD RACE PELHAM,** with Double Reins. Unstained bridle leather, nickel inlet buckles. Bit, extra. $\frac{5}{8} \times \frac{5}{8}$ in.

**No. 16. FULL QUEENSLAND HEAD RACE PELHAM,** with Double Reins. Unstained bridle leather, nickel inlet buckles. Bit, extra. $\frac{5}{8} \times \frac{5}{8}$ in.

**No. 3. FULL QUEENSLAND HEAD RACE PELHAM,** with Double Reins. Sam Brown bridle leather, with nickel inlet buckles. South-Eastern Pattern. $\frac{5}{8} \times \frac{5}{8}$ in. Bit, extra.

**No. 4. SINGLE QUEENSLAND HEAD RACE PELHAM,** with Double Reins. Sam Brown leather, nickel inlet buckles. South-Eastern Pattern. $\frac{5}{8} \times \frac{5}{8}$ in. Bit, extra.

**No. 17. SINGLE QUEENSLAND HEAD RACE PELHAM,** with Extended Throat Race with Double Reins. Unstained bridle leather, nickel inlet buckles. $\frac{5}{8} \times \frac{5}{8}$ in. Bit, extra.

**No. 18. GENT'S SPLIT HEAD PELHAM.** Sam Brown or stained bridle leather, nickel buckles. Double Reins, paten leather. Front, $\frac{3}{4} \times \frac{5}{8}$ in. Bit, extra.

**No. 1. SPLIT HEAD PELHAM,** with double reins. Unstained bridle leather, nickel whole bridle buckles. South-Eastern pattern. Bit, extra. $\frac{3}{4} \times \frac{5}{8}$ in.

**No. 2. SPLIT HEAD PELHAM,** with double rains. Sam Brown leather, N.P. inlet buckles, South-Eastern pattern, $\frac{3}{4} \times \frac{5}{8}$ in. Bit, extra.

**No. 20. WEYMOUTH BRIDLE.** Unstained bridle leather, nickel inlet buckles, double reins, $\frac{3}{4} \times \frac{5}{8}$ in., for curb and braddon as illustrated. Curb and braddon, extra.

# SADDLERY SUNDRIES

### HEAD COLLARS.

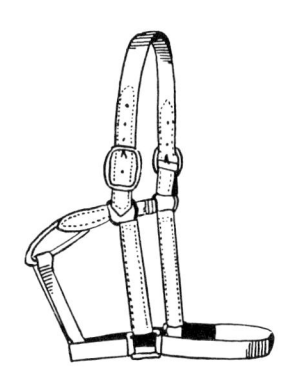

**ALBERT HEAD COLLAR**, with brass squares, rings, and buckles. Round throat, lined cheeks and points. 1⅛, 1¼ in.

**STALLION HEAD COLLAR**, with brass rings and buckles. Harness leather with lined cheeks. Very strong. For draught stallion. 1½ in.

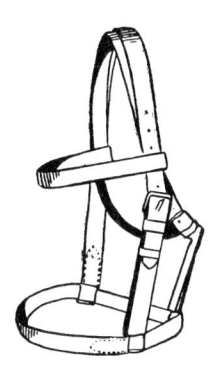

**NEWMARKET HEAD COLLAR**, with japanned gear buckles and rings. 1¼, 1½ in.

**FIGURE 8 COW HEAD COLLARS.** Harness leather, japanned gear buckles. 1¼, 1½, in. Common, 1¼ in. Single Top. Lined Top.

### HALTER ROPE, PLAITED.

White Cotton. Manilla and New Zealand. 1½ in. x 7 ft. 6 in.; 1¾ in. x 7 ft. 6 in.; 1¾ in. x 9 ft.; 2 in. x 7 ft. 6 in.; 2 in. x 9 ft.; 2¼ in. x 9 ft.; 2½ in. x 9 ft.

Shipping Halters, with coloured head piece and throat lash, 1¾ in. x 7 ft. 6 in. Adjustable Heads, extra.

### HORSE AND CATTLE TIES.

White Cotton and New Zealand. 1¼ in. x 9 ft., 1 snap; 1½ in. x 9 ft., 1 snap; 1¾ in. x 9 ft., 1 snap; 2 in. x 9 ft., 1 snap; 2¼ in. x 9 ft., 1 snap; 1½ in. x 11 ft., 1 snap; 1¾ in. x 11 ft., 1 snap; 2 in. x 11 ft., 1 snap; 2¼ in. x 11 in., 1 snap; 1½ in. x 9 ft., 2 snap; 1¾ in. x 9 ft., 2 snap.

# SADDLERY SUNDRIES

## GIRTHS.

Split Kip. 3 in. Double Buckle.

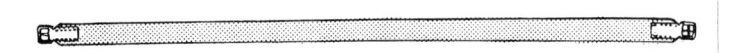

Plain Kip. Single Buckle. 1½, 1¾, 2 in.
Plain Sam Brown Leather. Single Buckle. 1½, 1¾, 2 in.
Plain Super Wool Web. 3, 3¼ in.
Plain White or Coloured Union. Single Buckle. 1¼, 1½, 1¾, 2, 2¼
Plain White or Coloured Wool, 3, 3¼ in.

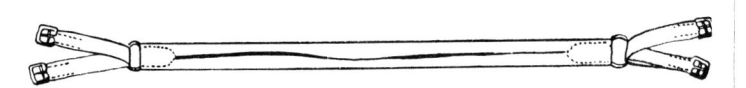

Folded Kip. Balance End.
Folded Kip. Split End.

## STIRRUP LEATHERS.

Colonial. Best hand sewn. ⅞, 1, 1⅛, 1¼, 1⅜ in.
Colonial. Machine sewn. 1⅛, 1¼ in.
English. 1⅛, 1¼ in.

Tubular Web.

Colonial. 3rd Quality. Machine sewn. Harness Leather, 1¼ in. only.

## CRUPPERS.

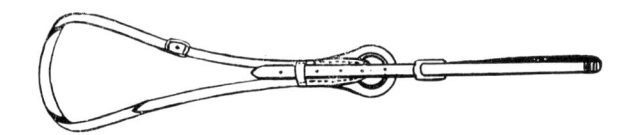

CRUPPERS. BREAKING. 1 in. harness leather, tin buckles, flat dock.

CRUPPERS. Flat dock, nickle buckles. ¾ in., pony size; ⅞ in., full size; and 1 in., full size.

## GIRTHS.

| KANGAROO | KANGAROO |
|---|---|
| Twisted. | Round Plaited Leather. |
| 12 strand | 12 strand |
| 14 strand | 14 strand |
| 16 strand | 16 strand |
| 20 strand | 20 strand |

## PATENT GIRTHS AND SURCINGLES.

GIRTHS. PATENT RACE, with Elastic Point. Made in Kip. 1¼, 1½, 1¾ in. and Web, White or Fawn.

SURCINGLES. Patent, with Elastic in Point. Made in Kip. 1¼, 1½, 1¾ in. and Web, White or Fawn.

HARRIS, SCARFE, LIMITED.　　　　　　　　　　　　　　　HF 31

# SADDLERY SUNDRIES
## SURCINGLES.

SURCINGLE, WEB, RACE. White or Fawn. 1½, 1¾, 2 in.

### SURCINGLES.
Bridle Leather. To lace. 1½, 1¾, 2 in.
Plain Leather. To lace or buckle. 2¼ x 2 ring; 2¼ x 3 ring; 2¼ x 4 ring.
Plain Leather. Folded Kip girth part. 2¼ x 4 ring.
Twisted kangaroo. 12 strand, 14 strand, 16 strand.

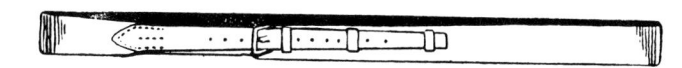

SURCINGLES KIP. 1½, 1¾, 2 in.

### SURCINGLES.
Plain Leather. To lace. 1½, 1¾, 2 in.
Plain leather, twisted kangaroo girth part. 2¼ x 4 ring.
Plain leather, plaited girth part. 2¼ x 4 ring.
Kangaroo Plaited. 10 strand, 14 strand, 16 strand.

## BREAST PLATE.

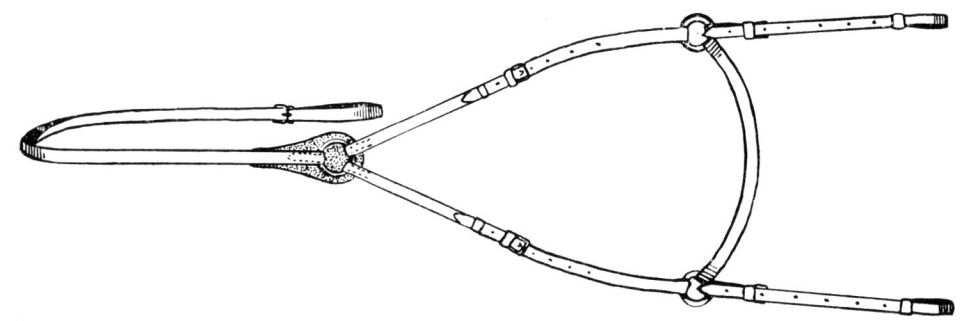

BREASTPLATES. With fork part Harness Leather　　　　　　　　　　　　　　　With tin buckles, ⅝ and ¾ in.
　　　　　　　　With fork part Stained Leather　　　　　　　　　　　　　　　With nickel buckles, ⅝ and ¾ in.
　　　　　　　　With fork parts Sam Brown Leather　　　　　　　　　　　　　With inlet buckles, ⅜ and ½ in.
　　　　　　　　　　Extra fork parts, tin buckles.　　　　Extra fork parts, nickel buckles.
BREASTPLATE STRAPS　　　　　　　　　　　　　　　　　　　　　　　　　　　　.. Nickel buckles.

## MARTINGALE.

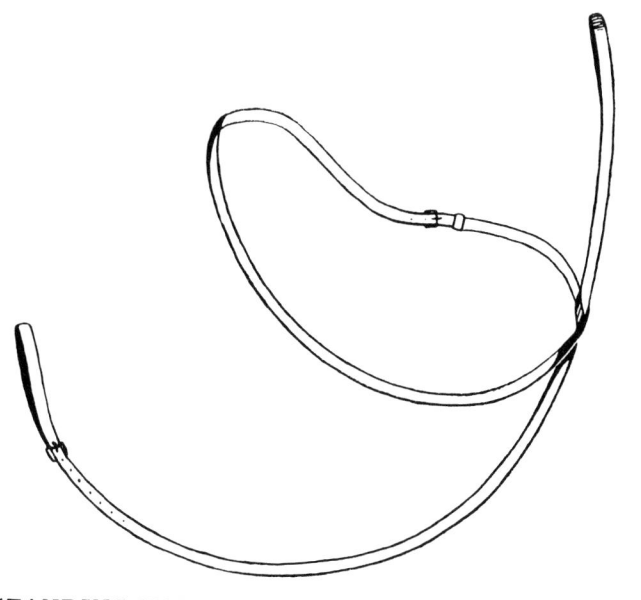

## PULLING NOSE BAND.

STANDING MARTINGALE. Bridle leather, nickel buckles.
RUNNING MARTINGALE. Bridle leather, nickel buckles, as illustrated, with fork part.

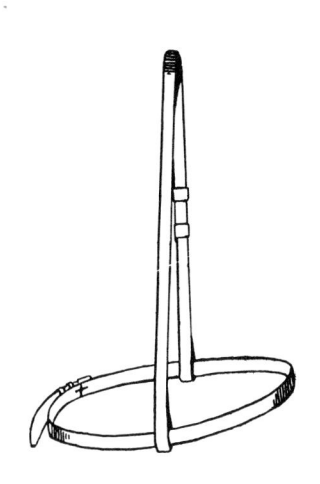

PULLING NOSEBAND. Bridle leather, nickel buckles.

# ENTIRE TACKLE

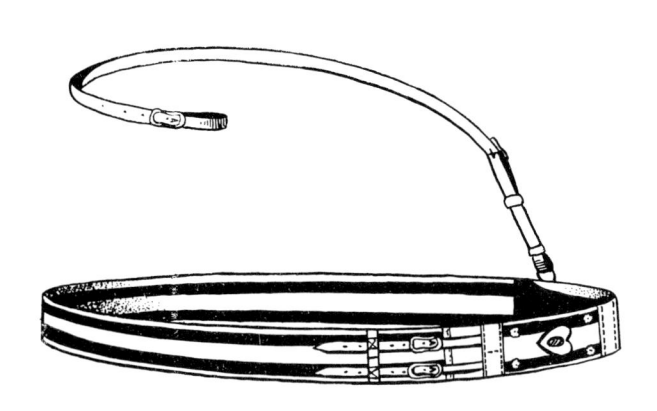

**ROLLERS. COLOURED WEB.** Padded, with serge lining. Heavy wool roller web. Bridle leather strapping, hand sewn.
With side rein. Size 5½, 6, and 6½ in. wide.
Without side rein. Sizes 5½, 6, and 6½ in. wide.
Side Rein for above. Bridle leather, nickel buckles.

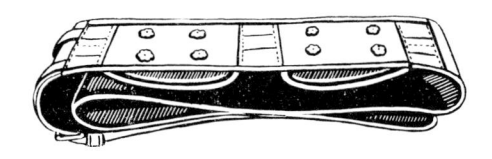

**ROLLERS. KIP.** Padded with serge lining. Only best selected kip used. All hand sewn. Size, 4 in. wide.

**ROLLERS. COMMON WEB.** For horse rugs. Felt padded. Size, 3 in. wide.

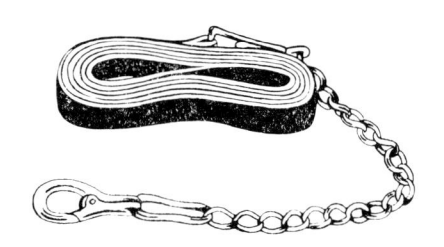

**REINS. STALLION.** Leading, with N.P. chain end. Selected bridle leather, strongly hand sewn. Sizes, 1, 1⅛, and 1¼ in.

**REINS. STALLION.** As above, with N.P. bar and chain. Sizes, 1, 1⅛, and 1¼ in.

**REINS. STALLION.** As above. Bridle leather. Nickel buckle only. Hand sewn. Sizes, 1, 1⅛, and 1¼ in.

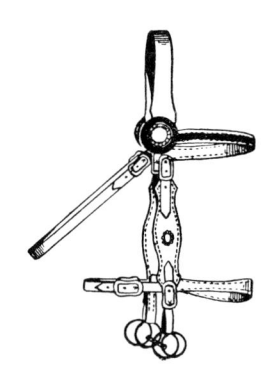

**STALLION BRIDLE.** Best selected stained bridle leather. Nickel whole harness buckles, nickel fancy rosettes. With and without nose band and patent leather forehead band. All strapping nicely shaped. Complete with lead rein. Sizes, draught, medium, and blood. Bit, Lead Chain, and Bar and Chain, extra.

No. 310. **N.P. STEEL STALLION LEAD BAR AND CHAIN**, with McCabe's hook, as used on stallion lead reins. Sizes, draught, medium, and blood.

No. 1106. **N.P. STEEL STALLION LEAD CHAIN**, with McCabe's hook as used on stallion lead reins. Sizes, Draught, medium, and blood.

STALLION BITS. SEE PAGE 48.
LINES NOT ILLUSTRATED ON THIS PAGE CAN BE MADE TO ORDER.

HARRIS, SCARFE, LIMITED. HF **33**

# TREES

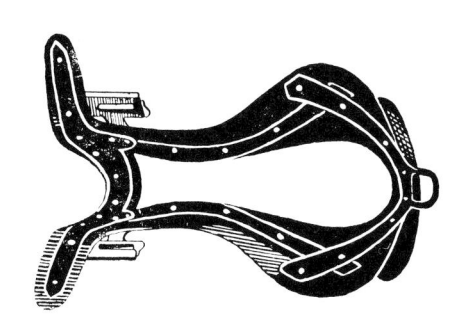

**RIDING SADDLE TREE.** Steel plated. 3 and 4 rivet.
**EDWARDS RIDING SADDLE TREE.** Steel plated. 3 and 4 rivet.

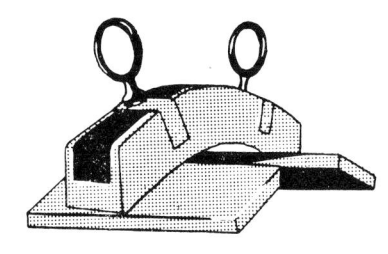

**SPRING CART SADDLE TREE AND BOARDS,** less fittings.
**SPRING CART SADDLE TREE AND BOARDS,** with nickel or brass fittings.
Tree only. Boards only.

**WAGGON SADDLE TREE AND BOARDS. CAMEL.**

**RIDING SADDLE TREE. CAMEL.**

**PACK SADDLE TREES.**

**RACE SADDLE TREE.** .. Steel plated. Straight head.

**CART SADDLE TREE AND BOARDS.** Single and Double end.
Tree only. Boards only.

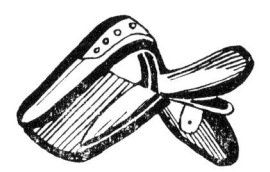

**BUGGY SADDLE TREE.** Old style, with cantle. New style, without cantle.

# TROTTING REQUISITES

**TROTTING HARNESS**, with Nickel, Brass, or Rubber and Gilt Mountings. As illustrated, less Hopples.

## SERVING HOPPLES.

No. 37. **SERVING HOPPLES**, which are an absolute preventative of the stallion being kicked.

## TROTTING BIKES OR GIG.

**SILVER STAR DE LUXE.** Solid hickory shafts, bow, cross pieces, etc. Best steel tubing, chromium plated. 26 in. x 1⅜ in. wheels with special pull out hubs and heavy spokes. Well balanced. Colours: Blue and Chrome, and Red and Chrome.

## HOPPLES.

PACERS. .. .. New Zealand pattern.

## BLOOMERS FOR HOPPLES.

Ordinary Bloomers .. .. .. Sets of 4.
High Bloomers .. .. .. Sets of 4.

## BELL BOOTS.

Rubber, for Trotters. Runwell or Ribbed .. 1, 2, 3, 4.

HARRIS, SCARFE, LIMITED. HF 35

# HORSE BOOTS

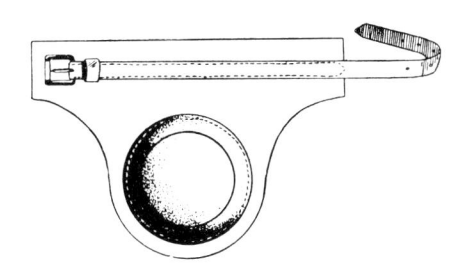

No. 18. **FETLOCK BOOT.** 1 strap. Felt or leather lined.

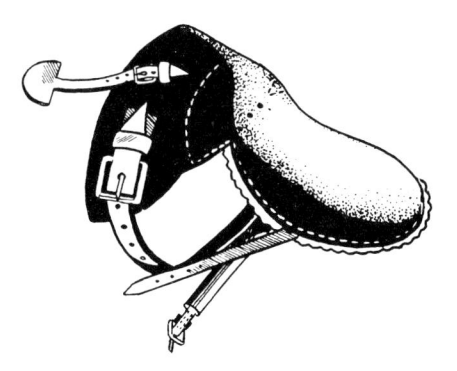

No. 24. **HIGH SCALPER.**

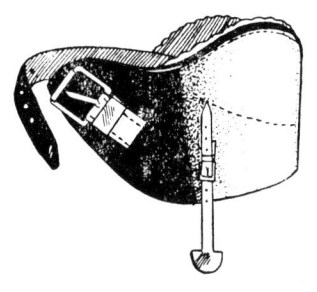

No. 22. **LOW SCALPER.**

No. 25. **PACER'S QUARTER BOOT.**

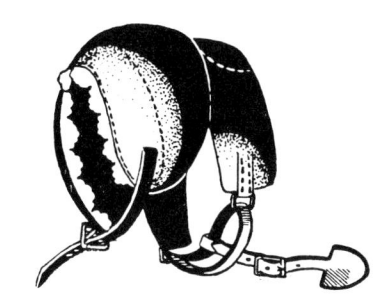

No. 23. **TROTTING QUARTER BOOT.** Hinged in two pieces.

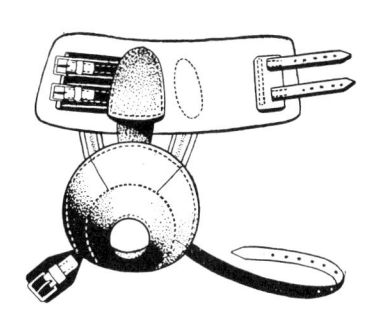

No. 26. **HEEL BOOT.** For ankles or back of joint protection.

# TROTTING AND RACING BOOTS

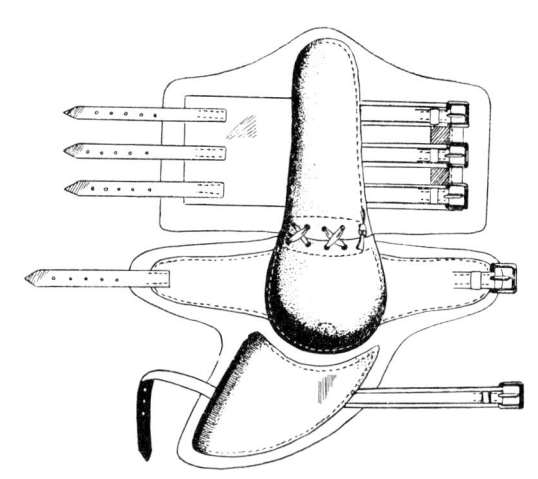

No. 16. **HIND SHIN, ANKLE, AND SPEEDY CUT BOOT.**

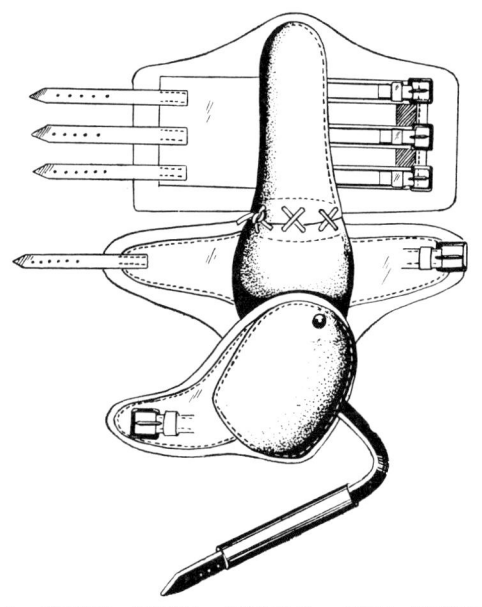

No. 17. **HIND SHIN, ANKLE, AND SPEEDY CUT BOOT.** In White or Brown.

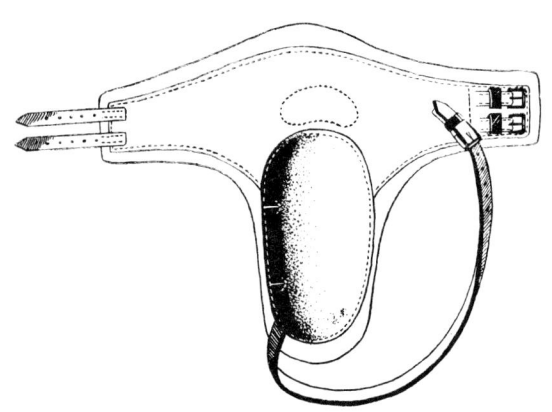

No. 36. **KNEE BOOTS** .. .. .. Felt lined.
No. 36A. **KNEE BOOTS** .. .. Leather lined.
No. 38. **KNEE AND HALF ARM BOOT.** Felt lined.
No. 38A. **KNEE AND HALF ARM BOOT.** Leather lined.

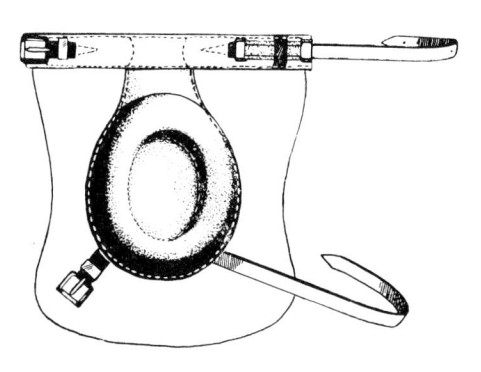

No. 20. **KNEE CAP.** Felt lined roll pad, with elastic in strap.

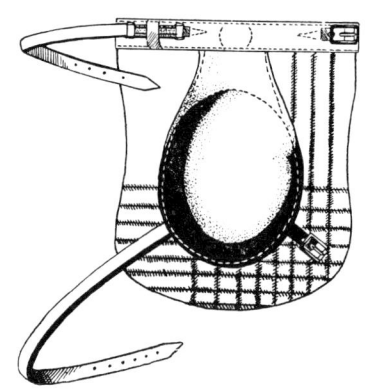

**KNEE CAP.**

No. 20A. **BLOCKED PAD.** Padded top, felt lined, elastic and leather top strap.
No. 20B. As 20 A, with plain leather riveted top strap.
No. 20C. .. .. As 20B, with plain not padded top.

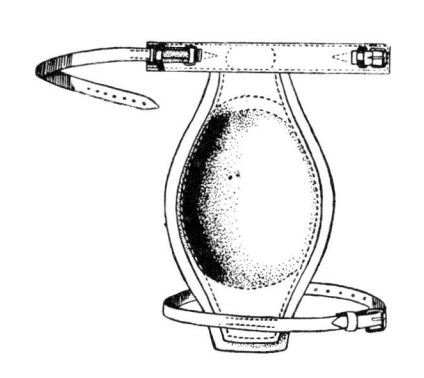

No. 21. **KILDAIRE KNEE CAP** .. Felt lined.

# TROTTING AND RACING BOOTS

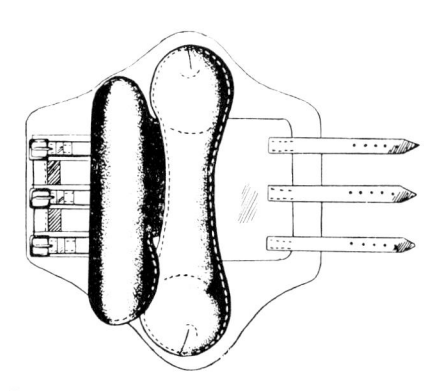

No. **14.** SPEEDY CUT BOOT, with back cord protection. 3 strap. Felt or leather lined. For Trotters only.

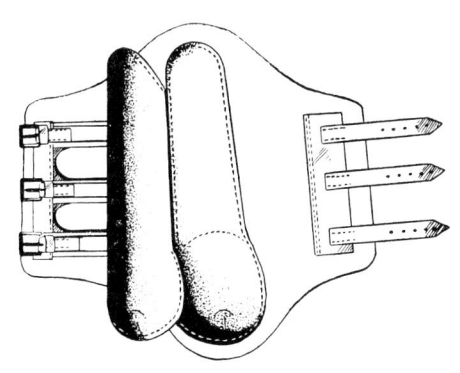

No. **108.** SHIN, ANKLE AND BACK CORD PROTECTION OR TENDON BOOT. 3 strap. Felt or leather lined.

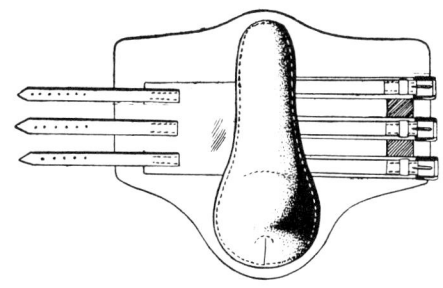

No. **92.** SHIN AND ANKLE BOOTS. 3 strap. Felt or leather lined.

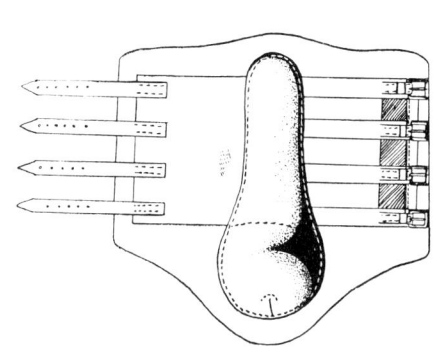

No. **110.** SHIN AND ANKLE BOOT. 4 strap. White or brown leather.

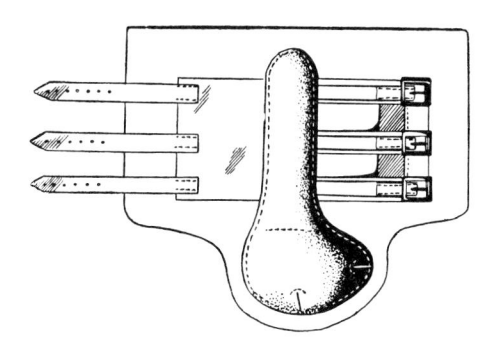

No. **120.** SHIN AND ANKLE BOOT. For front or hind leg. 3 strap. Felt or leather lined.

No. **120A.** SHIN AND ANKLE BOOT. For front or hind leg. 4 strap. Felt or leather lined.

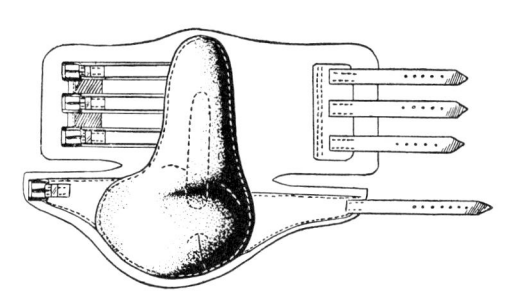

No. **130.** SHIN AND ANKLE BOOT. Leather lined. 4 strap.

# STRAPS

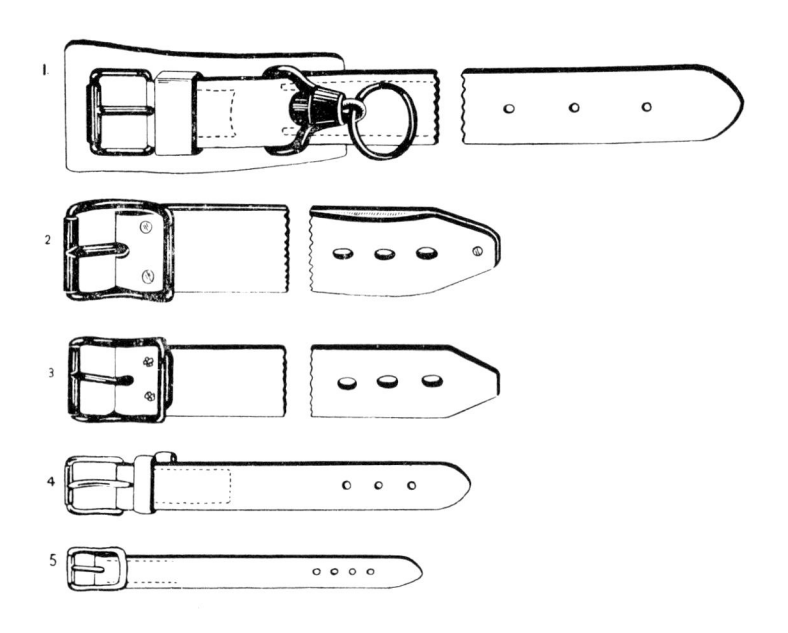

No. 1. **NECK STRAPS.** Harness leather. Japanned gear buckle. One fixed loop. Neck strap swivel. Leather safe to protect neck from buckle. All hand sewn. Sizes 1½ and 1¾ in. by 42 in. long.

Used for tethering animals, neck strap swivel prevents rope or chain from twisting.

No. 2. **HOBBLE STRAPS. DOUBLE.** Best harness leather. Strongly riveted, with japanned hobble buckle. For horses and camels.

Horse. Double. 1½ in. x 16 in. long; 1¾ in. x 17 in. long.
Camel. Double. 1¾ in. x 18 in. long; 2 in. x 18 in. long.

No. 3. **HOBBLE STRAPS. SINGLE.** Best harness leather, with japanned hobble buckle riveted on. For horses and camels.

Horse. 1½ in. x 16 in. long; 1¾ in. x 17 in. long.
Camel. 1¾ in. x 18 in. long.

No. 4. **BIT STRAP.** Harness leather, with nickel wire roller harness buckle. Hand sewn on, and two fixed loops. ⅞ and 1 in. wide x 10 in. long.

No. 4. **BIT STRAP.** Harness leather, with japanned gear buckles and two fixed loops. ⅞ and 1 in. wide x 10 in. long.

No. 5. **DEE STRAP.** Harness leather, with tinned bridle buckles hand sewn on, and one fixed loop. ⅝ and ¾ in. wide, 10 in. long.

No. 5. **DEE STRAP.** Bridle leather, with nickel bridle buckle hand sewn on, and one fixed loop. ⅝ and ¾ in. wide, x 10 in. long.

### BELL STRAPS.

**HORSE.** Harness leather, with japanned gear buckle hand sewn on. Size, 1¼ in. x 3 ft. 6 in. long.

**SHEEP.** Harness leather, with tinned bridle buckle riveted on. Size, 1 in. x 30 in. long.

# STRAPS

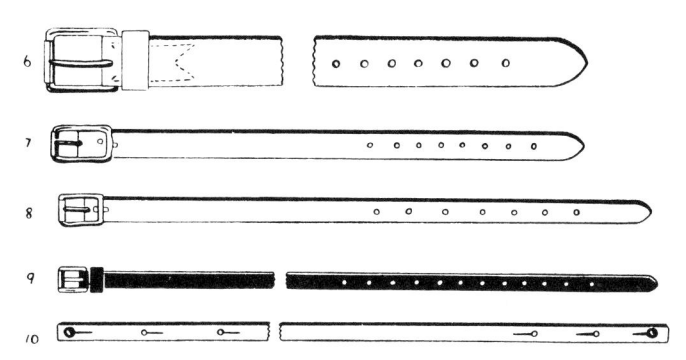

**No. 6. MOTOR STRAPS.** Harness leather, with nickel or brass harness buckle hand sewn on, and one fixed loop. Sizes, 1, 1¼, and 1½ in. wide x 48, 54, 60, and 72 in. long.

**No. 7. BLIND STRAPS.** Harness leather, with tinned bridle buckle riveted on. Sizes, ⅝, ¾, and 1 in. wide x 18 and 24 in. long.

**No. 7. BLIND STRAPS.** Harness leather, with tinned bridle buckle hand sewn on, and one fixed loop. Sizes, ⅝, ¾, and 1 in. wide x 18 and 24 in. long.

**No. 7. BLIND STRAPS.** Strap leather, N.P. gaiter buckle riveted on. Size, ½ in. wide x 12 in. long. For very light blinds.

**No. 8. SADDLE STRAPS.** Strap leather, with N.P. gaiter buckle riveted on. Sizes, ⅝ and ¾ in. wide x 24, 30, 36, 42, 48, 54, 60, 66, and 72 in. long.

**GLADSTONE BAG STRAPS.** Strap leather, with N.P. roller buckle hand sewn on, and fixed and sliding loop. Sizes, 1 in. wide x 60, 66, and 72 in. long.

**No. 9. FIELD GLASS CASE STRAPS.** Strap leather, with N.P. roller buckle hand sewn on, with one fixed loop. Size, ½ in. wide x 60 in. long.

**No. 10. FIELD GLASS STRAPS.** Black or brown strap leather, with stud fastenings. Size, ⅜ in. wide x 42 in. long.

**No. 3. PERAM OR MONKEY STRAP.** Strap leather waist and 2 shoulder straps and two side straps to fasten to dees on side of peram. Riveted.

**No. 4.** As No. 3, with adjustable shoulder straps, and all hand sewn.

**No. 0. PERAM STRAP.** Split leather strap, with buckle and billet each end to fasten across peram. Riveted.

**No. 1. PERAM STRAP.** Split leather waist strap, with two side straps to fasten to each side of peram. Riveted.

**PERAM SPRING STRAPS.** Strap leather, with N.P. gaiter buckle riveted on. Size, 12 in. long and 1 in. wide.

# LEATHER

### HARNESS.

For making Harness or Heavy Strapping, etc.

#### IN SIDES ONLY.

No. 1. Black or Brown, free from cuts and brands. 20 to 24 lb. per side.
No. 2. Black or Brown, slightly branded. 18 to 22 lb. per side.
No. 3. Brown only, slightly branded. .. 15 to 18 lb. per side.
Can be cut at extra cost full length of back only. Back measures approximately 6 ft.

When ordering to be cut, state what job it is wanted for, such as Reins, Traces, etc.

Note.—Leather cut to order cannot be returned.

### KIP.

For Saddle Bags, Light Strapping, and General Saddlery Work. In Sides only.

No. 1. Brown, free from cuts and brands. 8 to 11 lb. per side.
No. 2. Brown, slightly branded. .. 8 to 11 lb. per side.
If wanted cut, particulars as Harness Leather apply.

### BRIDLE.

For making Bridles, Reins, etc.

Melbourne. Stained. .. Approximately 15 lb. per side.
Camerons. Stained. Approximately 18 to 20 sq. ft. per side.
If wanted cut, particulars as above.

### BAG.

For making Bags of all descriptions. Also a light leather used extensively for Saddlery Work.

Camerons' self-colour, plain. 18 to 20 sq. ft. per side.
If wanted cut, particulars as above.

### STRAP.

For making all kinds of Strapping.

Camerons. 18 to 20 square feet per side.

### BASILS.

Nos. H and I. For general repairs, patching, etc.
J. For making small aprons.
K. For making medium aprons.
L. For making large aprons.
"Apron." For making small, light aprons.
"Glove." For making gardening and all classes of gloves.
"Bellows." For making and repairing bellows.
"Goat Skin." For making aprons. Will not tear.

### KANGAROO.

A light leather which has many uses. Full skins only, ¾ to 2½ lb. per skin.

### BOX HIDE.

A Black or Tan Hide used in the manufacture and repairing of footwear. Sides or cut.

### LEATHER APRONS WITH BIB.

No. 1. Light Small Basil, with Basil strapping. No Buckle.
No. 2. Large Basil, with Leather Strapping and Buckles.
GOAT. Large Basil, with Leather Strapping and Buckles.

# HORSE RUGS, ETC.

### HORSE RUGS.

**BLUE OR FAWN.** Wool, winter weight, with breast strap and plaited web fillet string. Bound red and blue. 5 ft. 6 in., 5 ft. 9 in., and 6 ft.

**COTTON CHECK,** with red and blue or yellow and blue stripe. With breast strap and plaited web fillet string. Bound red and blue or yellow and blue. 5 ft. 6 in., 5 ft. 9 in. and 6 ft.

**JAPARA.** Waterproof. Japara is a very light weight waterproof Rug or Sheet. To go over wool rug. 5 ft. 6 in., 5 ft. 9 in., and 6 ft.

**BEENIES PATENT.** Made in Manhattan White Duck and Khaki Chemical Duck. Beenies Patent Rugs when fitted has no tight straps, and when properly adjusted will not come off. Manhattan Duck, 5 ft., 5 ft. 6 in., 5 ft. 9 in., and 6 ft. Khaki Waterproof Duck, 5 ft. 6 in., 5 ft. 9 in., and 6 ft.

**HORSE RUGS OR SHEETS.** Fringed white or blue linen, with breast tape and fillet string.

**HORSE RUGS OR SHEETS.** Check Cotton. Brown and white, blue and white, and green and white check, with fringe, breast tape, and fillet string.

### DOG RUGS.

Blue or Fawn Serge and Kersey. Japara, waterproof lined, with collar check. Japara, waterproof lined, with blue rugging. These Rugs are complete with breast strap and girth. We only stock Dog Rugs to fit kangaroo or greyhound dogs. (If wanted for other dogs they will have to be made specially. We would also like a paper pattern with order. Prices on application.)

### HORSE CLOTHING.

**BLUE OR FAWN WOOL,** comprising winter weight wool rug with breast strap and plaited web fillet string. Hood and roller to match. 5 ft. 6 in., 5 ft. 9 in., and 6 ft. Other sizes made to order.

**HOODS** only, for Horse Clothing. Blue or fawn wool, bound red or blue.

### SADDLE CLOTHS.

Blue or Fawn Saddle Serge and Kersey. These cloths are saddle or full shaped. Bound red or blue, and with shaped backs. Ditto Felt Cloths made to order.

HF 42　　　　　　　HARRIS, SCARFE, LIMITED.

# HORSE AND COW RUGS

Plain Canvas Horse Rug
Fitted with Surcingle and Crupper

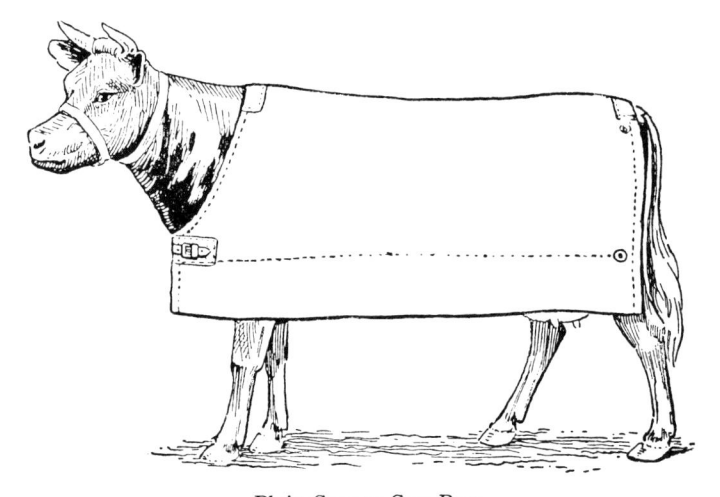

Plain Canvas Cow Rug
Fitted with Surcingle and Fillet Straps

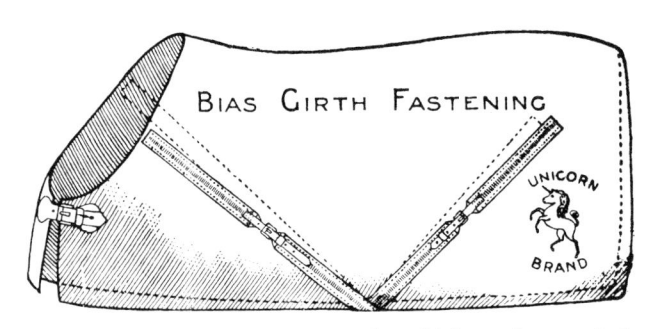

Illustration showing patent bias girths, which can be attached to any horse or cow rug at a little extra cost

**SHEEP RUGS**

# HORSE AND COW RUGS

## HORSE RUGS

"**UNICORN.**" Strongly made rugs to fit any size of horse. Manufactured from any of the following qualities of canvas

| | |
|---|---|
| H Canvas ... ... ... ... | Lined or Unlined |
| A Canvas ... ... ... ... | " " |
| AA Canvas ... ... ... ... | " " |
| Heavy Cotton Duck ... ... ... | " " |
| OM Duck ... ... ... ... | " " |
| No. 3608 ... ... ... ... | " " |
| Superfine Cotton Duck ... ... ... | " " |

Each rug is fitted with a surcingle and crupper securely attached. Also strong leather breast strap. Bias girths, as illustrated on this page, may be substituted for the ordinary girth with but a small increase in price. Leg straps, a feature necessarily enhancing the security of the rug, can also be provided at additional cost

### Specifications

| Length | To fit Horse | Length | To fit Horse |
|---|---|---|---|
| Ft. Ins. | Hands | Ft. Ins. | Hands |
| 4  6 | 13 | 6  0 | 15.2 |
| 4  9 | 13.2 | 6  3 | 15.3 |
| 5  0 | 14 | 6  6 | 16 |
| 5  3 | 14.2 | 6  9 | 16.2 |
| 5  6 | 14.3 | 7  0 | 17 |
| 5  9 | 15 | | |

Description of qualities of canvas used will be seen below

## COW RUGS

"**UNICORN.**" Similar to "Unicorn" horse rugs. Bias girths and leg straps can be supplied as desired. Length overall, 5 ft. 3 ins. Will fit most beasts. Special sizes can be made to order

### Qualities of Canvas in Cow Rugs

| | |
|---|---|
| H Canvas ... ... ... ... | Lined or Unlined |
| A Canvas ... ... ... ... | " " |
| AA Canvas ... ... ... ... | " " |
| Heavy Cotton Duck ... ... ... | " " |
| OM Duck ... ... ... ... | " " |

Breast straps, surcingle and crupper are fitted to each rug, which are all well and strongly made

### Description of Qualities of Canvas in Horse and Cow Rugs

| | |
|---|---|
| A Canvas | A brown canvas, mixture of flax and jute, medium weight |
| AA Canvas | A brown canvas, principally flax, heavier than A canvas, first class quality |
| H Canvas | A brown canvas, all jute, heavyweight |
| Heavy Cotton Duck | A white heavyweight cotton duck |
| OM Duck | Birkmyre's, white or khaki, chemically prepared standard British Duck, absolutely waterproof |
| No. 3608. Canvas. | All flax canvas. Approximately 26 oz. to the square yard |
| Superfine Cotton Duck. | Extra quality. Approximately 18 oz. to the square yard |

Veterinary experts advise that it is vital to an animal's existence that it be well covered during those months of the year when, owing to the changeable atmospheric conditions, derangements and sickness become prevalent. "Unicorn" horse and cow rugs are unequalled in quality and workmanship and are the direct means whereby thousands of beasts are saved from death yearly

# THREADS

### LINEN THREAD.

**KNOX'S.** For Sewing Machines. Colours: Whitey Brown, Black, Tan, and Drab. Nos. 10, 12, 16, 18, 20, 25, and 30, in 2-oz. reels; Nos. 35, 40, 50, and 60 in 1-oz. reels.
Pure White. Nos. 16, 18, 20, 25, 30, in 2-oz. reels; Nos. 40, 50, 60, 70, in 1-oz. reels

**FINLAYSON & BLOUSEFIELD.** Red Ink Ticket Label. For Sewing Machines. 3 Cord. Colours: Whitey Brown, Black, Nos. 18, 20, 25, 30, 35, and 40. Drab, No. 25. All 2-oz. reels.

**FINLAYSON & BLOUSEFIELD OR DUNBAR McMASTERS.** Machine Thread. For Pearson's Machine. Colours: Black and Whitey Brown. No. 18 x 3, 4, 5, 6, 7, and 8 cord.

**TALBOT MACHINE SILK.** Specially prepared to run smoothly in sewing machnes. Colours: Red, Nos. 10, 12, 16, and 24. Blue, Nos. 10, 12, 16, and 24. Black, Nos. 12, 16, and 24. White, No. 24. Orange, Nos. 16 and 24. 1-oz. reels.

**KERR'S LUSTRE TWIST.** The best substitute for Machine Silk. Colours: Black and Tan, Nos. 14, 16, and 18. In 400 yard reels.

**KERR'S UNBLEACHED COTTON. NINE CORD.** Glace finish Machine Thread. White. Nos. 40, 50, and 60. 1-oz. reels.

**DUNBAR McMASTER'S GREY SOLE SEWING THREAD.** Reverse twist. No. 3 x 3 fold. No. 3 x 4 fold. 1-lb. balls.

**FINLAYSON'S PLAITED PITCHED THREAD.** Grey. 6, 7, and 8 cord. In ¼-lb. balls.

**WAX THREAD.** On card, complete with needle. Barbours. Black and Tan.

# TEXTILES AND SUNDRIES

### COLLAR CHECK.
No. 1. With single orange and blue stripe. 44 in. wide. Heavy.
No. 2. With double orange and single blue stripe. 44 in. wide. Medium.
No. 3. With single red and blue stripe. 44 in. wide. Light.

### KERSEY.
All Wool.
Blue, with red stripe. .. .. 44 in. wide. Heavy.
Plain. Blue. .. .. .. 36 in. wide. Heavy.
Plain. Fawn. .. .. .. 72 in. wide. Heavy.

### SADDLE SERGE.
All Wool. Blue, Fawn, and White. C10, C12, and C14, x 44 in. wide.

### SADDLE FELT.
All Wool.
SUPERFINE QUALITY. .. $\frac{1}{8}$ in. and $\frac{3}{16}$ in. thick.
ORDINARY QUALITY .. $\frac{1}{4}$, $\frac{3}{8}$, $\frac{1}{2}$, $\frac{5}{8}$, and $\frac{3}{4}$ in. thick.

### COLLAR TWINE.
5 ply, $\frac{1}{2}$ and 1-lb. balls. 3 ply, $\frac{1}{2}$ and 1-lb. balls. 5 ply, 5-lb. balls.
BARBOUR'S. .. .. 5 ply, $\frac{1}{2}$ and 1-lb. balls.

### HORSE HAIR.
Curled and Teased. .. No. 00, Grey. No. C.B., Black.

### DOE HAIR.
For Padding.

### COLLAR LACES.
SCOTCH LACE OR GREENHIDE LEATHER. 6 ft. long.

### HEMP.
#### FOR MAKING WAX ENDS.
STEWART'S. Brown. No. 1. Common. .. 2-oz. balls.
BARBOUR'S. Brown. No. 1. Common. .. 2-oz. balls.
BENTLEY'S. Common Brown. .. .. 2-oz. balls.
STEWART'S. Fine White Scotch. .. .. 2-oz. balls.
FINLAYSON'S. White. No. 12 .. .. 2-oz. balls.
BARBOUR'S. White. No. 12. .. .. 2-oz. balls.

### WAX BLACK.
Winter and Summer use. For making Wax Ends.

# WEBBING

### SURGICAL ELASTIC.

**STRONG FLAT ELASTIC.** As used for patent Girths and Surcingles, all kinds of horse Boots and Trusses, for human use. Sizes: $\frac{3}{4}$, $\frac{7}{8}$, 1, $1\frac{1}{4}$, $1\frac{1}{2}$, $1\frac{3}{4}$ in.

### WEBBING.

**BRACE WEB UNION** (Cotton and Wool). For making Braces, and any job where a light and strong web is required. Sizes: $1\frac{1}{4}$, $1\frac{1}{2}$, $1\frac{3}{4}$, 2, $2\frac{1}{4}$, $2\frac{1}{2}$ in. wide, in pieces of 18 yards. Colours: White, Blue, Fawn, and Red.

**RACE GIRTH WEB UNION** (Cotton and Wool). For making light Race Girths and Surcingles. Sizes: $1\frac{1}{2}$, $1\frac{3}{4}$, 2, $2\frac{1}{2}$ in. wide, in pieces of 15 yards. Colours: White, Blue, and Fawn.

**GIRTH WEB.** All Wool. A strong and heavy wool web for making Girths for ordinary saddles. Sizes: 3, $3\frac{1}{4}$ in. Colours: White and Fawn.

**CIRCULAR WEB.** A white linen Circular Web for making White Web Riding Bridles, Handparts for Reins, Stirrup Leathers, etc., in pieces of 24 yards. Sizes: $\frac{3}{8}$, $\frac{1}{2}$, $\frac{5}{8}$, $\frac{3}{4}$, $\frac{7}{8}$, 1, and $1\frac{1}{4}$ in. wide.

**ROLLER WEB.** A heavy Wool Web used in the manufacture of Stallion and Rug Rollers. Sizes: 4, $4\frac{1}{2}$, 5, 6, and $6\frac{1}{2}$ in. Colours: Red and Fawn, Red, White and Blue.

**BELT WEB WORSTED.** A light Wool Web for making Men's Body Belts. Sizes: $4\frac{1}{2}$ and 5 in. Colour: White.

**STRAINING WEB.** A strong Linen Web for straining seats of Riding Saddles; also used in cemeteries for lowering coffins.

# HOOD MATERIALS AND SUNDRIES

## HOOD MATERIAL.
### FOR TOURERS AND ROADSTERS.

No. 35-11. Single Texture. Black, with mole backing. 34 oz. to yard. 54 in. wide.

No. 350. Single Texture. Black with khaki backing. 34 oz. to yard. 54 in. wide.

No. 353. Single Texture. Black with black and white backing. 34 oz. to yard. 54 in. wide.

No. 15-11. Double Texture. Black with mole backing. 38 oz. to yard. 54 in. wide.

No. 150. Double Texture. Black with khaki backing. 38 oz. to yard. 54 in. wide.

No. 255. Double Texture. Black with grey backing. 40 oz. to yard. 54 in. wide.

No. 250. Double Texture. Black with khaki backing. 40 oz. to yard. 54 in. wide.

No. 253. Double Texture. Black with black and white backing. 40 oz. to yard. 54 in. wide.

No. 955. Double Texture. Black with grey backing. 42 oz. to yard. 54 in. wide.

No. 950. Double Texture. Black with khaki backing. 42 oz. to yard. 54 in. wide.

### EVERBRIGHT DECKING FOR SEDAN CARS.

No. 554. Bright black, with white backing. 44 oz. to yard. 54 in. wide.

No. 554. Bright black with white backing. 48 oz. to yard. 63 in. wide.

### TEAL CLOTH FOR SPORTS CARS.

T5-D65. Grey back. .. .. 54 in. wide.
T5-D6-11. Mole back. .. .. 54 in. wide.
T5-W23. Black and white back. .. 54 in. wide.
T7-D60. Khaki back. .. .. 54 in. wide.

### BOW BINDING OR DRILL.
A light material for covering bows and pads on car hoods. In Colours: Khaki and Grey, and Black and White. 72 in. wide.

### HOOD WEBBING.
Grey or Khaki, Black and White. .. 2 in. wide.

### HIDEM OR CONCEALED BINDING.
A binding when fixed does not show any tacks. In Colours: Bright and Dull Black, also Red, Brown, Green, and Blue.

### CANVAS HOOD MATERIAL.
Waterproof. Colours: Lavender and Khaki. .. 72 in. wide.

### CROCKETT'S DUCK.
For buggy hoods, or for upholstery covering. 50 in. wide. In pieces of 12 yards.

### TUFTING BUTTONS.
For Crockett's Duck on cloth. Colours: Bright and Dull Black, Claret, and Green. In packets of 1 gross.

### TRIMMING TACKS.
A large head tack used mainly for trimming. Bright or japanned. No. 6 x ½ in.; No. 8 x $\frac{9}{16}$ in.; No. 10 x ⅝ in.; No. 12 x ¾ in. shank x ¼ in. raised head.

### LEATHERMET NAILS.
A large head nail which has many uses in any household. In packets of 1,000. ¾ in. shank, ⅝ in. head. Colours: Black, Green, Brown, Tan, and Grey.
As above, in packets of 50. ½ in. shank, ⅜ in. head. No. 96, Black; 4½, Maroon, No. 7, Tan; No. 9, Green; No. 12, Grey; No. 17, Blue.

## DRIVING BITS

No. 04. **POLISHED WILSON SNAFFLE.** Jointed Mouth. Full size; Cob size; Pony size.

No. 04. **N.P. WILSON SNAFFLE.** Jointed Mouth. Full size; Cob size; Pony size.

No. 06. **N.P. WILSON SNAFFLE.** Jointed Mouth. Full size.

No. 3660. **N.P. WILSON SNAFFLE.** Jointed Mouth. Full size.

No. 3660. **POLISHED WILSON SNAFFLE.** Jointed Mouth. Full size.

No. 2448. **N.P. WILSON SNAFFLE.** Jointed Mouth. Full size.

No. 2447. **N.P. WILSON SNAFFLE.** Jointed Mouth. Light. Full size.

No. 323. **N.P. WILSON SNAFFLE.** Double Jointed Mouth. Full size.

No. 211. **BRASS FLAT RING.** Jointed. Polished Mouth. Full size.

No. 211. **N.P. FLAT RING.** Jointed Mouth.

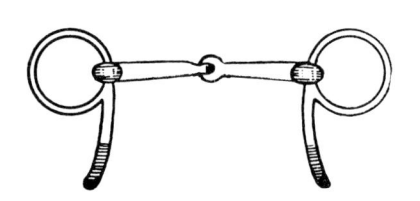

No. 661. **N.P. HALF SPOON CHEEK DRIVING SNAFFLE.**

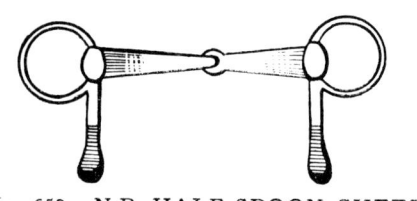

No. 659. **N.P. HALF SPOON CHEEK TROTTING SNAFFLE.** Taper Mouth.

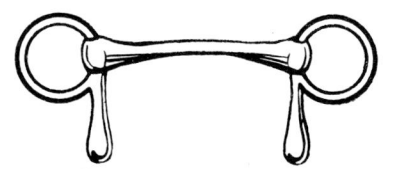

No. 662. **N.P. HALF SPOON CHEEK TROTTING SNAFFLE.** Mullen Mouth.

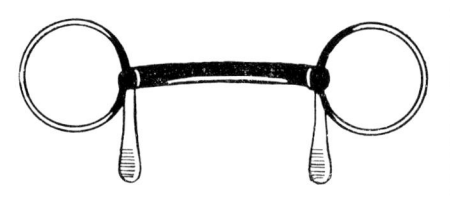

No. 768. **N.P. HALF SPOON CHEEK TROTTING SNAFFLE.** Rubber Mouth. Full size.

No. 809. **N.P. HALF SPOON CHEEK TROTTING SNAFFLE.** Rubber Mouth. Cob size.

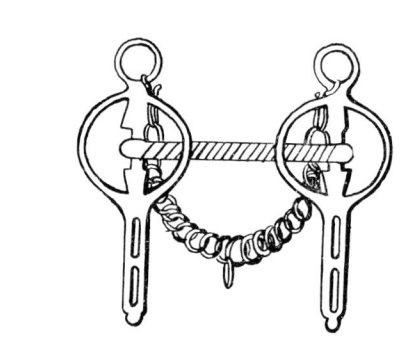

No. 25. **N.P. LIVERPOOL CURB, BIT AND CHAIN.** Bar Mouth. Gig size; Cob size; Pony size.

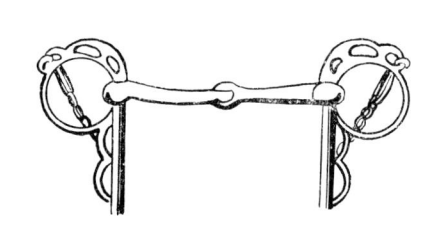

No. 1101. **N.P. SMITH & BEHREN'S DRIVING BIT AND CURB.** Jointed Mouth.

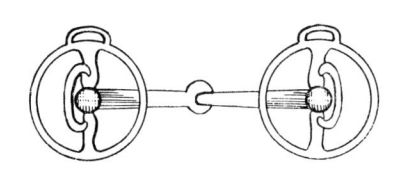

No. 1513. **N.P. LOOP ON CHEEK METROPOLITAN BIT.** Jointed Mouth.

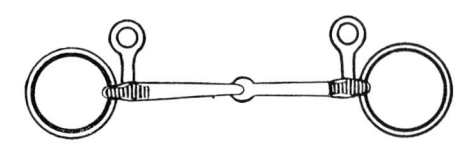

No. 666. **N.P. HANOVARIAN BUGGY BIT.** Loose Ring. Jointed Mouth.

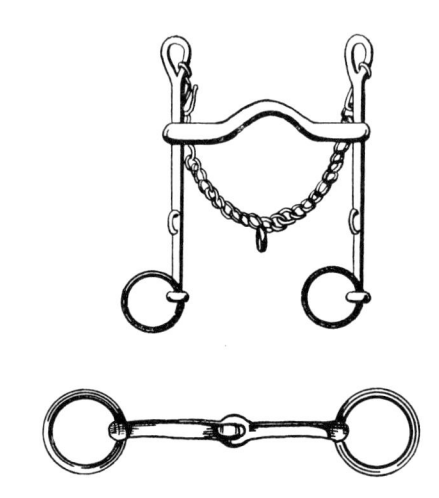

No. 22. **N.P. HACKNEY BIT AND CURB.** With Bradoon.

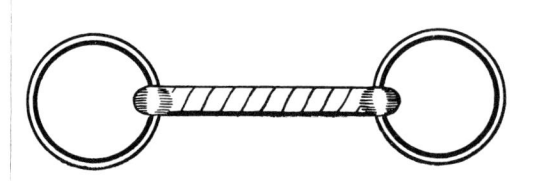

No. 1219. **N.P. STALLION BRADOON.** ½ in. Bar Mouth. Blood and medium. ⅝ in. Bar Mouth. Draught.

No. 2250. **N.P. WILSON'S SNAFFLES.** Bar Mouth. Stallion. Medium, ½ in. mouth; Draught, ⅝ in. mouth.

HARRIS, SCARFE, LIMITED.  HF 49

# RIDING BITS

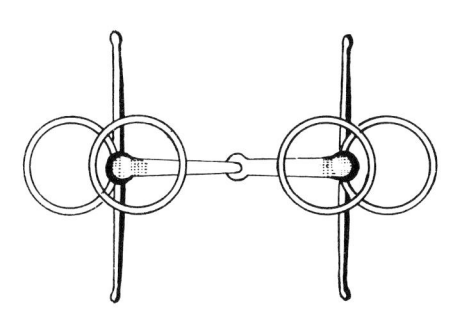

No. 239. **N.P. NEWMARKET SNAFFLE.** Jointed Mouth. Full size.

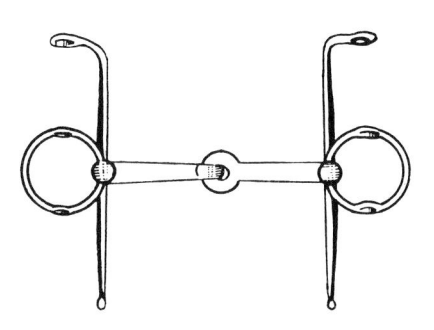

No. 241. **N.P. NELSON'S GAG SNAFFLE.** Full size.

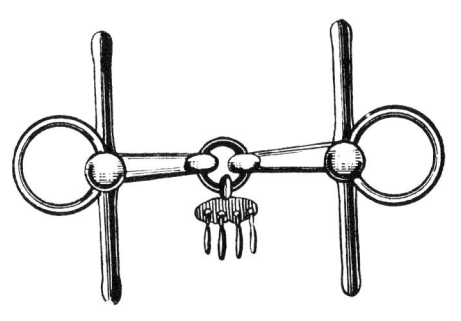

No. 182. **TINNED BREAKING BIT.** With keys. Without keys.

No. 192. **N.P. COLT RING.**

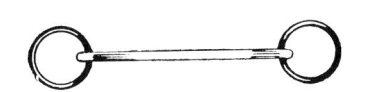

No. 321. **N.P. CHECK BRADOON.** For Trotters.

No. 1068. **N.P. GENT'S PELHAM.** Bar Mouth. Full size.

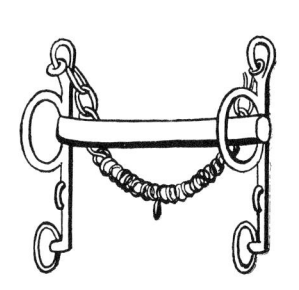

No. 1134. **N.P. GENT'S PELHAM.** Mullen Mouth. Full size.

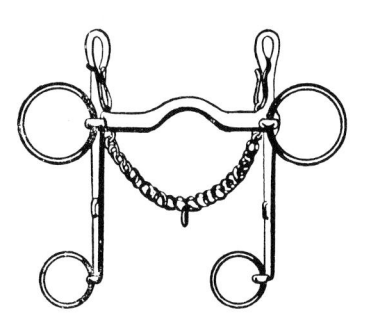

No. 231. **N.P. PELHAM.** Low Port Mouth. Pony size.

No. 243. **N.P. 9th LANCERS POLO BIT.** Low Port Mouth. 2 loop.

No. 1665. **N.P. 3 in 1 RIDING BIT.** Low Port Mouth.

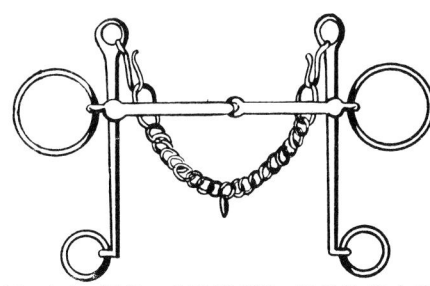

No. 75. **N.P. GENT'S PELHAM.** Jointed Mouth. Full size.

No. 74. **N.P. GENT'S PELHAM.** Jointed Mouth. Cob size; Pony size and Full size.

No. 242. **N.P. GENT'S PELHAM.** Jointed Taper Mouth. Full size. Short cheek.

**N.P. NOSEBAND BIT.** Bit only. Strapping extra.

# RIDING BITS AND BRADOONS

**A 50. N.P. BRADOONS.** Jointed Mouth, Wire Ring. Full size, 3½ x 7/16 in. mouth; pony size, 3 x 7/16 in. mouth; full size, 3½ x ½ in. mouth; full size, 4 x ½ in. mouth.

**No. 4838. N.P. BRADOONS.** Jointed Mouth. Wire Ring. Full size, 3½ x ½ in. mouth.

**No. 8730. N.P. BRADOONS.** Jointed Mouth. Wire Ring. Cob size, 3 x 7/16 in. mouth.

**No. 6407. N.P. BRADOONS.** Jointed Mouth. Wire Ring. Cob size, 3 x 7/16 in. mouth.

**No. 781. N.P. BRADOONS.** Jointed Mouth. Wire Ring. Full size, 3½ x ½ in. mouth; full size, 4 x ½ in. mouth; pony size, 3 x 7/16 in. mouth; cob size, 3½ x 7/16 in. mouth. Mullen, full size, 3½ x ½ in. mouth.

**No. 081. N.P. STEEL BRADOONS.** Jointed Mouth, Wire Ring. Full size, 3½ x ½ in. mouth; full size, 4 x ½ in. mouth; full size, 3½ x ⅜ in. mouth. Mullen, full size, 3½ x ⅜ in mouth.

**No. 1610. N.P. DOUBLE MOUTH BRADOON.** Jointed. mouth.

**No. 675. N.P. EGG BUTT BRADOON.** Turn Ring. Jointed Mouth. Full size, 3½ x ⅜ in. mouth.

**No. 753. N.P. EGG BUTT BRADOON.** Turn Ring. Mullen Mouth. Full size, ⅜ in. mouth.

**No. 1041. N.P. EGG BUTT BRADOON.** Turn Ring. Taper Jointed Mouth. Full size.

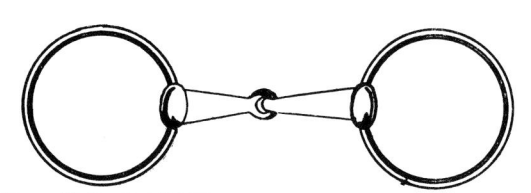

**No. 523. N.P. BARREL BUTT BRADOON.** Jointed Taper Mouth. 3½ in. ring.

**No. 771. N.P. RUBBER MULLEN MOUTH BRADOON.** Full size, ⅝ in. mouth.

**No. 1527 N.P. ON STEEL DEE RING BRADOON.** Jointed Mouth. Straight Butt. Turn Ring. Full size, ⅜ in. mouth.

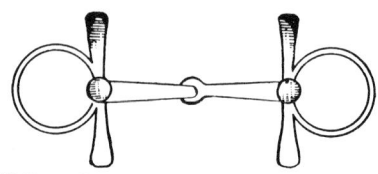

**N158. N.P. TOM THUMB SNAFFLES** .. Full size.
**No. 1008. N.P. TOM THUMB SNAFFLES** .. Full size.

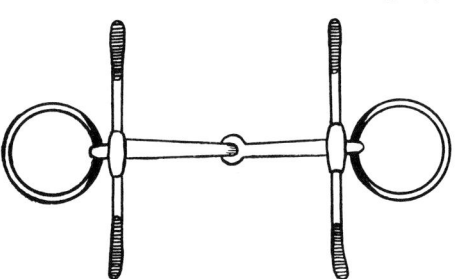

**No. 67. N.P. ON STEEL. SNAFFLE BARREL BUTT.** Full size.

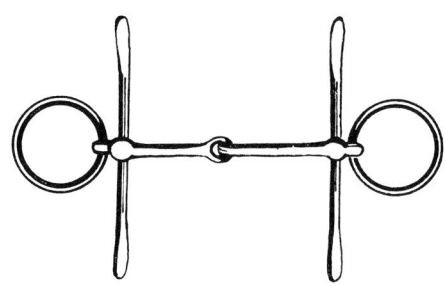

**No. 9002. N.P. JOINTED MOUTH SNAFFLE.** Full size.
**No. 9003. N.P. JOINTED MOUTH SNAFFLE.** Full size.
**No. 04. N.P. JOINTED MOUTH SNAFFLE.** Full size. 9/16 in. mouth.
**No. 04 or 1772. N.P. JOINTED MOUTH SNAFFLE.** Full size. ⅝ in. mouth.

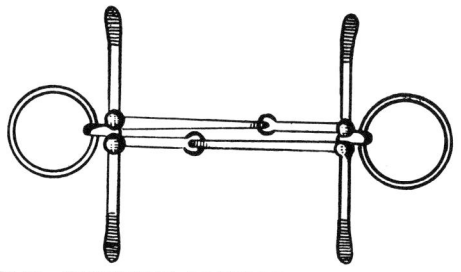

**No. 360. N.P. DOUBLE JOINTED MOUTH SNAFFLE.** Weymouth.

HARRIS, SCARFE, LIMITED.     HF 51

# SADDLERS' IRONMONGERY

## BUCKLES

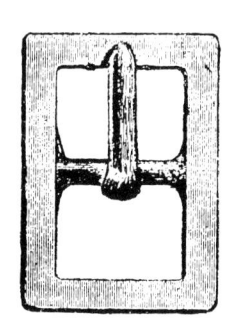

No. 4854. HARNESS. Nickel silver. Whole. Square. $\frac{1}{2}$, $\frac{5}{8}$, $\frac{3}{4}$, $\frac{7}{8}$, 1, 1$\frac{1}{8}$, and 1$\frac{1}{4}$ ins.

No. 4854. HARNESS. Brass. Whole. Square. $\frac{1}{2}$, $\frac{5}{8}$, $\frac{3}{4}$, $\frac{7}{8}$, 1, 1$\frac{1}{8}$, and 1$\frac{1}{4}$ ins.

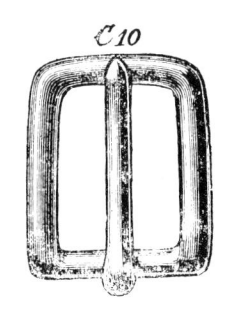

No. 3390. HARNESS. Nickel silver. Wire. Half. $\frac{1}{2}$, $\frac{5}{8}$, $\frac{3}{4}$, $\frac{7}{8}$, 1, 1$\frac{1}{8}$, and 1$\frac{1}{4}$ ins.

No. 3390. HARNESS. Brass. Wire. Half. $\frac{1}{2}$, $\frac{5}{8}$, $\frac{3}{4}$, $\frac{7}{8}$, 1, 1$\frac{1}{8}$, and 1$\frac{1}{4}$ ins.

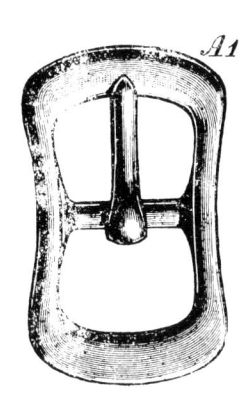

No. 5852. HARNESS. Nickel silver. Whole. Swell front. $\frac{1}{2}$, $\frac{5}{8}$, $\frac{3}{4}$, $\frac{7}{8}$, 1, 1$\frac{1}{8}$, and 1$\frac{1}{4}$ ins.

No. 5852. HARNESS. Brass. Whole. Swell front. $\frac{1}{2}$, $\frac{5}{8}$, $\frac{3}{4}$, $\frac{7}{8}$, 1, 1$\frac{1}{8}$, and 1$\frac{1}{4}$ ins.

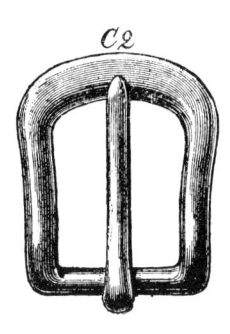

No. 5851. HARNESS. Nickel silver. Half. Swell front. $\frac{1}{2}$, $\frac{5}{8}$, $\frac{3}{4}$, $\frac{7}{8}$, 1, 1$\frac{1}{8}$, and 1$\frac{1}{4}$ ins.

No. 5851. HARNESS. Brass. Half. Swell front. $\frac{1}{2}$, $\frac{5}{8}$, $\frac{3}{4}$, $\frac{7}{8}$, 1, 1$\frac{1}{8}$, and 1$\frac{1}{4}$ ins.

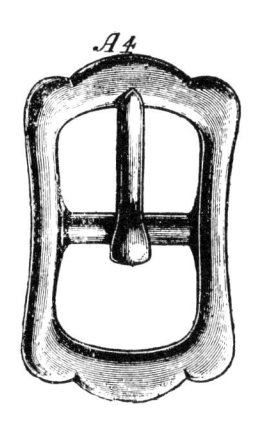

No. 2990. HARNESS. Nickel silver. Whole. Victoria pattern. $\frac{1}{2}$, $\frac{5}{8}$, $\frac{3}{4}$, $\frac{7}{8}$, 1, 1$\frac{1}{8}$, and 1$\frac{1}{4}$ ins.

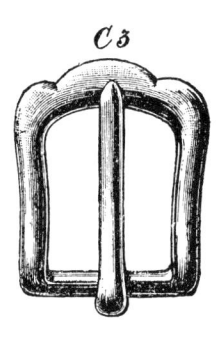

No. 2989. HARNESS. Nickel silver. Half. Victoria pattern. $\frac{1}{2}$, $\frac{5}{8}$, $\frac{3}{4}$, $\frac{7}{8}$, 1, 1$\frac{1}{8}$, and 1$\frac{1}{4}$ ins.

# SADDLERS' IRONMONGERY

## BUCKLES

*B13*

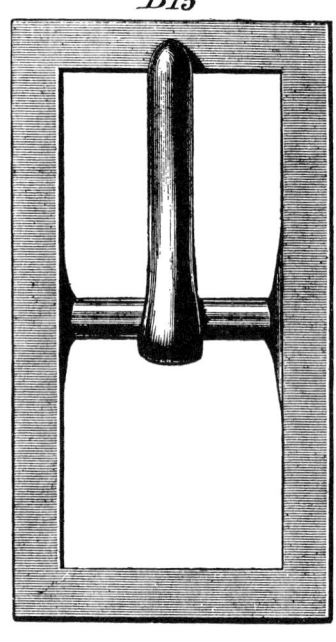

No. 4854. **TUG.** Nickel silver. Whole. Square. 1, 1⅛, 1¼, 1⅜, and 1½ ins.

No. 4854. **TUG.** Brass. Whole. Square. 1⅛, 1¼, 1⅜, and 1½ ins.

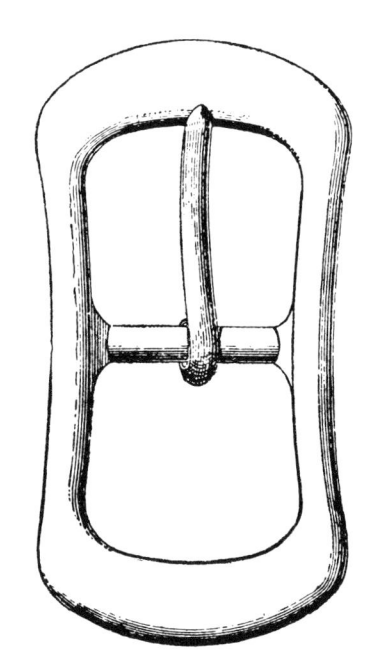

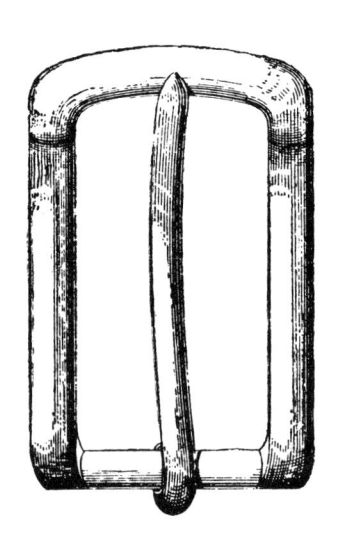

No. 3390. **TUG AND TRACE.** Nickel silver. Wire. Half. 1, 1⅛, 1¼, 1⅜, and 1½ ins.

No. 3390. **TUG.** Nickel silver. Wire. Half. 1¾ and 2 ins.

No. 3390. **TUG AND TRACE.** Brass. Wire. Half. 1, 1⅛, 1¼, and 1⅜ ins.

No. 3390. **TUG.** Brass on iron. Half. 1½, 1¾, and 2 ins.

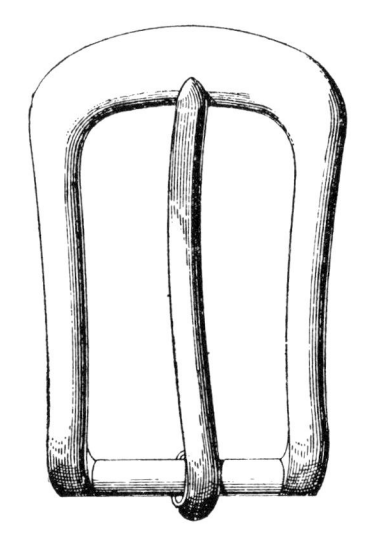

No. 5852. **TUG.** Nickel silver. Whole. Swell front. 1⅛, 1¼, 1⅜, and 1½ ins.

No. 5852. **TUG.** Brass. Whole. Swell front. 1⅛, 1¼, 1⅜, and 1½ ins.

No. 5851. **TUG AND TRACE.** Nickel silver. Half. Swell front. 1⅛, 1¼, 1⅜, and 1½ ins.

No. 5851. **TUG.** Nickel silver. Half. Swell front. 1¾ and 2 ins.

No. 5851. **TUG AND TRACE.** Brass. Half. Swell front. 1¼ and 1⅜ ins.

No. 5851. **TUG.** Brass. Half. Swell front. 1½, 1¾, and 2 ins.

HARRIS, SCARFE, LIMITED. HF 53

# SADDLERS' IRONMONGERY

## BUCKLES

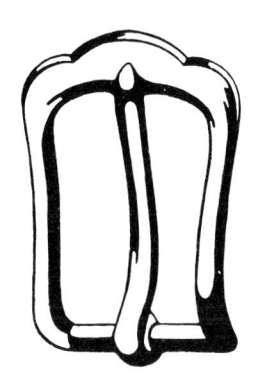

No. 2989. TUG AND TRACE. Nickle silver. Half. Victoria pattern. 1¼, 1⅜, and 1½ ins.

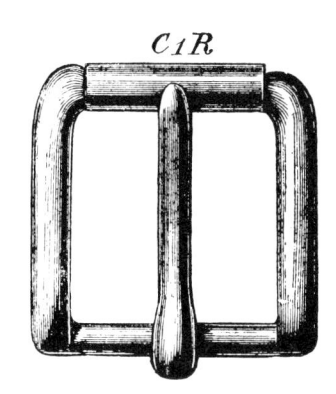

*C₁R*

No. 267. HARNESS. Nickel silver. Wire roller. ⅝, ¾, ⅞. 1, 1⅛, 1¼, 1⅜, 1½, 1¾, and 2 ins.

No. 267. HARNESS. Brass. Wire roller. ⅝, ¾, ⅞, 1, 1⅛. 1, 1⅛, 1⅜. 1½, 1¾, and 2 ins.

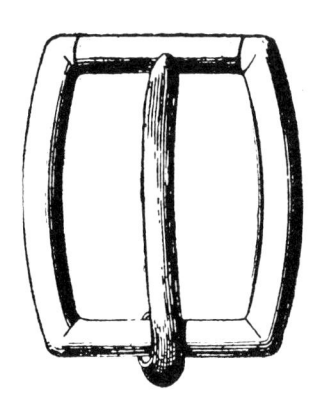

No. 1790R. BARREL POLEPIECE. Nickel plated. Nickel silver or brass on iron finish. 1¼, 1⅜, and 1½ ins.

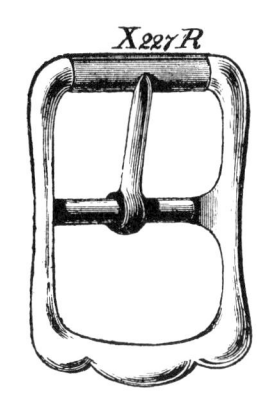

*X227R*

No. 6137R. BRIDLE. Nickel silver. Whole crown, roller. ⅜, ½, ⅝, ¾, ⅞, 1, and 1⅛ ins.

No. 6137R. BRIDLE. Tinned. Whole crown, roller. ½, ⅝, ¾, ⅞, 1, and 1⅛ ins.

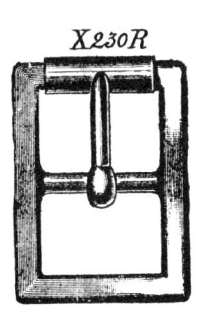

*X230R*

No. 6138R. BRIDLE. Nickel silver. Whole. Square. Flat top. ⅜, ½, ⅝, ¾, ⅞, 1, and 1⅛ ins.

# SADDLERS' IRONMONGERY

## BUCKLES

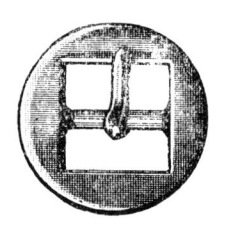

No. 020. CART. Nickel silver. Whole. ⅞, 1, 1⅛, 1¼, 1½, 1¾, 2, 2½, and 3 ins.

No. 020. CART. Brass. Whole. ⅞, 1, 1⅛, 1¼, 1½, 1¾, 2, 2½, and 3 ins.

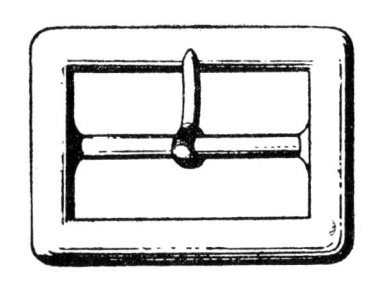

No. 538. BELT. Nickel plated. 1, 1¼, 1½, 1¾, and 2 ins.

## DOG COLLAR BUCKLES

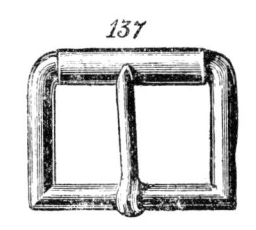

No. 2128. Nickel plated. ½, ⅝, ¾, ⅞, 1, 1⅛, 1¼, and 1½ ins.

No. 2128. Brass. ½, ⅝, ¾, ⅞, 1, 1⅛, 1¼, and 1½ ins.

No. 2128. Tinned. ½, ⅝, ¾, ⅞, 1, 1⅛, 1¼, and 1½ ins.

## GIRTH BUCKLES

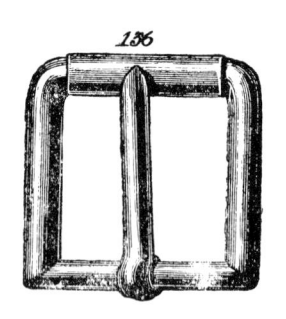

PLAIN. Tinned .. .. .. .. Size, 1 in
PLAIN. Steel. For race girths .. Sizes, ¾ and ⅞ in.

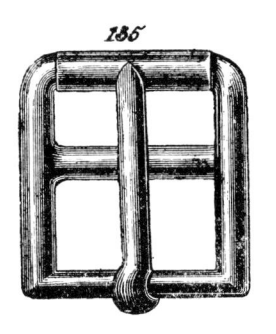

BARRED. Tinned .. .. .. Size, 1 in
BARRED. Nickel plated .. .. .. Size, ¾ in.

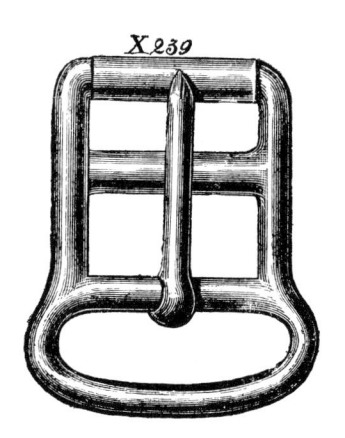

BARRED WITH LOOP. Tinned. Barred. 1½ in. Loop 1 in

HARRIS, SCARFE, LIMITED.     HF 55

# SADDLERS' IRONMONGERY

### GAITER BUCKLES

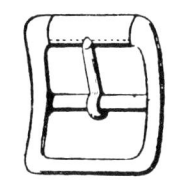

No. 0153A. Nickel plated. With roller. ½, ⅝, and ¾ in.

### INLET BUCKLES

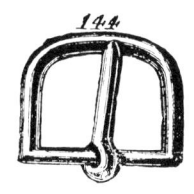

*144*

No. 504. Nickel silver, and tinned. ⅜, ½, ⅝, ¾, ⅞, and 1 in.

### STIRRUP LEATHER BUCKLES

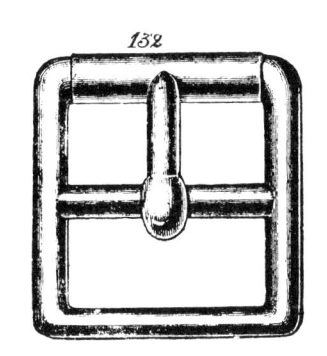

*132*

| | |
|---|---|
| POLISHED | ⅞, 1, 1⅛, 1¼, and 1⅜ in. |
| NICKEL PLATED | ⅞, 1, 1⅛, 1¼, and 1⅜ ins |

### BREECHING DEES

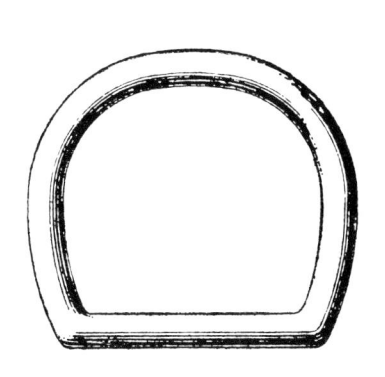

| | |
|---|---|
| BRASS. Deep | 1⅜, 1½, 1¾, 2, 2½, and 3 ins. |
| NICKEL SILVER. Deep. | 1⅜, 1½ 1¾, 2, 2½, and 3 ins. |

*A558*

No. 7724. TUG. Nickel silver and brass. ⅝, ¾, ⅞, and 1 in

### SADDLE DEES

*120*

| | |
|---|---|
| NICKEL PLATED | ⅝, ¾, and 1 in. |
| BURNISHED TINNED | ⅝, ¾, ⅞, and 1 in. |
| BURNISHED TINNED, STOUT | 1 in. only |

U 8

# SADDLERS' IRONMONGERY

## DOG COLLAR DEES

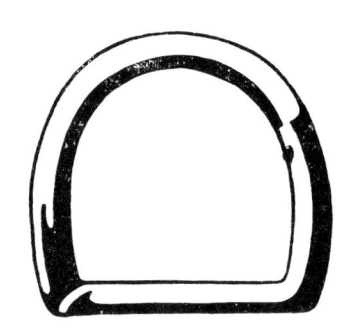

**NICKEL PLATED.** Stout　　..　　1, 1⅛, 1¼, and 1½ ins.
**BRASS.**　　..　　½, ⅝, ¾, ⅞, 1, 1⅛, 1¼, 1½, and 1¾ ins.

## FLAP LOOPS

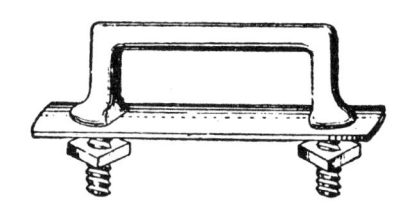

**PLAIN WIRE.** Nickel silver and brass.　1, 1⅛, 1¼, 1⅜, and 1½ ins.

## TUG LOOPS

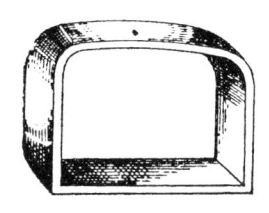

**No. 311S.** Nickel silver　..　..　1¼, 1½, 1¾, and 2 ins.
**No. 311S.** Brass　..　..　..　1½, 1¾. and 2 ins.

**TO RIVET.** Nickel silver and brass　..　1½, 1¾, and 2 ins.

## BREECHING RINGS

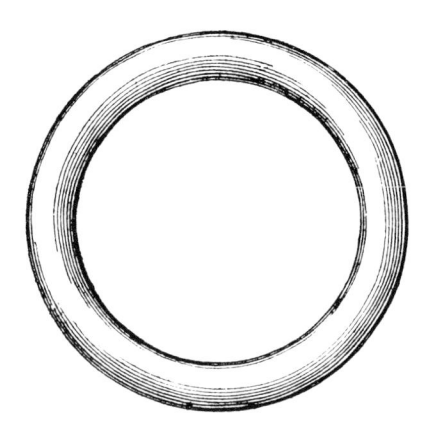

**NICKEL SILVER**　..　1, 1⅛, 1¼, 1⅜, 1½, 1¾, 2, 2½, and 3 ins.
**BRASS**　..　..　1¼, 1⅜, 1½, 1¾, 2, 2½, and 3 ins.

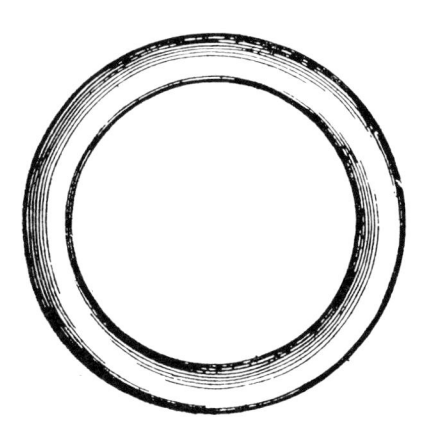

**TINNED**　..　..　..　1½, 1¾, and 2 ins.

## MARTINGALE RINGS

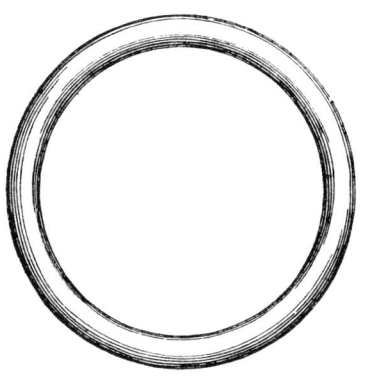

**NICKEL SILVER**　.　⅝, ¾, ⅞, 1, 1⅛, 1¼, 1⅜, 1½ and 1¾ ins.
**TINNED**　..　..　⅝, ¾, ⅞, 1, 1⅛, 1¼, 1⅜, 1½, and 1¾ ins.

HARRIS, SCARFE, LIMITED. HF 57

# SADDLERS' IRONMONGERY

## SADDLE STAPLES

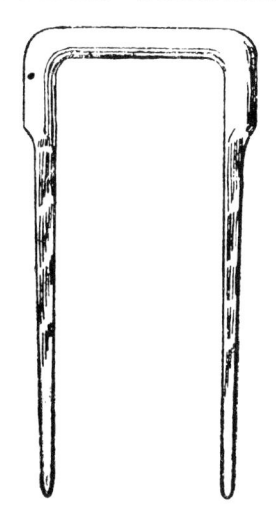

No. 6310. Nickel plated Race. Sizes ⅝ x 2 ins., ¾ x 2¼, ⅞ x 2¼, and 1 x 2¼ ins.

TINNED.    Sizes ¾ x 2¼, ⅞ x 2¼, and 1 x 2¼.

## STAPLE PLATES

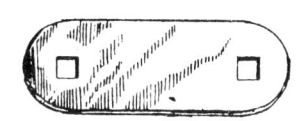

NICKEL PLATED    ¾, ⅞, and 1 in.

## ROSETTES

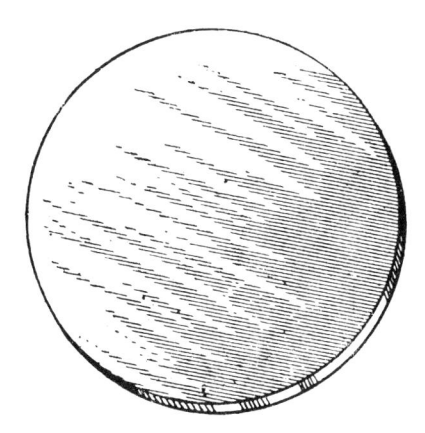

No. 657. Plain. Nickel silver.    1½, 1¾, 2, and 2¼ ins.
No. 657. Plain. Brass    1½, 1¾, 2, and 2¼ ins.

## ROSETTES

No. 3621    Fancy Brass    1½, 1¾, 2, and 2¼ ins.

## OVALS

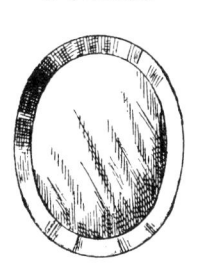

NICKEL SILVER    ⅞, 1, 1¼, 1½, 1¾, and 2 ins.
BRASS    ⅞, 1, 1¼, 1½, 1¾, 2, 2¼, and 2½ ins.

## CIRCLES AND KNOBS

BRASS    1⅛, 1¼, 1½, and 1¾ ins.

HF 58  HARRIS, SCARFE, LIMITED.

# SADDLERS' IRONMONGERY

## FACEPIECES

No. 2563. Fancy pattern. Brass or nickel silver finish.

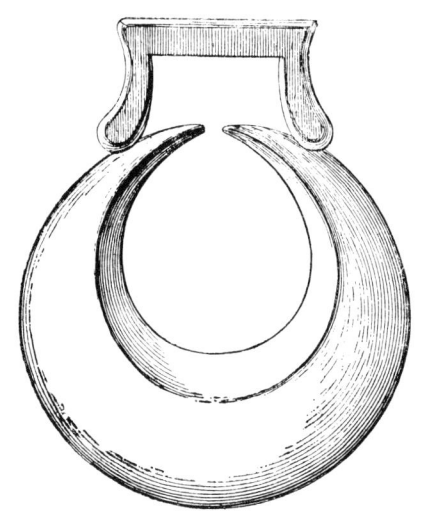

No. 1172. Crescent pattern. Brass or nickel silver finish.

## FACEPIECE STUDS

| No. 3177. | Nickel silver | .. | ⅜, ½, ⅝, ¾, and ⅞ ins. |
| No. 3177. | Brass | .. .. | ⅜, ½, ⅝, ¾, and ⅞ ins. |

## NOSEPIECES

No. 7482. .. .. .. Brass or nickel silver.

## TERRETS

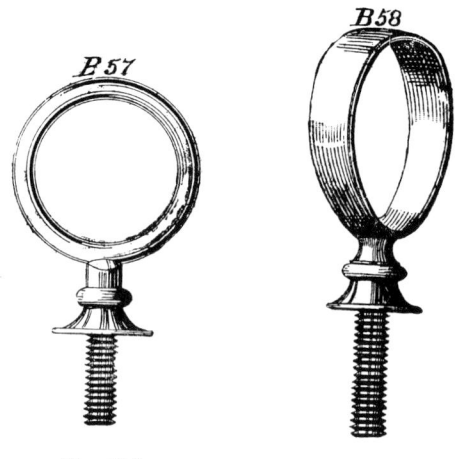

No. 806.  No. 4297.

| No. 806. | Nickel silver. Plain. | 1½, 1⅝, 1¾, and 1⅞ ins. |
| No. 806. | Brass. Plain .. | 1½, 1⅝, 1¾, and 1⅞ ins. |
| No. 4297. | Nickel silver. Plain swage. | 1⅝, 1¾, 1⅞, and 2 ins. |
| No. 4297. | Brass. Plain swage. .. | 1⅝, 1¾, and 1⅞ ins. |

No. 537.

SPRING CART. Plain swage with bridge sockets. Brass. 1⅞ and 2 ins.

SPRING CART. Plain wire with bridge sockets. Brass. 1⅞ and 2 ins.

No. 537. Square. Nickel silver or brass. 1⅝ and 1¾ ins.

HARRIS, SCARFE, LIMITED — HF 59

# SADDLERS' IRONMONGERY

**TERRETS**

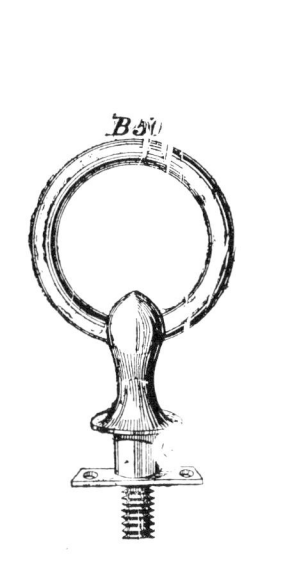

No. 1233.

No. 2454. One Bell.

No. 2454. Two Bell.

No. 2454. Three Bell.

No. 1233. Wire Bell. Nickel silver .. $1\frac{5}{8}$, $1\frac{3}{4}$, and $1\frac{7}{8}$ ins.

No. 2454. Single Bell Terret. .. Brass or nickel silver.

No. 2454. Two and Three Bell. Nickel silver or brass.

**PAD HOOKS**

No. 1158. .. .. .. Nickel silver and brass

HF 60　　　　　　　HARRIS, SCARFE, LIMITED.

# SADDLERS' IRONMONGERY

## BEADED NAILS

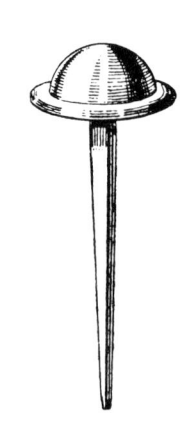

No. **3165.** Nickel silver and brass. Buggy, express, gig, and cab sizes.

## SADDLE NAILS

**NICKEL PLATED.** .. Race, exercise, and stock sizes.

## CAB BOLTS

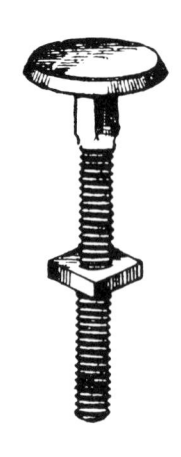

No. **644.** Nickel silver and brass. .. .. Size, ⅛ in

## CAB CANTLES

**NICKEL SILVER OR BRASS** .. .. Size 6 in

## FRONT CHAINS

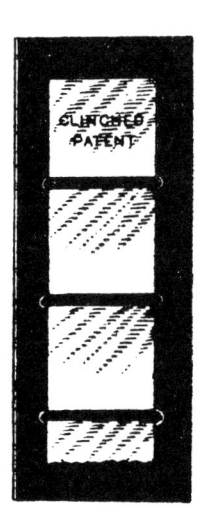

**CLINCHED.** On Patent Nickel silver on white, black, red, and blue. Brass on black.

HARRIS, SCARFE, LIMITED.  HF 61

# SADDLERS' IRONMONGERY

## GEAR WORK.

### BUCKLES.

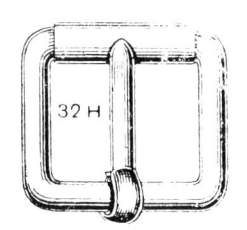

**No. 32.** GEAR. Japanned. Roller. ¾, ⅞, 1, 1⅛, 1¼, 1½, 1¾, 2, 2½, and 3 in.

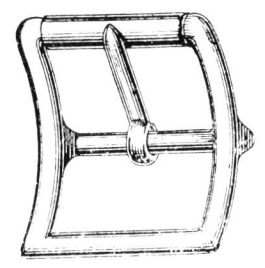

**No. 7.** HOBBLE BUCKLES. Japanned. Single. Roller. ¾, ⅞, 1, 1¼, 1½, 1¾, 2 in.

### BITS AND RINGS.

BITS and RINGS. Mullen Japanned. Jointed mouth.

### DEES.

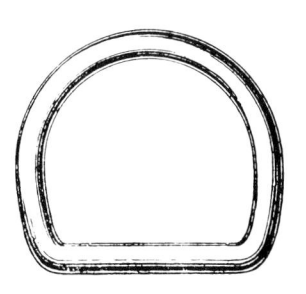

No. 52. GEAR DEES. Japanned. .. 1¼, 1½, 1¾, 2 in
HEAVY DEES. .. .. 2½ and 3 in

### RINGS.

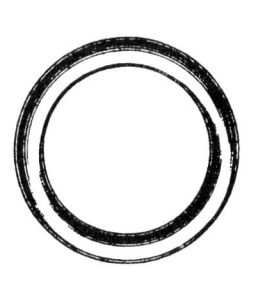

GEAR RINGS. Japanned. .. 1¼, 1½, 1¾, 2 in
GEAR RINGS. Japanned. Heavy. .. 2½ and 3 in

### CHAINS.

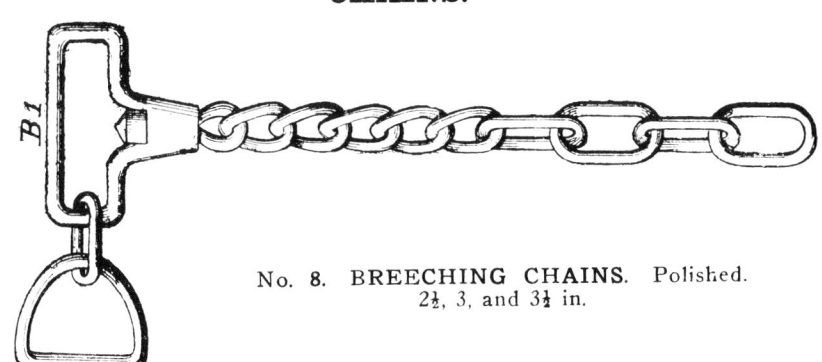

No. 8. BREECHING CHAINS. Polished. 2½, 3, and 3½ in.

**HOBBLE CHAIN.** Plain. Polished. 1¾ x 5/16 x 5, 2 x 5/16 x 5, 2 x 5/16 x 6 in.

No. 1116. POLISHED BREAST CHAINS. ¼, 5/16, and ⅜ in.

# SADDLERS' IRONMONGERY

## CHAINS

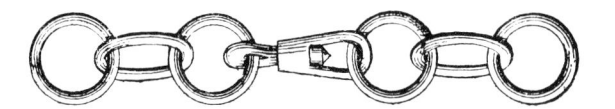

**SWIVEL HOBBLE CHAINS.** Polished. 1¾ x 5⁄16 x 5
1¾ x 5⁄16 x 6, 2 x 5⁄16 x 5, 2 x 5⁄16 x 6, 1¾ x ¼ x 5, 2 x ¼ x 5,
2 x ¼ x 6, 2¼ x ⅜ x 5, 2¼ x ⅜ x 6.

## GEAR WORK. CHAINS.

| | |
|---|---|
| **PLOUGH CHAINS.** Hand-made. | 8 lbs., 10 lbs., and 12 lbs |
| **PLOUGH CHAINS.** Australian P. & W. Electric welded. Tested Steel | 8 lbs., 10 lbs., 12 lbs., and 14 lbs. |

## LEADING CHAINS

| | |
|---|---|
| **LEADING CHAINS.** Australian P. & W. Electric welded. Tested Steel | 14 lbs., 16 lbs., 18 lbs., and 20 lbs. |
| **LEADING CHAINS.** Hand-made | 14 lbs., 16 lbs., 18 lbs., 20 lbs., and 22 lbs. |
| **LEADING CHAINS.** Jones. English. | 16 lbs., 18 lbs., and 20 lbs. |

## BODY CHAINS

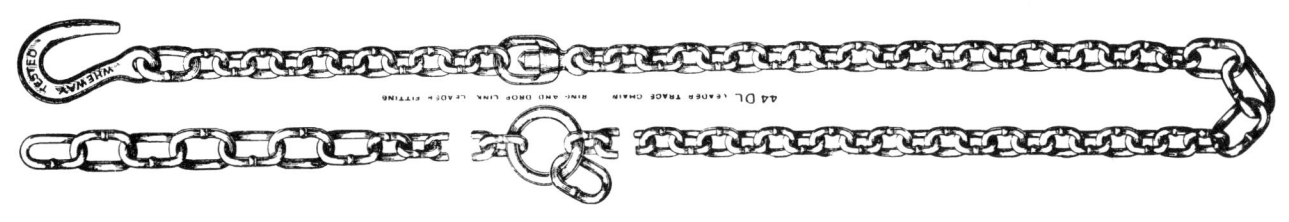

| | |
|---|---|
| **BODY CHAINS.** Hand-made | 17 lbs., 18 lbs., 24 lbs., 26 lbs., and 28 lbs. |
| **BODY CHAINS.** Australian P. & W. Electric welted. Tested Steel | 22 lbs., 24 lbs., 26 lbs., and 28 lbs. |
| **BODY CHAINS.** Jones. English | 26 lbs. |

| | |
|---|---|
| **BACK CHAINS.** Single link. | 4 to 6 lbs. |

# SADDLERS' IRONMONGERY

### GEAR WORK.  CHAINS.

SPRING CART, WITHOUT HOOKS.

TROLLY, WITH RINGS.

### TRACE END CHAINS.

No. 101. PLAIN TRACE END CHAIN. Polished. 1½, 1¾, 2, 2½, and 3 in.

No. 101T. TRACE END CHAIN. T end. Polished. 1½, 1¾, 2, 2½, and 3 in.

No. 11.  TRACE END CHAIN, WITH CURLED HOOK  ..  ..  ..  ..  2, 2½, and 3 ins.

HF 64          HARRIS, SCARFE, LIMITED.

# SADDLERS' IRONMONGERY

### GEAR WORK.     TUG CHAINS.

No. 110. PLAIN TUG CHAIN.    5/16 in.     No. 111. PLAIN TUG, WITH SWIVEL. Swivels: 5/16 and 3/8 in.

SPRING TUG CHAIN. 3/8 in.

No. 333. WHEEL CHAIN. 1/4 in.

### HOOKS.

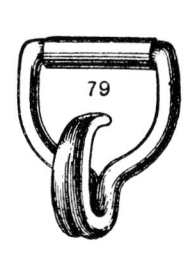

No. 79. BELLYBAND ROLLER. 1½ and 1¾ in.

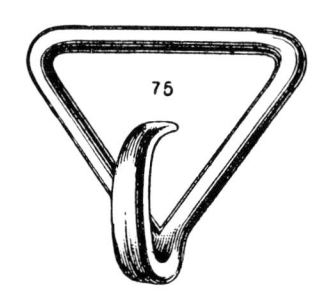

No. 75. BACKBAND HOOK 2½, 3, and 3½ in.

HAME HOOKS. Closed eye 1½ and 1¾ in.

No. 136. SWIVEL NECK STRAP. 1¼, 1½, 1¾, and 2 in.

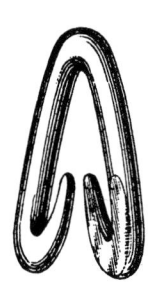

SPLIT LINKS. Polished. 1¼ x ¼, 16 x 5/16, 1½ x 3/8, 2 x ⅝, 2½ x ¾, and 3 x ⅞ in.

# SADDLERS' IRONMONGERY

## GEAR WORK.  SPIDER FITTINGS.

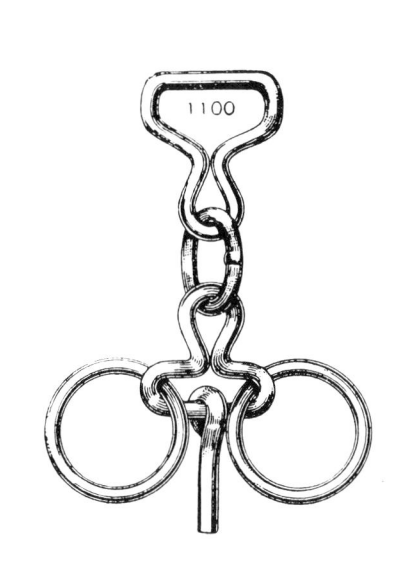

No. 1100. **LOOP LINK A1.**

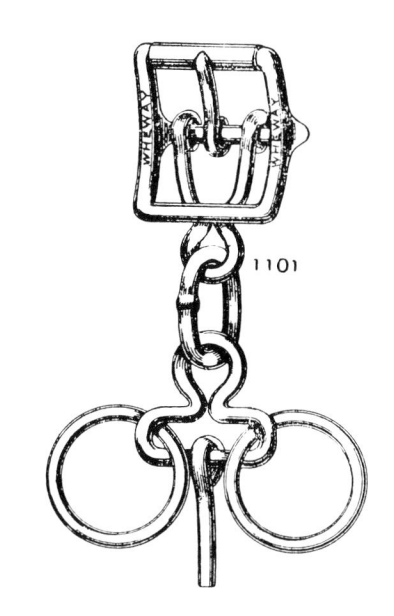

No. 1101. **BUCKLE LINK A1.**

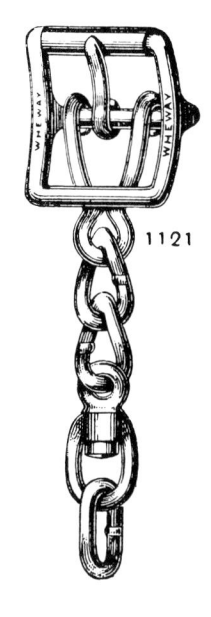

No. 1121. **BUCKLE CHAIN AND SWIVEL.**

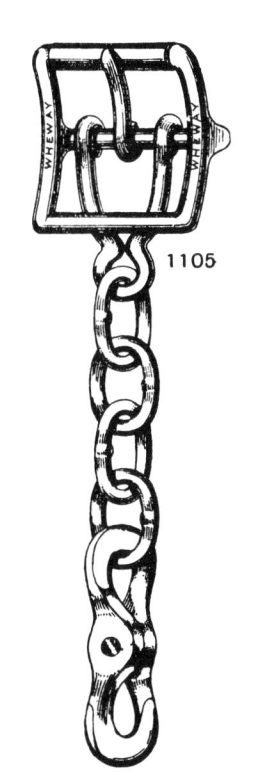

No. 1105. **BUCKLE CHAIN AND FIG. 8.**

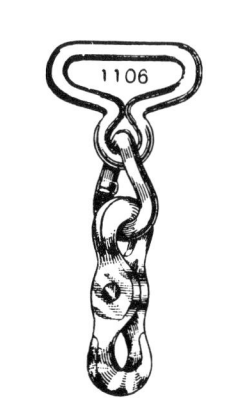

No. 1106. **LOOP LINK AND FIG. 8.**

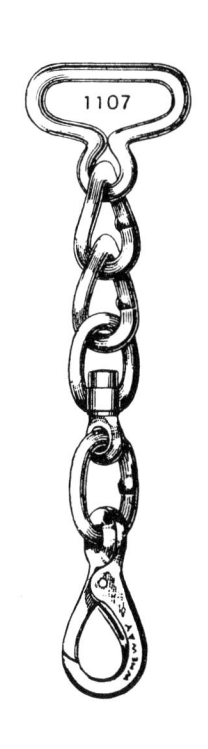

No. 1107. **LOOP CHAIN AND SPRINGLESS HOOK.**

HF 66          HARRIS, SCARFE, LIMITED.

# SADDLERS' IRONMONGERY

## GEAR WORK.    SPIDER FITTINGS.

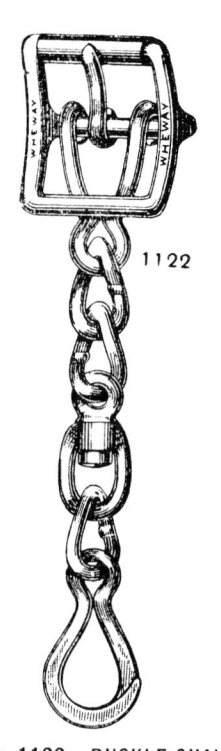

No. 1122. BUCKLE CHAIN AND SPLIT LINK

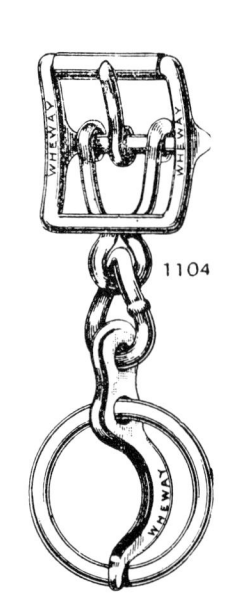

No. 1104. BUCKLE LINK, RING, AND TONGUE

No. 1123. BUCKLE CHAIN, RING, AND TONGUE

No. S61 x 1¾. LOOP LINK, RING, AND TONGUE

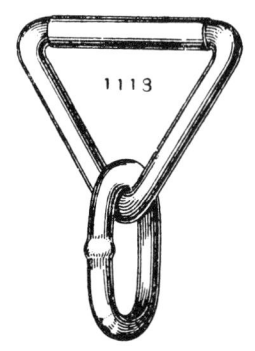

No. 1113 x 2½ x 3 in. TRIANGLE AND LINK FOR HARVESTER TRACES

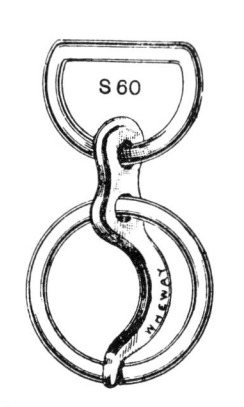

No. S60 x ¾. LOOP RING AND TONGUE. Holdfast

## MENDING LINKS

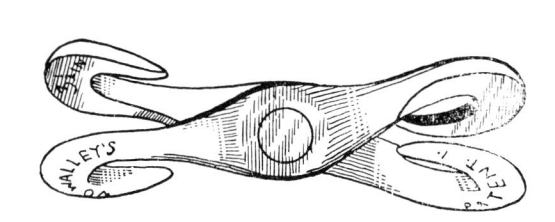

WALLY, OR FIG. 8 HOOK.

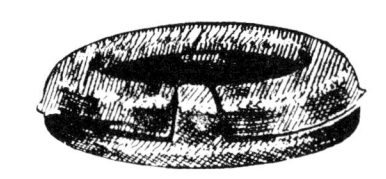

Patent Links for Chain Mending (Japanned)

| | | | | | | | |
|---|---|---|---|---|---|---|---|
| 1⅛ in. long | x | 3/16 in. | thick | 2⅝ in. long | " | 9/16 in. | thick |
| 1¼ | " | ¼ | " | 3 | " | ⅝ | " |
| 1½ | " | 5/16 | " | 3½ | " | ¾ | " |
| 1¾ | " | ⅜ | " | 4¼ | " | ⅞ | " |
| 2 | " | 7/16 | " | 4¾ | " | 1 | " |
| 2⅜ | " | ½ | " | | | | |

HARRIS, SCARFE, LIMITED.  HF 67

# SADDLERS' IRONMONGERY

**COVERT SNAPS.**

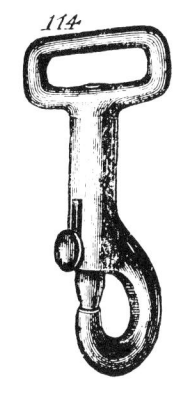

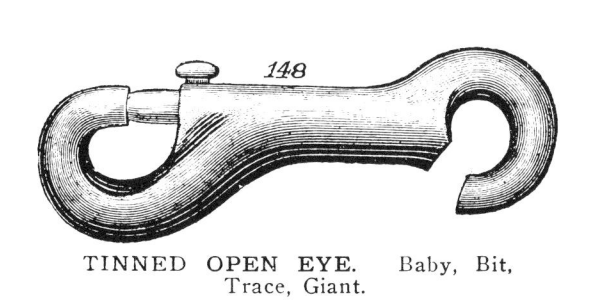

*114*

*148*

TINNED OPEN EYE.  Baby, Bit, Trace, Giant.

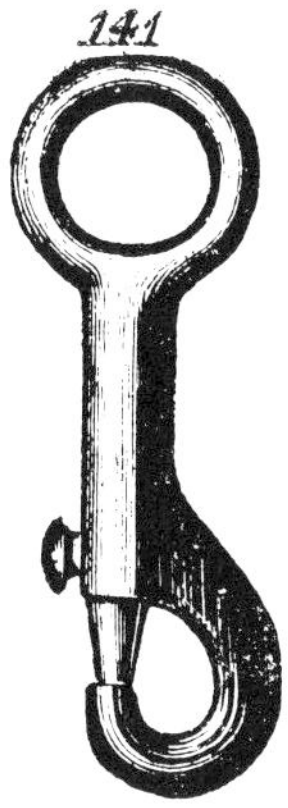

*141*

**TINNED SQUARE EYE.** ¾, ⅞, 1, 1¼. 1¼, 1½, and 1¾ in.

**TINNED ROUND EYE.** ⅝, ¾, ⅞, 1 in.

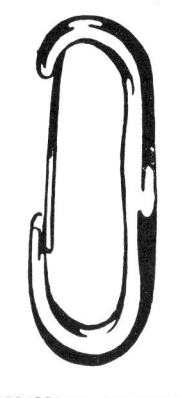

TINNED ROUND SWIVEL EYE
¾, ⅞, and 1 in.

**TINNED DERBY BIT.**

**TINNED LINK BIT.**

NATIONAL ROLLER. 1½, 1¾, and **2 in.**

# SPURS AND CHAINS

N.P. CURB CHAIN.

N.P. SPUR CHAINS. In pairs.

BURNISHES BIT. Leather back. No. 758, Single, and No. 501 Double Link.

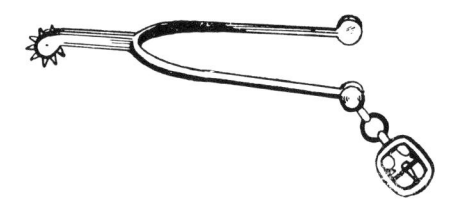

NICKEL PLATED STEEL RACE SPURS. $\frac{1}{2}$, $\frac{3}{4}$, and 1 in. necks. Upright and cross rowels. Assorted length necks.

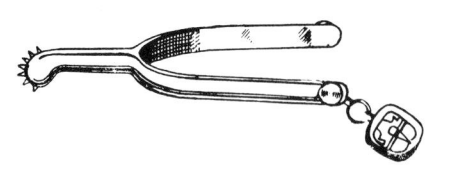

No. 5132. N.P. SPURS .. Assorted length necks.
No. 5139. N.P. SPURS .. Assorted length necks.
No. 5182. SOLID NICKEL SPURS. $\frac{3}{4}$ in. sides. Assorted length necks.
No. 5139. TINNED SPURS. Assorted length necks.
No. 5139. N.P. DUMMY POLO SPURS. Assorted necks.

All Spurs Complete with straps.

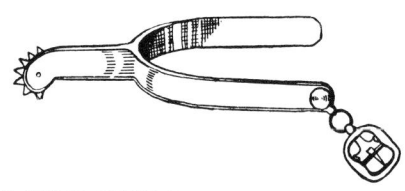

N.P. FLAT SIDE SPURS. $\frac{1}{2}$, $\frac{5}{8}$, $\frac{3}{4}$, and $\frac{7}{8}$ in. With straight and goose neck. Assorted length necks. Complete with spur straps.

N.P. DRESS SPURS. Complete with Boxes.
No. 529. N.P. DRESS SPURS, with Side Screw.
SPUR STRAPS. In Sets. Strap Leather. Kangaroo.
SPUR ROWELS. In Pairs. $\frac{5}{8}$, $\frac{3}{4}$, $\frac{7}{8}$, 1, $1\frac{1}{4}$ in.

# STIRRUPS AND CLOGS

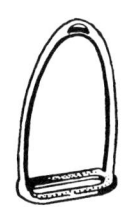

No. 8333A. Polished. Open bottom, Shook quality. 4 in. tread.

No. 8333A. N.P. Open bottom, Shook quality, 4 in. tread.

No. 8333A. N.P. Open bottom, 3rd quality, 4 in. tread.

No. 2145. N.P. on Forged Steel. Open bottom, 4 in. x 12 oz., 4¼ in. x 14 oz., 4½ in. x 16 oz.

N.P. Open Bottom Race Stirrups with flat bottom, 4, 6, 8, 10 oz.

N.P. Cradle Bottom Race Stirrups. 4, 6, 8, 10 oz.

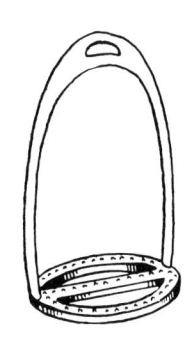

No. 8452. Polished. 3-Bar. Shook quality. 4¼ in. tread.

No. 8452A. N.P. 3-Bar. Shook quality. 4½ in. tread.

No. 8452A. N.P. 3-Bar. 3rd quality. 4½ in. tread.

N.P. 3-Bar. Straight side. 4¼ in. and 4½ in. tread.

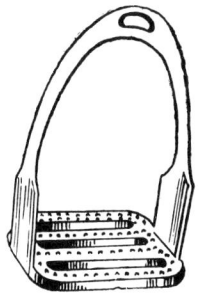

No. 1724. N.P. Simplex Safety Stirrups, 4, 4¼, 4½ in. tread.

No. 1724. N.P. Steel Simplex Race Safety Stirrups.

No. 506A. N.P. 4-Bar. 2nd quality. 4½ in. tread.

No. 4040A. N.P. 4-Bar. 2nd quality. 4¾ in. tread.

## SAFETY STIRRUPS.

Open.      Closed.

No. 21051. N.P. Scott's Patent Safety Stirrups. Reversible.
Gent's sizes, 5, 6, 7.     Ladies' sizes, 3, 4, 5.

### CLOGS, CHILDREN'S RIDING.
Basil, Bag Leather, Kip.

# BUGGY AND WAGGON LAMPS

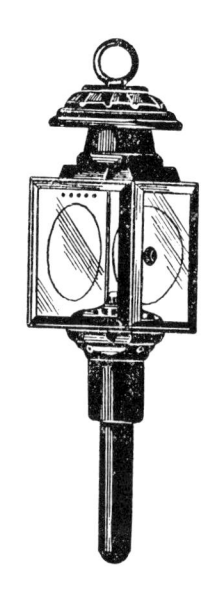

**No. 2104T. PONY AND BUGGY.** Japanned bayonet; wire fastening; bevelled glass. In pairs or R. and L.H.

**No. 2104T.** As above, with patent fastening. In pairs or R. and L.H.

**N35.** As above. Patent fastening. Pony and Buggy. In pairs.

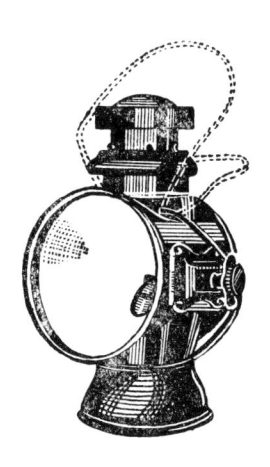

**No. 2108T. PONY AND BUGGY.** Bevelled glass; fiddle bell; N.P. patent fastening. In pairs.

**N2106. PONY AND BUGGY.** Bevelled glass; oval bell; patent bolt. N.P. In pairs.

**N26. PONY AND BUGGY.** Bevelled glass; shield bell; patent bolt. N.P. In pairs.

## EXPRESS CART OR TROLLY LAMPS.

| | |
|---|---|
| No. 1. | With bevelled glass. |
| No. 2. | With plain glass. |
| TAIL LAMPS. | With red glass. Regulation size. |

## LAMPS SUNDRIES.

| | |
|---|---|
| LAMP SPRINGS. | 12 x ⅞ in. Covered. |
| LAMP BARRELS. | 1, 1 1/16, 1 ⅛, 1 3/16, 1 ¼ in. |

**DIETZ UNION DRIVING LAMPS.** In pairs. Full size.

**DIETZ EUREKA DRIVING LAMPS.** In pairs. Small size.

Extra Fonts, Burners, Glasses and Frames, or Glasses only.

## CANDLES.

**BURFORD'S.** 8, 10, and 12 candles to 1b. In 1-lb. packets or 50-lb. case lots.

HARRIS, SCARFE, LIMITED.  HF 71

# WHIPS AND CROPS

No. 2335. **JOCKEY.** Steel lined and thread. Nickel mount.

DEALER'S CROPS. .. .. 2½, 3, and 3½ ft.

No. S1. **JOCKEY.** Steel lined and thread, turk's head mount.
No. S2. .. .. .. As above.

TWISTED WILLOW CROP. .. .. 3, 3½, 4 and 4½ ft.

No. S22. **JOCKEY.** Whalebone and Flax. Turk's head mount.
No. S23. .. .. .. As above.

No. 5713. **STOCK CROP.** Plaited. Steel lined and thread. Nickel mount.

No. 2686½. **JOCKEY.** Whalebone and Gut. Nickel mount.
No. 2713½. .. .. .. As above.

No. A7335. **STOCK CROP.** Steel lined and thread. Nickel mount.

**KANGAROO PLAITED RIDING FLOGGER.** Steel lined. 4, 6, and 8 plait.

**STOCK CROP CANE.** With plaited hand part and turk's head.

No. HA/1½. **POLO.** Whalebone and Gut. Turk's Head mount.

S111½ x 4 ft. **TROTTING.** Raw hide lined and thread.

No. 6326 x 4 ft. **TROTTING.** Whalebone lined and flax.
No. 5979 x 4 ft. **TROTTING.** Steel lined and thread.
S113½ x 4 ft. **TROTTING.** Raw hide lined and flax, with leather hand part.
**CANES. BULLOCK.** Approximately 7 ft. 6 in. long x 1 in. diameter, with root on end.
**CANES. NILGARI.** Approximately 3 ft. long x ¾ in. diameter, with knob end. Used for making stockwhips.

**STOCK CROP.** .. Kangaroo plaited, with turk's head.

No. 7068. **MALACCA CART CROPS.** 2½, 3, 3½, 4, and 4½ ft.

B913. **STOCK CROP.** Steel lined and thread. Leather hand part. Nickel mount.

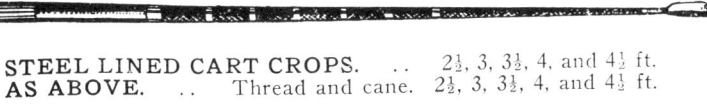

**STEEL LINED CART CROPS.** .. 2½, 3, 3½, 4, and 4½ ft.
**AS ABOVE.** .. Thread and cane. 2½, 3, 3½, 4, and 4½ ft.

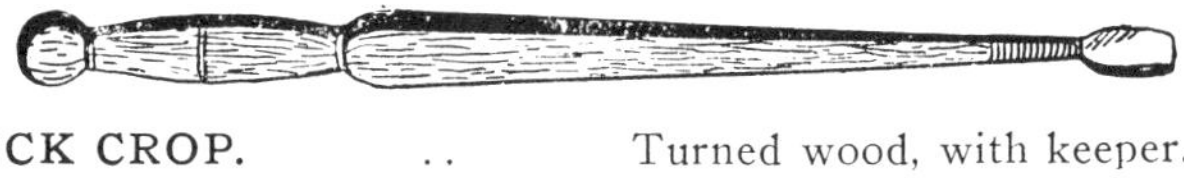

**STOCK CROP.** .. Turned wood, with keeper.

# WHIPS AND THONGS

BINDER CROP. Malacca. .. .. .. .. .. .. .. 7 ft. and 8 ft.

### WHIP CORD.

WHITE. .. .. 4, 6, 8, 10, and 12 dozen knots to lb.
COLOURED. .. .. 6, 8, 10, and 12 dozen knots to lb.
Each knot measures about 4 ft. 6 in.

CROP AND THONG. As above .. .. .. .. .. .. .. .. 7 ft. and 8 ft.
WHIPS. BUGGY. Straight top. Steel lined. .. .. .. .. .. .. Self hand part.

WHIPS. BUGGY. Straight top. Steel lined. .. .. .. .. .. .. Leather hand part.
WHIPS. BUGGY. French top. Thread and cane. .. .. .. .. .. .. With self hand part.
WHIPS. BUGGY. French top. Steel lined. .. .. .. .. .. With leather hand part.

# CURRYCOMB AND BRUSHES

## DANDY BRUSHES.

| | | |
|---|---|---|
| RENOWN UNION. | Brass wire drawn. | Colonial. |
| RENOWN UNION. | | Colonial Pocket. |
| No. 45. RENOWN. Kitool. | | Colonial. |
| No. 65. KITOOL | | Colonial. |
| No. 45. WHISK | | Colonial. |
| No. 1. RACIOR. Quill. | | English. |
| BONQUILLO. Kitool and Quill. | | English. |
| No. 1. INDESTRUCTIBLE. Kitool and Fibre. | | English. |
| XL. INDESTRUCTIBLE. Kitool and Fibre. | | English. |
| No. F12. Fibre. | | English. |
| INDESTRUCTIBLE. | Fibre. Colonial. | Glued. |
| MAGPIE. | Fibre. Colonial. | Glued. |
| BASSINE. | Fibre. Colonial. | Glued. |

## BODY BRUSHES.

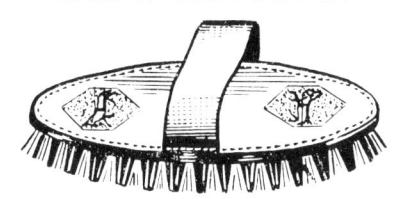

No. RA. Leather Back Body Brush. English. Excelsior hair. RD, DB, BC, A, RACIOR, H3, H4, H5, H32.

COMPO BRUSHES. In pairs or single. V45, V60, V52, V54.

No. 0106/10T. MANE DRAGS. .. With wood handle.

IRON MANE COMBS.
BONE MANE COMBS.
ALUMINIUM MANE COMBS.

## CURRY COMBS.

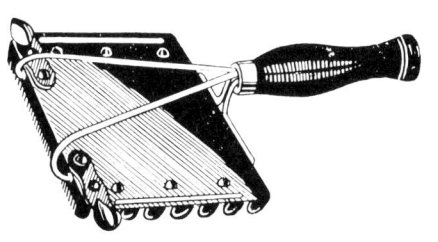

No. 0224. JAPANNED BACK SOLID CURRY COMB. 8 bar, with 2 knockers.
No. 0107B. JAPANNED SOLID BACK CURRY COMB. 8 bar, 2 knocker, with Mane Comb on back.
No. 0107B. JAPANNED SOLID BACK CURRY COMB. With Mane Comb and Brass Roller.

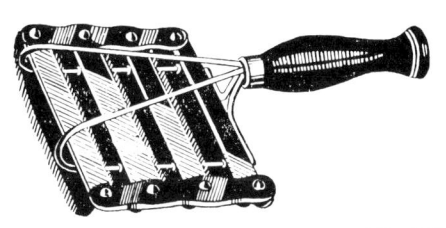

No. 0228. JAPANNED OPEN BACK CURRY COMB.
No. 0228. TINNED OPEN BACK CURRY COMB.

No. 043B. JAPANNED SOLID BACK THUMB CURRY COMB.
No. 043B. TINNED SOLID BACK THUMB CURRY COMB.

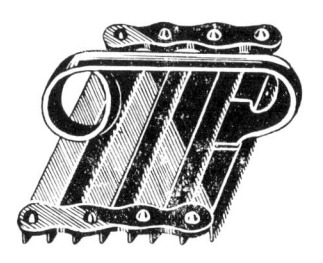

No. 0164. JAPANNED OPEN BACK CURRY COMB. Thumb.
No. 0164. TINNED OPEN BACK CURRY COMB. Thumb.
No. 49826J. JAPANNED. As above. .. Continental.
No. 49826J. TINNED. As above. .. Continental.
SPRATT'S REVERSIBLE CURRY COMBS. Spiral handled. 4 Coil.
No. 033C. COW CURRY COMB. 3 Bar, 2 Knocker, Wing Back, Half Round, Japanned. 6 in.
No. 0299. REFORM CURRY COMB, with Leather Strap across back.

# SADDLERS' TOOLS

No. 96. SADDLER'S SEAT STEEL.

SADDLER'S COLLAR ROD.

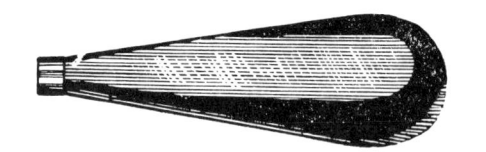

AWL HAFT,
BOXWOOD, HARNESS.
With Blade.
PATENT SCREW
SEAT AWL.
With Blade.

SEAT AWL BLADE. 3½ to 7 in.
STRAINING AWL BLADE. Assorted.

SADDLER'S HARNESS AWL BLADE. 3, 4, 5, 6, 7, 8 Cord.

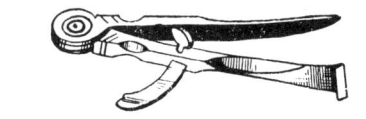

SADDLER'S COMPASS RACE.

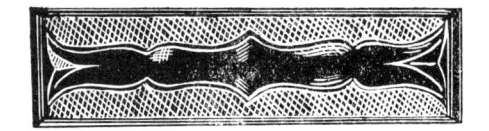

SADDLER'S LOOP DIE.

COLLAR NEEDLES. Half Moon and Straight. 4, 4½, 5, 5½, 6, 6½, 7, and 8 in.
PANEL NEEDLES. As above. Half Moon and Straight. 1¼, 1½, 1¾, 2, 2¼, 2½, and 3 in.
HARNESS NEEDLES. In packets of 25. 00, 0, 1, 2, 3, 4, 5, 6, and assorted 1-6.
SADDLER'S SHARP NEEDLES. In packets of 25. 3 and 4.
GLOVER'S NEEDLES. .. In packets of 25. 00, 0, 1.
QUILTING NEEDLES. In packets of 25. Assorted sizes.

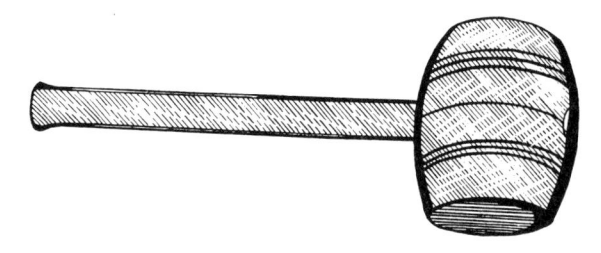

SADDLER'S PUNCHING MALLET. Lignumvitae. 2½ lb.

SADDLER'S COLLAR MALLET.

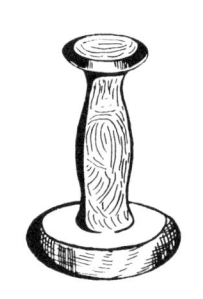

SADDLER'S SMASHER.

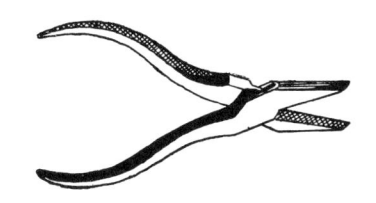

SADDLER'S PLIERS. Nos. 1, 2, 3.

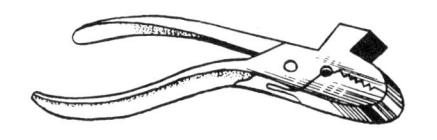

SADDLER'S BULLDOG PLIERS.
SADDLER'S BLUCHER PLIERS.

## SADDLERS' TOOLS

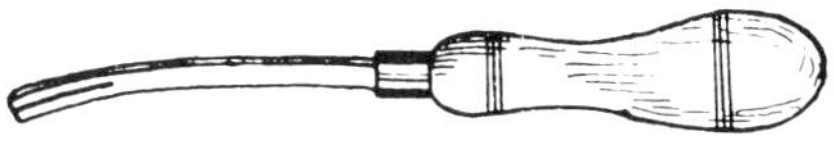

No. 83. SADDLER'S EDGE TOOLS. Nos. 1, 2, 3, 4, and 5.

No. 77. SADDLER'S SINGLE CREASE. Nos. 1 and 2.

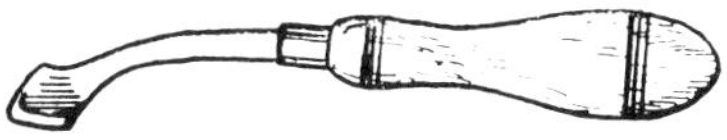

No. 78. SADDLER'S BEVEL CREASE.

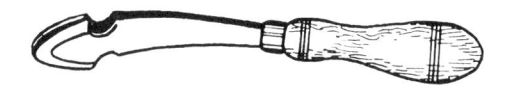

SADDLER'S SCREW CREASE.
No. 81. Small.   No. 82. Large.

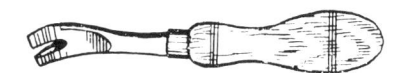

SADDLER'S NAIL CLAW.

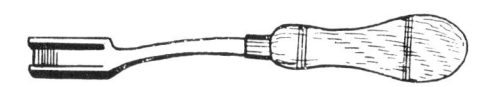

No. 108. SADDLER'S SKIRT SHAVE. Assorted sizes.

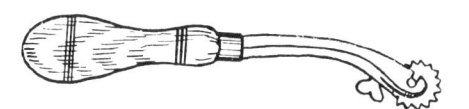

SADDLER'S OVERSTITCH FRAME AND WHEEL. Complete.

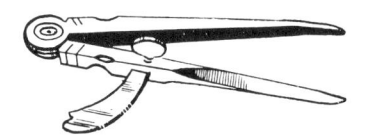

No. 117. SADDLER'S SCREW COMPASS. 6 in. and 7 in.

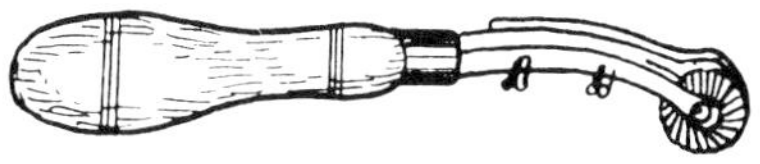

No. 167. SADDLER'S PRICKING WHEEL. Frame only.

No. 93. PRICKING WHEEL ONLY. Nos. 7, 8, 9, and 10.

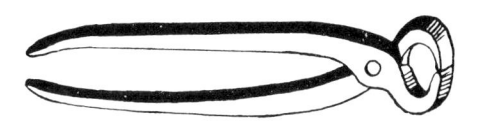

CUTTING NIPPERS. 6, 8, and 10 in.

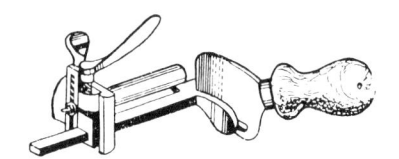

SADDLER'S PLOW GUAGE. Dixon's. Birch's. Extra Knives for Dixon's.

SADDLER'S SPOKE SHAVE.
No. 139. Large.   No. 138. Small.
No. 139. Large.   No. 138. Small.

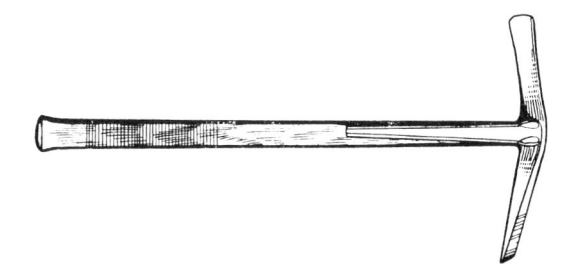

SADDLER'S HAMMER.
No. 101. Rosewood.   No. 99. With claw.

PERFECT STITCHER.

HARRIS, SCARFE, LIMITED.

# SADDLERS' TOOLS

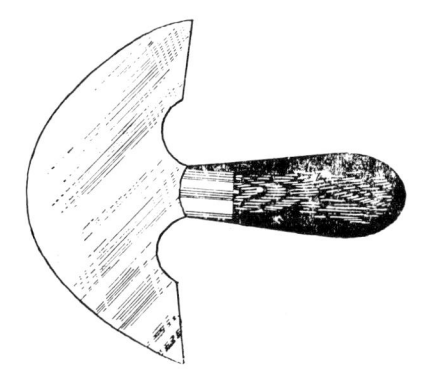

**No. 131. SADDLER'S ROUND KNIFE,** with flat handle. 6 in.

**SADDLER'S ROUND KNIFE,** with round handle. 5½ and 6 in.

**SADDLER'S DOUBLE HEAD KNIFE.**

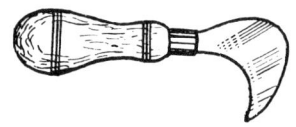

**SADDLER'S SINGLE HEAD KNIFE.**

**FRENCH HEAD KNIVES.** 4 in. x 2 in. blade, with curved end.

**SADDLER'S COLLAR KNIFE.** 6 in. blade, ¾ in. at handle, 1½ in. at end, 10 in. overall.

**SADDLER'S HAND KNIFE,** 4 in. x ¾ in. blade, with round handle. Overall, 7¾ in.

**DIXON'S ROUND LEATHER PUNCH**
Nos. 0, 1, 2, 3, 4, 5, 6, 7, 8, 9, 10, 11, 12, 13, 14, 15, 16.

**PUNCHES. BLECKMAN'S ROUND.**
No. 4965 x $\frac{1}{8}$, $\frac{3}{16}$, $\frac{1}{4}$, $\frac{5}{16}$, $\frac{3}{8}$, $\frac{7}{16}$, $\frac{1}{2}$, $\frac{9}{16}$, $\frac{5}{8}$.

**PUNCHES. ON CARDS. BLECKMAN'S.** Round. 1 each $\frac{1}{16}$, $\frac{1}{8}$, $\frac{3}{16}$, $\frac{1}{4}$, $\frac{5}{16}$, $\frac{3}{8}$.

**DIXON'S BUTTONHOLE.**

**DIXON'S OVAL LEATHER PUNCHES.**
Nos. 17, 18, 19, 20, 21, 22, 23, 24, 25, 26, 27, 28, 29.

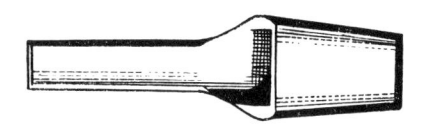

**DIXON'S CREWS PUNCHES.** Nos. 33, 34, 35, 36, 37, 38, 39, 40.

**DIXON'S TRACE PUNCH.** 1½ in.

**PUNCHES. DIXON'S WAD.**
$\frac{5}{8}$, $\frac{3}{4}$, $\frac{7}{8}$, 1 in.

**PUNCHES. BLECKMAN'S WAD.**
No. 4957 x ½, $\frac{5}{8}$, $\frac{3}{4}$, $\frac{7}{8}$, 1, 1¼, 1⅜, 1½ in.

HARRIS, SCARFE, LIMITED.                                  HF 77

# SADDLERS' TOOLS

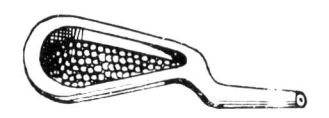

SADDLER'S PALM IRON.

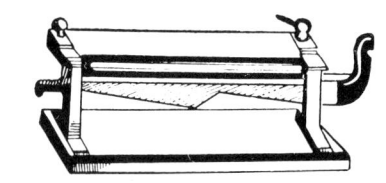

SADDLER'S SPLITTING MACHINE.
7 in.

### PLIERS REVOLVING PUNCH.

No. 384 x 4 tube.   No. 386 x 6 tube.
No. 24 x 4 tube.    No. 26 x 6 tube.

**BLECKMAN'S.**
No. 55089A x 4 tube.   No. 55089 x 6 tube.

**BARNARD'S.**
No. 186 x 6 tube.

### IRONS, PINKING.
DIXON'S. Half round.           $\frac{1}{2}, \frac{5}{8}, \frac{3}{4}, \frac{7}{8}, 1$ in.

### SADDLERS' RIVET SETS.
DIXON'S.

### SADDLERS' THIMBLES.
DIXON'S ASSORTED.

### SADDLERS' BELLY STUFFERS.
DIXON'S.

### SADDLERS' HOLLOW BONES.
Assorted sizes.

### DIXON'S SADDLERS' SEWING CLAMPS.

### WASHER CUTTERS.

**WYNN'S PATTERN.** Double Cutter to fit brace. Will cut washers up to $5\frac{1}{2}$ in. diameter.

No. $656\frac{1}{2}$. **MARPLE'S.** To fit brace. Rule marked. Double, with adjustable blades. Will cut washers up to 6 in. diameter.

**DIXON'S.** Double, with handle. Rule marked. Will cut washer up to 10 in. diameter. With adjustable blade.

**DIXON'S.** Single, with handle. Rule marked. Will cut washer up to 10 in. diameter. With adjustable blade.

**DIXON'S.** Single, with handle. Rule marked. Will cut washer up to 10 in. diameter. With adjustable blade.

No. 114. **DIXON'S COMPASS WASHER CUTTER.** Single. Will cut up to 16 in. diameter.

HF 78  HARRIS, SCARFE, LIMITED.

# Veterinary Instruments and Sundries
## SPECULUM.

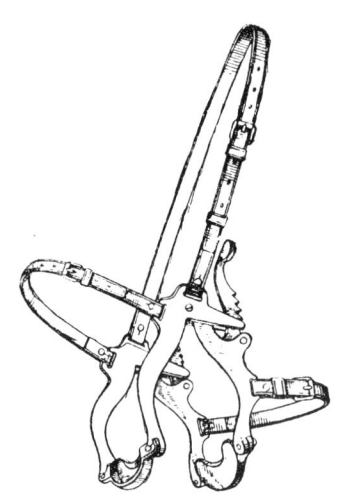

No. 1525. **CLIMAX SPECULUM.** With rubber covered plate No. 1703.
No. 1703. **EXTRA RUBBER COVERD PLATE.**

Showing Speculum in use.

## DRENCHING BIT.

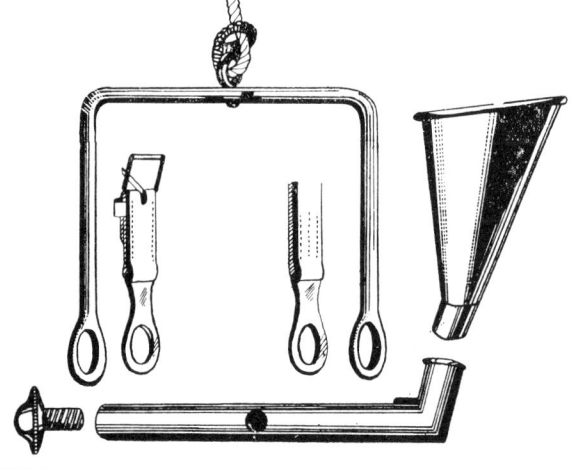

DRENCHING BITS. N.P., Cattle. Galvanised, Cattle.

## MOLAR CUTTER.

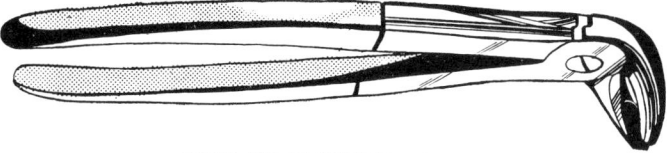

MOLAR CUTTER. N.P.

## PIG RING.

WOLVERINE. Small, medium, large. In packets 1 gross.

## PIG RING PLIERS.

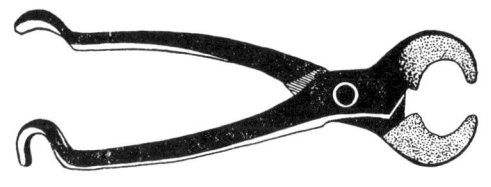

SINGLE.

DOUBLE.

## SHEEP TALLIES.

3 Figure.  4 Figure.

HARRIS, SCARFE, LIMITED.     HF 79

# VETERINARY INSTRUMENTS

## SAYERS' PISTOLET DRENCHING GUNS.

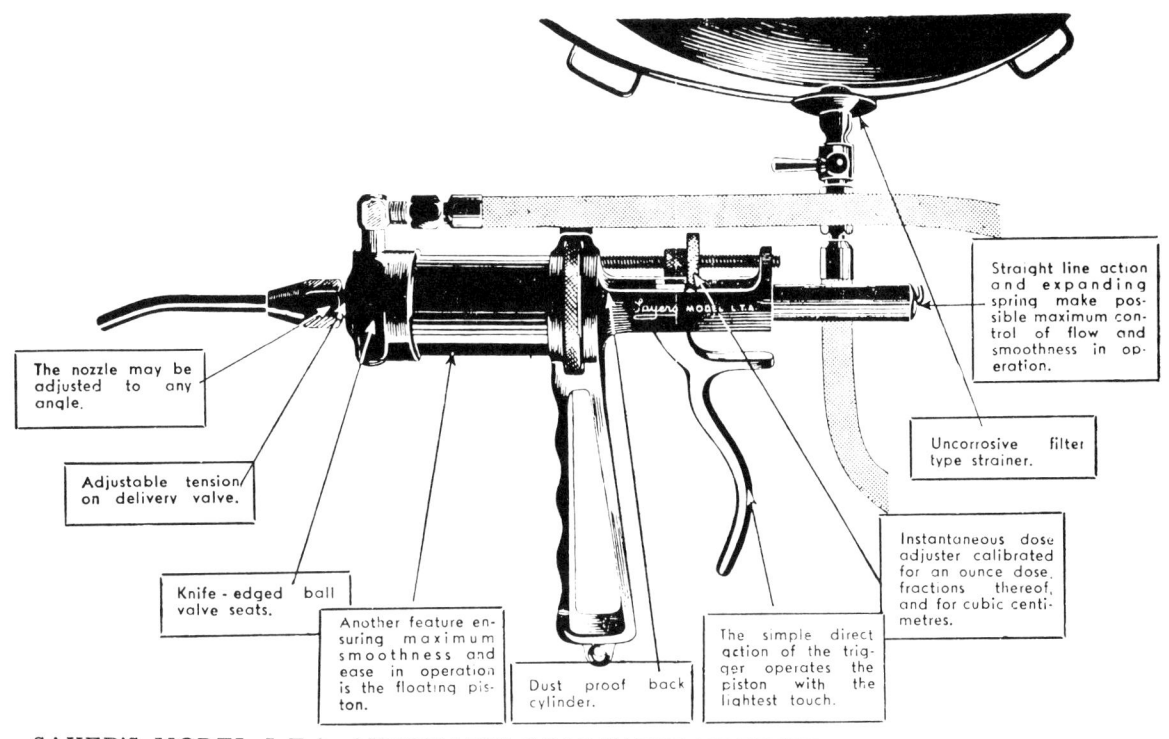

Labels on diagram:
- Straight line action and expanding spring make possible maximum control of flow and smoothness in operation.
- The nozzle may be adjusted to any angle.
- Uncorrosive filter type strainer.
- Adjustable tension on delivery valve.
- Instantaneous dose adjuster calibrated for an ounce dose, fractions thereof, and for cubic centimetres.
- Knife-edged ball valve seats.
- Another feature ensuring maximum smoothness and ease in operation is the floating piston.
- Dust proof back cylinder.
- The simple direct action of the trigger operates the piston with the lightest touch.

**SAYER'S MODEL L.T.A. AUTOMATIC GRADUATED DRENCHING GUN, FOR SHEEP, ETC.**

This Gun is an all purpose Drencher with which any dose from 5 c.c. to 1 oz. can be administered with perfect accuracy. It is solidly constructed of the very finest materials to withstand the corrosive effects of carbon tetrachloride, tetrachlorethylene, bluestone, arsenic, and nicotene sulphate.

The barrel is detachable, and there is not a single washer used in its construction. Every part is a separate unit, and all parts are interchangeable. They may be replaced should the necessity arise, at a very low cost. Complete as above, with Gun, Tubing, and ¾-gallon container.

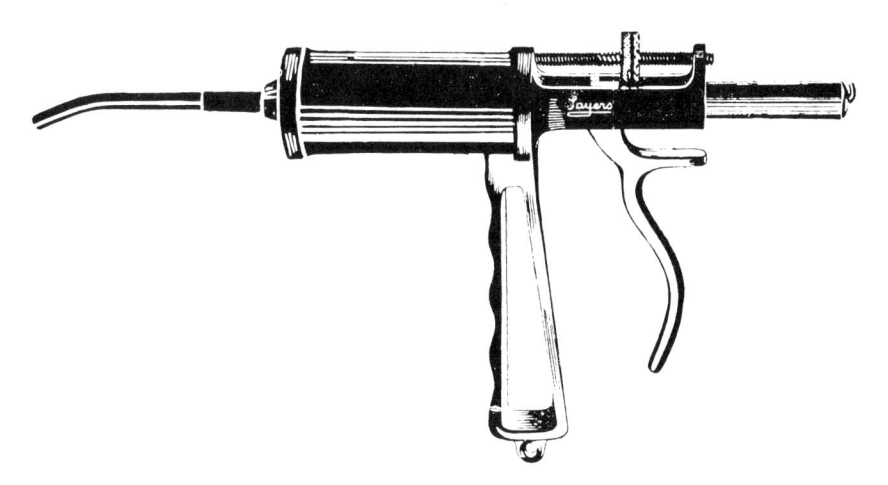

**SAYER'S. MODEL ZA PISTOLET.** Graduated Drenching Gun. For Sheep, etc.    ..    ..    Dose, 5 c.c. to 1 oz.

## IMPERIAL DRENCHING GUN.

A precision instrument that has all the advantages of the ordinary automatic type, but in addition has a number of other exclusive features. It is lighter and more compact; is simple to operate and maintain. The size of the dose is visible, and adjustable from 1 to 10 c.c. It can be used for all types of drenches, including Bluestone and Nicotine. Sheep can be drenched either facing or behind the operator, by a simple adjustment of nozzle. The whole outfit is well finished, with heavy nickel plating, and each outfit is supplied complete with gun, tank straps, neatsfoot oil and packed in neat fibre case.

# VETERINARY INSTRUMENTS

## VETERINARY OUTFITS.

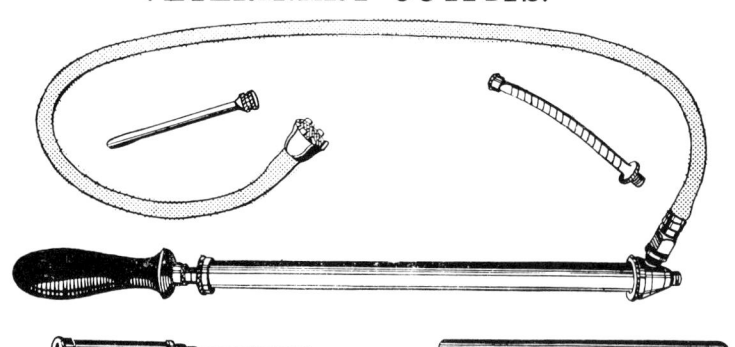

**REGA VETERINARY OUTFIT.** Complete as above, with self supplying injection syringe, metal cattle needle, bull needle, milk fever needle. With air purifiers, M. & F. flexible connector, strainer, and 5 ft. surgical rubber tube.

**No. 2. REGA MILK FEVER OUTFIT.** With air pump, purifier, metallic flexible needle, rubber teat, syringe, milking tube, teat expander, and absorbent cotton.

## SYRINGES.

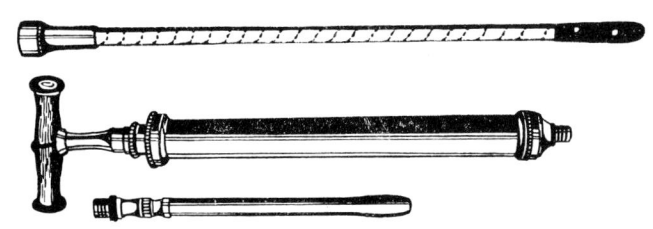

**CATTLE.** With flexible and metal needle. No. 8 x ½ pt.; No. 8 x 1 pt.; No. 8 x 2 pt.

## HORSE TOOTH RASPS.

**No. 4. HORSE TOOTH RASPS** .. .. As above.

**EXTRA FLOATS OR RASPS** for above. No. 7, Rasp and File. No. 7A, File. No. 7B, Rasp.

**DEWSBURY'S.** Horse Tooth Rasps with concave float. Extra Concave Floats.

## DILATORS.

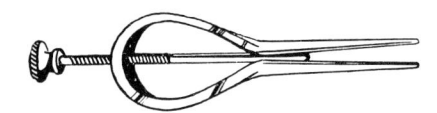

TEAT DILATORS
TEAT EXPANDERS .. Plunger and Screw type.

## BULL RINGS.

COPPER BULL.

| Sargent's. | Bleckman's. | English. |
|---|---|---|
| No. 21 x 2½ x 5/16 in. | 2½ x 5/16 in. | No. 4559. |
| No. 22 x 3 x 5/16 in. | 3 x 5/16 in. | 2½ x 3/8 in. |
|  | 3 x 3/8 in. | 3 x 3/8 in. |

## SPEYING NEEDLES.

## MILK FEVER TUBES.

## TRIUMPH PLIERS.

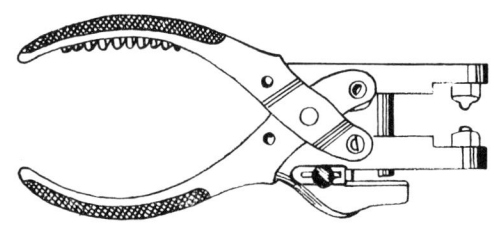

No. 190. TRIUMPH COMBINATION SHEEP EAR AND EYELETTING PLIERS.

## SHEEP EAR LABELS.

**HARD METAL.** Ordinary shape.
**ALUMINIUM.** New Eyeletted.

## SHEEP EAR PLIERS.

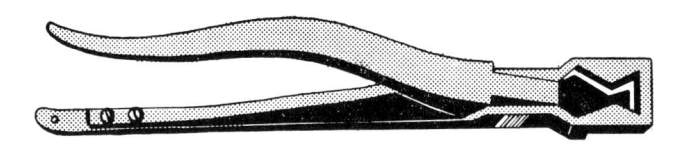

SHEEP OR CATTLE EAR PLIERS.

# VETERINARY INSTRUMENTS

### CALF WEANERS.

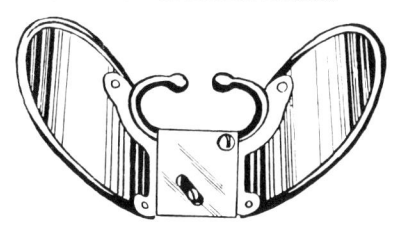

Small and Large.

### BURDIZZO PLIERS.

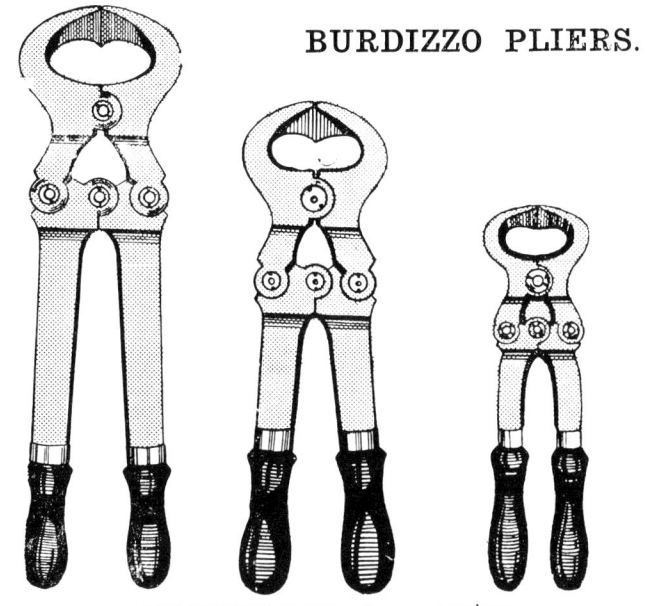

**BURDIZZO PAT.** For castrating.

| | | | |
|---|---|---|---|
| Small. For Lambs | .. | .. | 9 in. overall. |
| Medium. For Sheep | .. | .. | 12¼ in. overall. |
| Large. For Cattle | .. | .. | 17½ in. overall. |

### DEHORNERS.

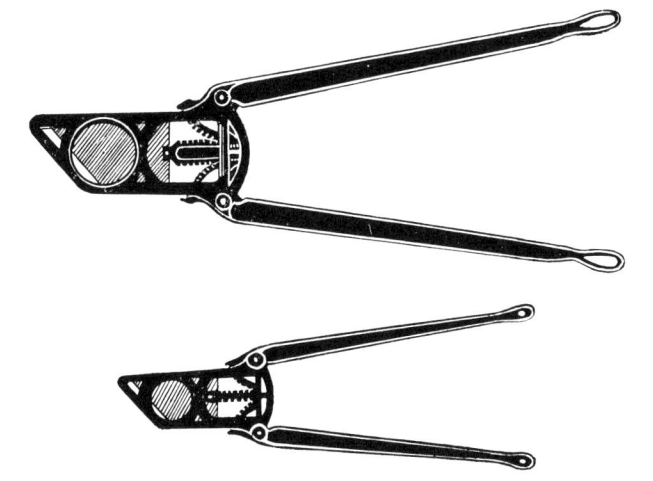

**NEWTON'S.** .. Draw cut. For Calves and Rams.
No. 1. No. 3.
Exert Knives, Nos. 1 and 3.
**H.S.L. PATTERN.** .. .. Small and Large.

### EMASCULATORS.

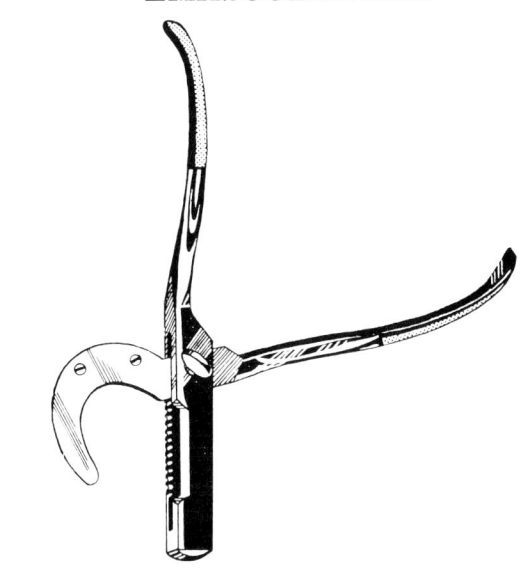

No. T5627. EMASCULATORS. .. Triple Crusher.

### TATTOO OUTFITS.

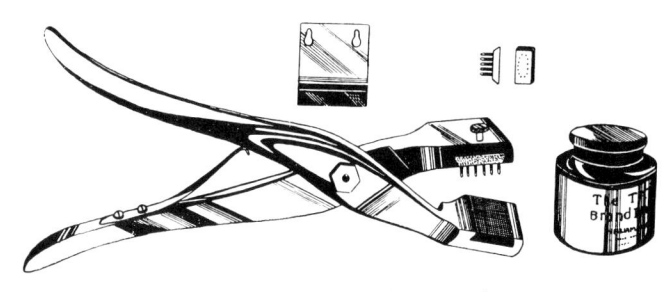

**TATTOO OUTFITS.** Complete.

No. 0. Four Figure. For rabbits, lambs, dogs, and small animals.
No. 1. Private Brand or Design. .. Short neck.
No. 2. Three Figure Brand. .. .. Short neck.
No. 2A. Three Figure Brand .. .. Long neck.
No. 3. Five Figure Brand. .. .. Short neck.
No. 4. Four Figure Brand. .. .. Long neck.
No. 5. Six Figure Brand. .. .. Long neck.

All above instruments complete with set figures 0-9; bottle ink, inkwell, and spacers; packed in fibre case, with the exception of No. 1, which is fitted with private design instead of figures.

**KATANA.** Three Figure. Short neck. Complete as above, with special brand.

**EXTRA LETTERS.** For above.

#### SPECIAL PIG BODY TATTOO.

**PIG ROOTER CLINCH.** This instrument cuts instead of ringing the pig's nose.

Extra bottles Tattoo Ink.

# VETERINARY INSTRUMENTS

## HORSE CLIPPERS.

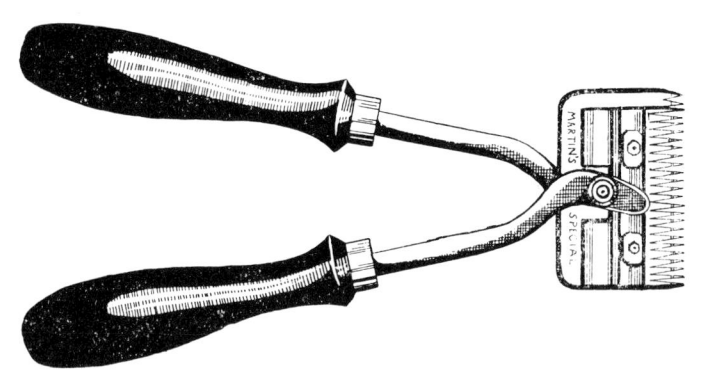

A. MARTIN'S. No. 1. .. .. .. Improved.
A. MARTIN'S. No. 11. .. With centre adjustment.
A. MARTIN'S. Special. .. .. .. Horse.
CLARK'S. No. 7. .. Toilet. Hand, with spring.

## BANDAGES.

**NEWMARKET HORSE LEG.** 2½ in. White and Fawn, 5 in. White and Fawn. These are made of a stockingette material, and are 6 ft. long, with tape. Suplied in ½ sets = 2 bandages, or full sets = 4 bandages.

## TROCAR.

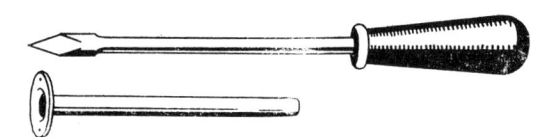

With 2 Canulas. For blown cattle.

## BULL NOSE PLIERS.

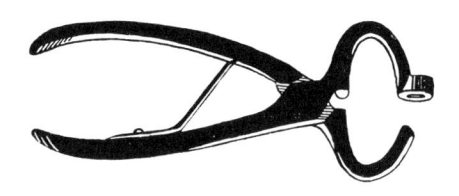

No. 125. For cutting hole for Bull Ring.

## SNAPS, BULL LEAD.

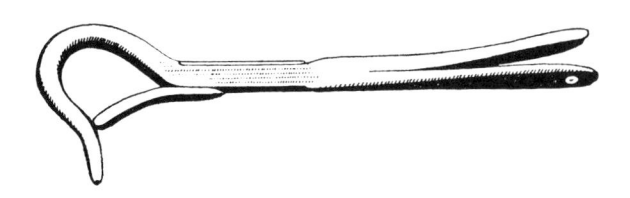

HAND FORGED. .. With or without handles.

No. 500. Tinned, with chain. .. With or without handles.

## BRANDS.

FIRE OR TAR. .. .. For Sheep and Cattle.

# CATTLE DRENCHES, ETC.

## GIFFWELL PRODUCTS.

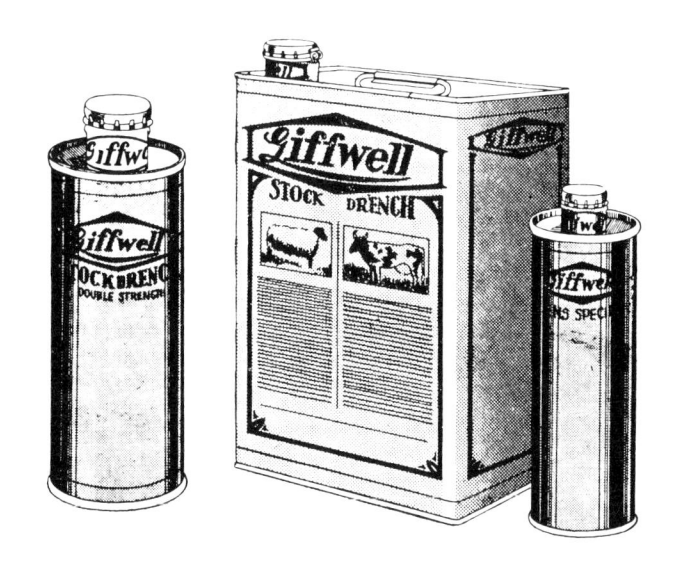

**GIFFWELL STOCK DRENCH.** In ½ pt., 1 pt., ½ gall., 1 gall.

**STEVENS SPECIFIC.** For Mamitus and Garget. In ½ pt. tins. Sufficient for 5 cows.

**GIFFWELL STOCK COMPOUND.** In 20-lb. and 140-lb. bags and ton lots.

**GIFFWELL TEAT SALVE.** .. .. In 1-lb. tins.

### WAGSTAFF'S STOCK DRENCH.

Double strength. ½ pt., 1 pt., ½ gall.

# VETERINARY REMEDIES

### REDUCENE.

**THE ABSORBENT BLISTER.** Reducene, which is the greatest absorbent ever discovered, discounts firing and blistering as obsolete and barbarious. The application of Reducene is the most humane treatment known. Reducene acts rapidly, and removes pain more quickly than any other preparation. Reducene will cure lameness and relieves inflamation quickly and permanently. Reducene will leave no scar or twisted hairs. Directions with every can. In 1-lb. cans only.

### SOLOMAN SOLUTION.

**A PAINLESS SWEATING BLISTER.** For horses and cattle. Cure for splints, curbs, sprains, swellings, windgalls, sore shoulders, sore backs, fistulas, greasy heels, and all kinds of wounds, sores, etc. Directions with every jar. Small and large jars.

### LIEUT. JAMES' BLISTERING OINTMENT.

**FOR HORSES.** Directions with every jar. In small jars only.

### RADIOL.

**FOR HORSES, CATTLE, AND DOGS.** For dispersing soft swellings in horses, cattle, and dogs; also windgalls, bog spavin, thorough pin, capped elbow, capped hock, sprained tendon, enlarged glands, etc. It fines down a worn horse's legs, and relieves lameness. Used in conjunction with Leg Wash Powders.

**FOR RUNNING GREYHOUNDS AND WHIPPETS.** Radiol quickly relieves soreness and pain, braces muscular and tendon tissues, etc. .

**FOR CATTLE.** It is valuable in mammitis and other inflammatory troubles.
Directions with every tin. In 1 size tins only, complete with 1 packet of Leg Wash Powders.

### RADIOL LEG WASH POWDERS.

In boxes of 6 Powders. Used in conjunction with Radiol.

### BONE RADIOL.

**FOR HORSES, CATTLE, AND DOGS.** Relieves lameness from hard, bony enlargements, such as splints, spavin, sore shins, ringbone (except low ringbone) without blistering, laying up the horse, or blemishing. Also old curbs, thickened tendons, joints, and other fibrous swellings. Directions with every bottle. In 4 fl. oz. bottle only. Complete with brush.

### KENDALL'S SPAVIN TREATMENT.

A counter irritant method for treating bone spavin, ringbone, splint, curb, swelling, sprains, lameness. Also for all cases requiring a stimulating, healing, or absorbent liniment. No blistering or sores made by its use. Directions with every bottle. In one size bottle only.

### PENETRENE.

**HAGLEY'S. FOR ANIMAL USE.** A safe and effective remedy for sprains, strains, splents, wind puffs, big knee, capped hock, sprung tendons, curbs, soft bunches, swellings, throat troubles, rheumatism, shoe boils, thorough pin, and lameness of all kinds. Directions with every bottle. In 10-oz. and 20-oz. bottles.

**HAGLEY'S. FOR HUMAN USE.** A safe and certain external remedy for rheumatism, sore muscles, sprains, lumbago, neuritis, varicose veins, sore throat, headache, toothache, and sciatica. A healing liniment possessing great penetrating and absorbing powers. Relieves swelling and allays pain. Contains no alcohol. Directions with every bottle. In 4 and 8-oz. bottles.

# VETERINARY REMEDIES

### LARYNGINE.
DOYLE'S. Prevents and cures coughs, colds, influenza, and strangles. Prevents roaring, whistling, and broken wind. Directions with every can. In 2-lb. cans only.

### EURYTHMIC.
**HEALING LOTION OR HOPPLE CHAFE.** Heals hopple chafe, boot chafe, sore backs, sore shoulders, girth galls, and other affections requiring healing astringents. Directions with every bottle. In 3 fluid oz. bottles, complete with brush.

### HAGLEY'S HOPPLE CHAFE SPECIFIC.
For cuts, chafes, scalds, cracked heels, collar and saddle galls, etc. A liquid gall cure, non poisonous, non irritating, rapid in its action, marvellous in its curative effects. Stops bleeding instantly. Directions with every botle. In bottles, complete with brush.

### BICKMORE'S GALL CURE.
For healing wounds and sores upon horses and cattle. Directions with every tin. In tins, 2 oz., 6 oz., 16 oz.

### FLINT'S MEDICATED OIL.
**THE OCCULT CURE.** For cuts, wounds, and galls on horses, cattle, and humans. Directions with every bottle. In one size bottle only.

### FLINT'S CURE FOR SAND IN HORSES.
Directions with every tin. In one size tin only.

### FLINT'S WORM POWDERS.
**FOR HORSES.** Directions with every packet. Packets contain 4 powders.

### FLINT'S VERMOLINE.
**THE OCCULT CURE.** For worms in sheep. Directions with every tin. This tin contains sufficient doses for 480 sheep, 600 weaners (6–8 months), or about 1,000 lambs.

### BERG OIL.
**HEUZENROEDER'S.** For horses, cattle, sheep, pigs, etc. For colic, bladder, kidney, sand, worms, stomach, hoven, fevers, poisoning, redwater. Directions with every bottle. In packets containing 6 small bottles.

### SAND AND COLIC POWDERS.
**HEUZENROEDER'S.** For horses and cattle. Directions with every tin. In small and large tins.

# VETERINARY REMEDIES

### CARBOX.

**A CLEANSER AND HEALER.** For horses, cattle, sheep, pigs, and dogs, and general domestic use.

**FOR HORSES.** Itch, greasy heel, sore shoulders, green wounds, mud fever, lice or stick flea.

**FOR CATTLE.** Mammitus, sore teats, udders, ringworm, lice, contagious abortion, and general uterine douche.

**FOR PIGS.** Lice and scale.

**FOR SHEEP.** Fly blow, cuts at shearing and at lamb marking, bad pizzles, and foot rot. Carbox will not stain the wool.

**FOR DOGS.** Mange, itch, and fleas.

Also has many uses in the home for the hair, feet, and laundry. Directions with every tin. In quarts, half gallon, and 1-gallon tins.

### SALVITIS COMPOUND.

**FOR HORSES.** Renders the coat fine and attractive, strengthens muscle and bone, brightens the spirit, enriches the blood, improves digestion, corrects humors, braces the nerves, induces appetite, and a never failing remedy for bots, worms, etc. Directions with every tin. In 2-lb. and 6½-lb. tins.

**FOR DAIRY CATTLE.** "Salvitis" greatly assists digestion by inducing a free flow of saliva, thus preventing impaction of the stomach. It provides against stoppage of the bowels, promotes the fullest absorption of nutrition, and thereby profitably increases the quality and richness of the milk yield. It is invaluable in the cure and prevention of such cattle ailments as cripples, bone weakness, wasting, or other ill conditions. "Salvitis" in fact protects, restores, animates, and strengthens by contributing the elements necessary to the maintenance in healthy soundness of blood, bone, flesh, and milk. Cattle take it readily. Directions with every tin. In 2-lb. tins.

### HOPLEMUROMA HOOF DRESSING.

For the improvement of the Growth of horses' feet, and to prevent and cure brittle or shelly feet, cracked heels, sand cracks, seedy toes, and diseased frogs. Directions with every tin. Made in one size tin only.

### DUNNING'S HOOF OINTMENT.

Used as a daily dressing to prevent all diseases, and for founderings, sandcrack, thrush, quitton, and other complaints of a running nature, greasy heel, stopping, brittle and contracted feet, cracked heels, wind galls, sidebones, wrung shoulders, corns, sores, cuts, and wounds of every description. Directions with every tin. In one size tin only, 9¼ oz.

### EMBROCATION.

**ELLIMAN'S ROYAL.** For horses and cattle. For sprains, curbs, splints, when forming for overreaches, chapped heels, wind, rheumatism, bruises, galls, broken knees, wounds, capped hocks, sore throats, influenza, sore shoulders, sore backs, sore mouth. And foot rot in sheep. Directions with every bottle. In small and large bottles.

**ELLIMAN'S UNIVERSAL.** For human uses. For rheumatism, lumbago, sprains, bruises, chest colds, sore throat, and odd stiffness. Directions on every bottle. In one size bottle only.

# LEATHER DRESSINGS, ETC.

## HARNESS COMPOSITIONS.
OR WATERPROOF LEATHER POLISHES.

SUPREEM. .. .. .. .. Black or Tan.
LYDDY'S O.B.B. .. .. Black. 5¼-oz. tins.
HARRIS'S. .. .. .. .. .. Black.

## HOOD DRESSING.
OR WATERPROOF DRESSING.

Supreme composition. .. For Motor or Buggy Hoods.

## FAT BACK.
**LYDDY'S O.B.B.** For preserving, renewing, and waterproofing harness and leather goods of every description. In 6¼-oz. tins. Directions on every tin.

## DUBBIN.
**LYDDY'S.** A superior preparation for waterproofing, softening, preserving boots, harness, leggings, etc. Black and Tan.

## HARNESS LIQUID.
**LYDDY'S O.B.B.** Is especially prepared for all kinds of harness, buggy and motor hoods, travelling bags, etc. It is perfectly harmless and especially adapted for giving to old harness a fresh and beautiful gloss equal to new. Can be put on with a sponge or brush. It preserves and renovates. Contents, 1 pt.

## HARNESS OIL.
A wonderful reviver and preserver for all kinds of leather. Black or Brown.

**HOLDFAST.** Black, pints and quarts. Brown, pints and quarts.

**GARGOYLE.** .. .. 1 and 4-gallon tins.

## COACHOLINE.
Is a dressing and waterproof preservative for harness, carriage tops, boots, and all kinds of leather. Is warranted superior to castor oil for carriage axles. Will not gum, drip, or waste. Same consistancy all weathers. Can also be used as a hoof ointment, and also for healing sores, scratches, and all skin diseases on horses and cattle. In 12-oz. tins.

## SADDLE SOAP.
**LYDDY'S O.B.B.** Specially prepared. For cleaning and renovating saddles. Can also be used for preserving all leather ware, cases, boots, etc. Will not rub off. In 5½-oz. and 12-oz. tins.

## BLACK DYE POWDER.
**LYDDY'S.** For dyeing all kinds of leatherware. Contents, 2 oz. This is sufficient to make one gallon of dye.

## BOSCO DYE.
A liquid dye used in the boot trade for dyeing footwear. Can be used for dyeing any leather goods. Can be applied with a sponge. In 4-oz. bottles. Colours: Black, Medium Tan, and and Nigger Tan.

## HOOD DRESSING.
**HOWE'S BLACK.** Will make your old hood look like new. In ½ pt., 1 pt., and quart tins.

**ROGERS BLACK.** Specially manufactured for black patent hoods, tarpaulins, and oilskins. Will not crack when the hood is folded, and finishes with a good black film. In ½ pt., 1 pt., and quart tins.

## UPHOLSTERY REVIVER.
**HOWE'S.** Makes any kind of leather or imitation leather look like new. Can be brushed or sprayed on. We recommend spraying with a spray gun or a small fly spray. In tins, ½ pt., 1 pt., and quart. Colours obtainable: Neutral or Clear, Red, Blue, Brown, Green, Grey, and Black. Dries practically instantly.

## LEATHER COAT DYE.
**SUPREME.** A permanent dye for restoring and recolouring all faded leather coats, boots, shoes, all leather travelware, and all leather goods. Made in one colour: Nigger Brown. In 6-oz. bottles.

## LEATHER COAT DRESSING.
**SUPREME.** Liquid Wax Brown. Produces a brilliant permanent wax finish on all types of leather coats, is thoroughly waterproof, and the colour will not run. The finish can be renewed from time to time by merely polishing briskly with a clean cloth. If colour of coat is faded, we recommend Supreme Leather Coat Dye. In 8-oz. bottles.

# SADDLERY DEPARTMENT

### BULLOCK BELLS

No.06 ... Oblong. Cast bell metal. 4, 5 and 6 ins. across base

### COW OR CATTLE BELLS

"**KENTUCKY.**" A well sounding and durable bell, made for rough usage

Nos. ... ... 1 2 3 4 5 6 7 9
Height (without loop) ... 6¼ 5⅛ 4¾ 4⅜ 3½ 2¾ 2 and 1½ ins.

### HORSE BELLS

No. 016. Oblong shape. Cast bell metal. 3¼ and 3½ ins. across base

### SHEEP BELLS

No 01. Round. Cast bell metal. 2½ and 3 ins. in diameter

# LEGGINGS

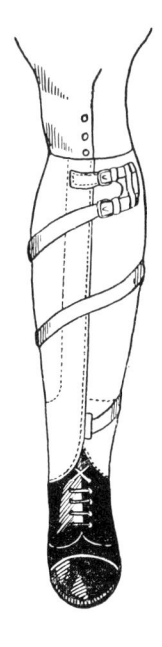

**STRAP PUTTEE.**
Split leather, Blocked.
Military strap leather, Blocked.
Holdfast strap leather, Blocked.

**SPRING PUTTEE.**
Split leather.
Strap leather.
Blocked calf, simplex.

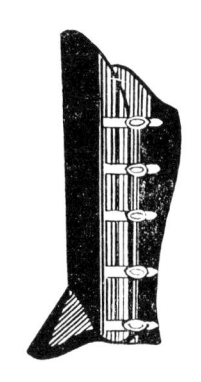

**FARM.**
Split or tweed leather.
Strap and buckle or spring.

**CONCERTINA.**
Wrinkled centre.
Plain centre.

**GAITERS, BICYCLE.**
With J.L.T. Clips.
6 in. x 3 clips.  9 in. x 4 clips.

With Studs.
6 in. x 3 stud.  9 in. x 4 stud.

HF 90    HARRIS, SCARFE, LIMITED.

# FOOTWEAR

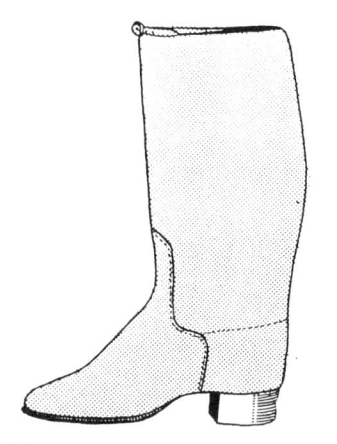

**LADIES' POLO OR PULL ON BOOTS.** Brown. Nos. 1 and 2.

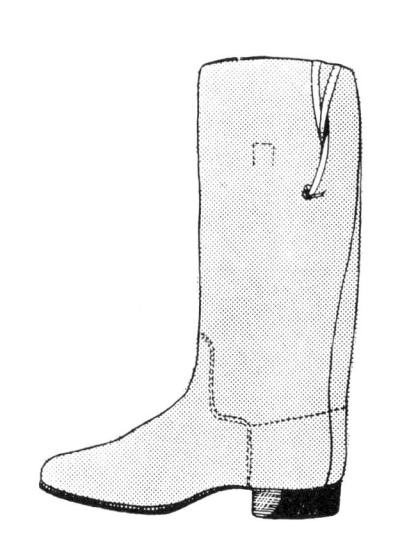

**GENT'S POLO OR PULL ON BOOTS.** Brown. Nos. 1 and 2.

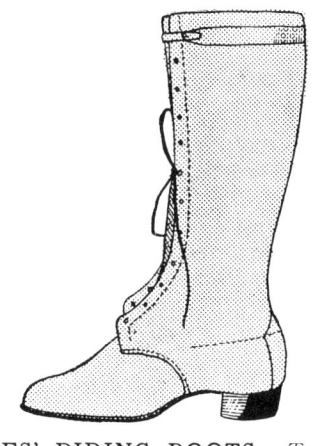

**LADIES' RIDING BOOTS.** To lace. Brown.

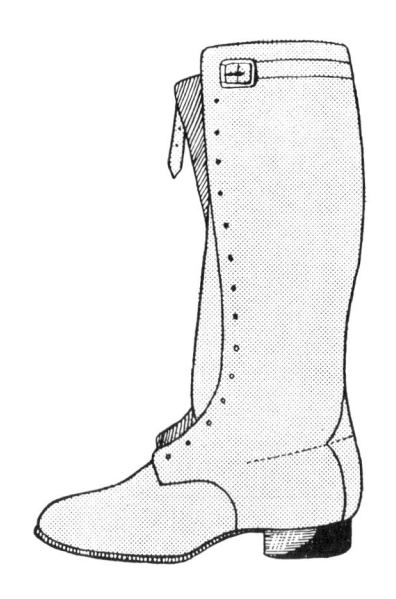

**GENT'S RIDING BOOTS.** To lace. Brown.

**GENT'S BOOTS. ELASTIC SIDES.** Black or Brown.

**GENT'S TRANSPORT BOOTS.** A good heavy waterproof boot for motor cycling, shooting, etc.

**MEN'S I-R KNEE BOOTS.**

No. 1030. .. Plain edge. Black.
No. 1001. .. Rolled edge. Black.
No. 1028. .. Rolled edge. Black, With white soles and heels.

**LADIES' I-R KNEE BOOTS.**

No. 1040. .. Plain edge. Black.
No. 1015. .. .. Fleecy lined.

No. 1014. **MEN'S I-R JACKEROO.** Black.

**I-R THIGH BOOTS.**

Rolled edge, all black.
Rolled edge, with white soles and heels.

## WADERS.

For duck shooting, etc.

No. 1029. Cloth, with 1004 Goloshes. Men's. All sizes.

No. 1029. Cloth. Stocking Feet. All sizes.

HARRIS, SCARFE, LIMITED.  HF 91

# SUNDRIES

## CHAMOIS.

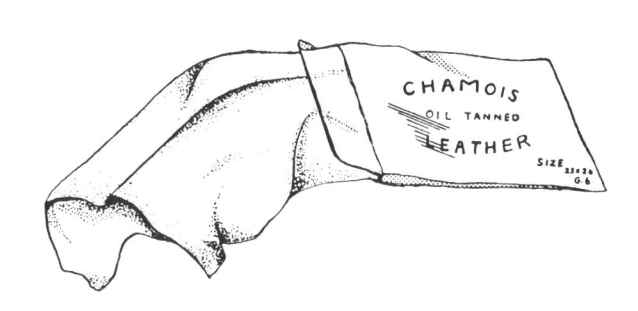

**CHAMOIS LEATHER. OIL TANNED AUSTRALIAN.**
Each packed in envelope.

G1.  17 in. x 16 in.         G2.  18 in. x 17 in.

G3.  20 in. x 19 in.         G4.  22 in. x 22 in.

G5.  23 in. x 24 in.         G6.  24 in. x 25 in.
          G8.  26 in. x 28 in.

**CHAMOIS LEATHER. OIL TANNED ENGLISH.**
A13.  22 in. x 21 in.        A15.  24 in. x 33 in.
          A16.  25 in. x 24 in.

## POLISHING CLOTHS.

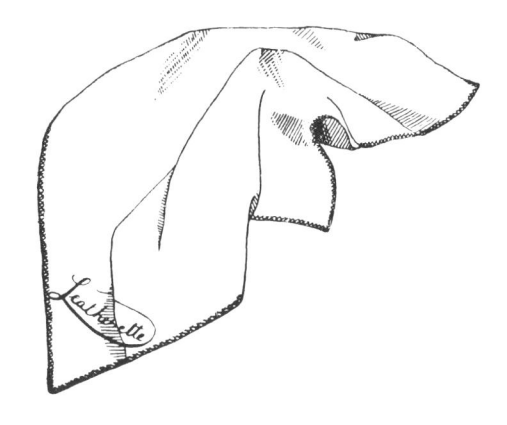

**LEATHERETTE POLISHING CLOTHS.** Yellow. 20 in. x 20 in.

B8NSG.  Check Polishing Cloth.  ..  24 in. x 24 in.
B8NC.   Check Polishing Cloth.  ..  27 in. x 27 in.

## SHIELD DUSTLESS DUSTERS.

28 in. x 17 in. These dusters have a dressing in them which holds and dissolves the dust. Ideal for furniture, motor cars, etc.

## SPONGE CLOTHS.

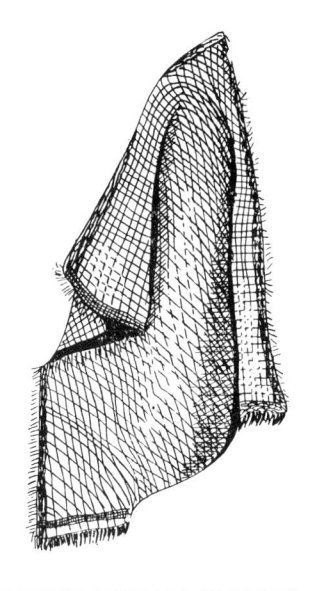

**SPONGE SWEAT CLOTHS.**
HOYLE'S.  ENGLISH.  22 x 18, 22 x 20, 22 x 22, 24 x 24.

## SPONGES.

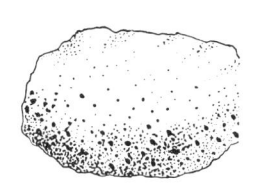

**SEA SPONGES.** Assorted sizes.

**BATH AND MOTOR.** On cards. No. X, 12 on card; No. 0, 12 on card; No. 1, 12 on card; No. 2, 12 on card; No. 3, 12 on card; No. 4, 12 on card; No. 6, 12 on card; No. 12, 6 on card.

# SUNDRIES

## FLAGS.

Flags made of best bunting.

**UNION JACK** or **AUSTRALIAN.** Blue or Red. 3 ft. x 1 ft. 6 in.; 4 ft. x 2 ft.; 4 ft. 6 in. x 2 ft. 3 in.; 6 ft. x 3 ft.; 7 ft. x 3 ft. 6 in.; 8 ft. x 4 ft.; 9 ft. x 4 ft. 6 in.; 12 ft. x 6 ft.

## LUGGAGE LABELS.

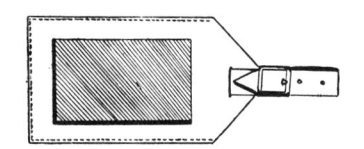

**LEATHER LUGGAGE LABELS.** Common, Single and Double. Best, Single and Double.

## WATCH POUCHES.

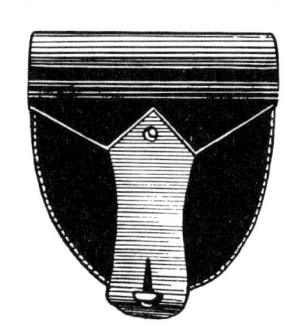

**LEATHER WATCH POUCHES.** Lined, Unlined, Foldover.

## AIR CUSHIONS.

**I-R CIRCULAR AID CUSHIONS.** 14, 16, 18, 20 in.
Square, 14, 16, 18 in.

## HOT WATER BAGS.

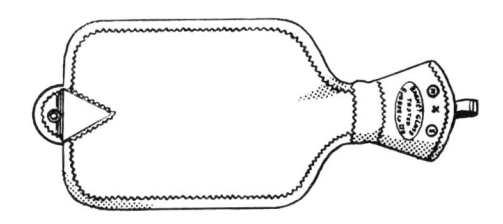

**DUNLOP OR BARNET GLASS HOT WATER BAGS.**
2 years' guarantee. 10 x 8, 12 x 8, 12 x 10, 13 x 9.

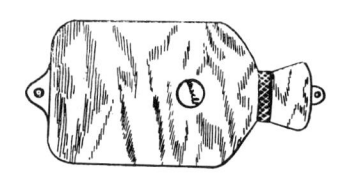

**DUNLOP, BARNET GLASS, OR ANSELL MOULDED HOT WATER BAGS.** Coloured. Size about 9 x 7.

## COVERS FOR HOT WATER BAGS.

**SWANDOWN OR BEST.** 10 x 8, 12 x 8, 12 x 10, 13 x 9.
**ORDINARY.** .. .. 10 x 8, 12 x 8, 12 x 10, 13 x 9.

# SUNDRIES

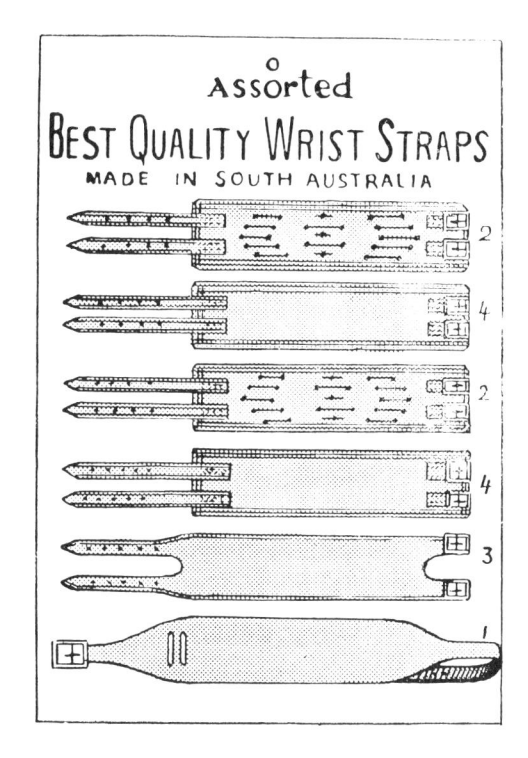

**Assorted BEST QUALITY WRIST STRAPS MADE IN SOUTH AUSTRALIA**

**WRIST STRAPS ON CARDS.** As illustrated.

No. 1. 7 in. x 2 in. Body Buckles riveted on. Overall measurement, 16 in.

No. 2. 6¾ in. x 2 in., with buckles and points hand sewn on. Overall measurement, 8¾ in.

No. 3. 6 in. x 1¾ in., with buckles riveted on. Overall measurement, 9 in.

No. 4. 6¾ in. x 3 in., with buckles and points hand sewn on. Overall measurement, 8¾ in.

No. 5. 8 in. x 2 in., with 2 buckles, sewn chamois (lined).

No. 6. As No. 5 .. .. .. .. .. (Unlined).

## WAIST BELTS.

GENT'S. On cards of 6 belts. Two 1¼ in.; two 1½ in.; two 1¾ in. These are strap leather with N.P. belt buckles riveted on. 1¼ x 42 in.; 1½ x 42 in.; 1¾ x 42 in.

## HANDLES.

RUG STRAP. N.P. .. To take rug straps ¾ in and ⅞ in.

## FINGER STALLS.

LEATHER. With Tape. .. On cards, 12 assorted.

## POUCHES, BUTCHERS.

SOLID SOLE LEATHER. Hand sewn with waist strap. With ring and billet for steel. Size of pouch, 7½ x 3½ x 2½. With 4 in. reinforced back.

## BIFURCATED RIVETS.

### N.P. OR COPPERED ON IRON.

No. 6. Coppered. Assorted. .. 1 dozen tins to carton.
No. 9. Coppered. Assorted. .. 1 dozen tins to carton.

In boxes of 1,000.

| | |
|---|---|
| No. 9 x 4/16 | No. 9 x 9/16 |
| No. 9 x 5/16 | No. 9 x 10/16 |
| No. 9 x 6/16 | No. 9 x 12/16 |
| No. 9 x 7/16 | No. 6 x 14/16 |
| No. 9 x 8/16 | No. 6 x 16/16 |

Bifurcated Rivets are for repairing leather goods such as harness, cases, and any other job where a split rivet can be used.

## COIL AXLE WASHERS.

These washers can be made to fit any axle coils. About 3 in. long. 5 coils to box. Sizes. 1⅛ and 1¼.

## MIRRORS.

BUSH. A Bevelled Mirror, leather bound and backed. In strong leather case as used by bushmen, drovers, etc. Size of mirror, 6 in x 3 in.

# SUNDRIES

### FIRE BEATERS.

Cane handle, with chrome sole leather blade bolted on with plates. Handle 6 ft. to 7 ft. long by about 1 in. diameter. Blade, 20 x 13 in. Specially tanned. Cane handle, with basil beater. Chrome leather will not burn.
Cane handle, with basil beater.

### FIRE LIGHTERS.

**BRASS KEROSENE TORCH.** Used for burning firebreaks, scrub, etc. Size, 36 in. x 1 in. diameter barrel, 12 in. x ½ in. nozzle

Showing Brass Firelighter with tap so as kerosene supply can be turned off.

# LEATHER SUIT CASES

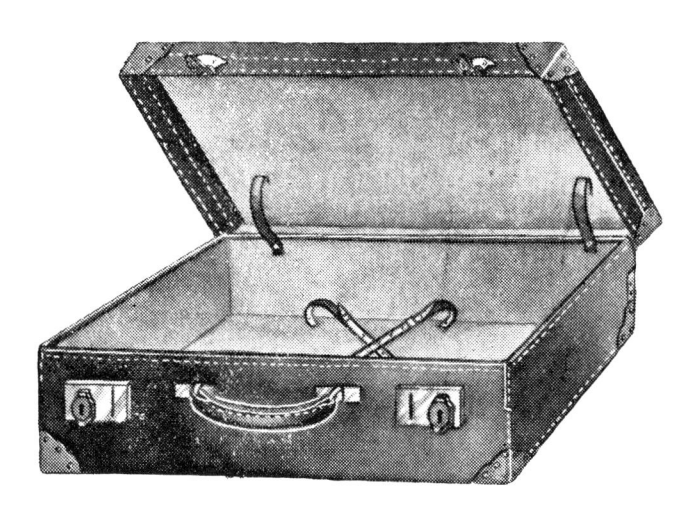

No. 30. **SUIT CASE.** Solid leather, with leather handle and lid stays. Straps in bottom. Drill lined. Two N.P. English safety locks, leather corners, strong steel frame stitched around top. All strongly sewn. Sizes: 24 x 15 x 7¼; 26 x 15 x 7¼; 28 x 16¼ x 7¼.

No. 9. **SHALLOW SUIT CASE.** Solid leather, with leather handle and lid stays. Watered silk lined, with drawn pocket on back. Two strong English safety locks. Strong steel frame stitched around top of case. All edges strongly butted together and hand sewn. Best selected leather. Sizes: 22 x 15 x 7; 24 x 15½ x 7; 26 x 16 x 7; 28 x 16 x 7; 30 x 16½ x 7.

No. 9. **DEEP SUIT CASE.** Solid leather. As No. 9 Shallow. Sizes: 24 x 15½ x 8; 26 x 16 x 8; 28 x 16 x 8; 30 x 16 x 8.

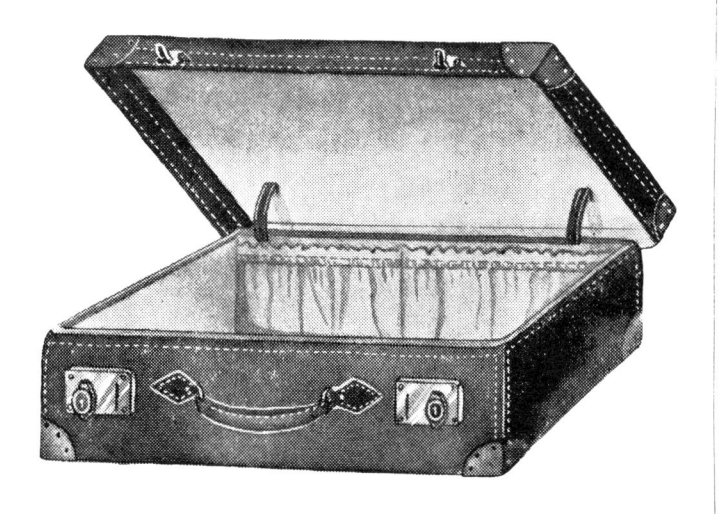

No. 29. **SUIT CASE.** Solid leather, with leather handle and lid stays. Drill lined, with drawn pocket on back. Two strong English safety locks, and leather cap corners. Strong steel frame stitched to top of case. All hand sewn. Sizes 22 x 14 x 7½; 24 x 15 x 7½; 26 x 15½ x 7½; 28 x 15½ x 7½; 30 x 16 x 7½.

No. 10. **SUIT CASE.** Solid leather. Strong leather handle, leather handle chapes, hand sewn and riveted, leather lid stays. Drill lined, with leather straps in bottom. Two English lever locks. Strong steel frame stitched around top of case. All edges strongly butted together and hand sewn. Built on fibre foundation. Best selected leather. Sizes: 24 x 16 x 8; 26 x 16½ x 8; 28 x 17 x 8; 30 x 17½ x 8.

**ALL LEATHER CASES MADE IN OUR OWN FACTORY.** Any sizes not specified can be made to order. Can also be made in colours.

# LEATHER SUIT CASES

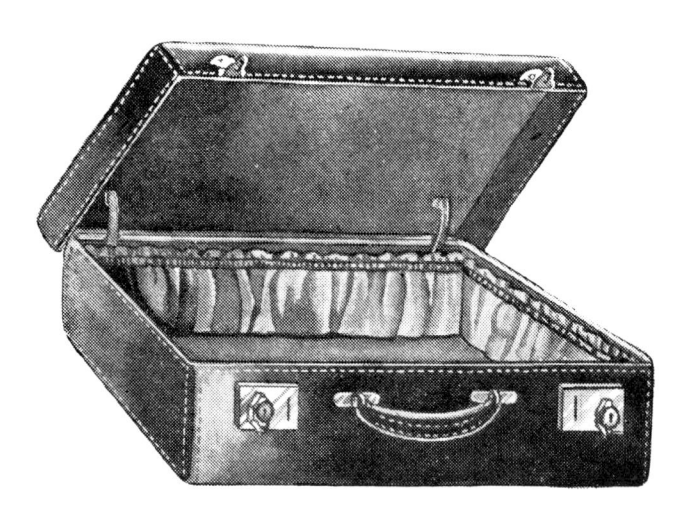

**AIRWAY CASE.** Solid leather. Best solid leather flat handle, leather lid stays. Two English safety locks. Watered silk linings with drawn pockets back and sides. Strong steel frame stitched around top of case. All edges strongly butted together and hand sewn. Best selected leather on fibre foundation. Specially light constructed for air travel, where weight of luggage is limited. Weight, approximately 7½ lb. Size: 22 x 14 x 7½.

**WEST END SUIT CASE.** With Tray. Solid leather. Best leather flat handle on leather chapes sand sewn and riveted. Two best quality English lever locks. Watered silk or best drill padded lining. Tray with sliding divisions for shirts, ties, handkerchiefs, with boot division in bottom. Straps in lid for papers, etc. Strong steel frame stitched around top of case, also around inside of lid. All edges strongly butted together and hand sewn throughout. Best selected leather on strong reinforced fibre foundation. First and second quality. Sizes: 24 x 15 x 9; 26 x 15 x 9; 28 x 16 x 9; 30 x 16½ x 9.

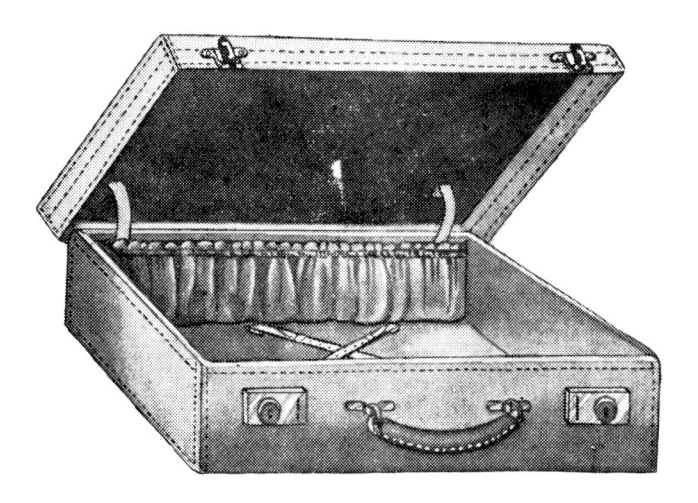

**CORONATION SUIT CASE.** Solid leather. Best solid leather round handle on strong metal plates or leather chapes hand sewn and riveted. Two best quality English lever locks. Watered silk or strong drill lined, with drawn pockets at back. Straps in bottom. Steel frame stitched around top of case. All edges turned, strongly butted together, and hand sewn. Best selected coronation leather (light or dark brown) on strong fibre foundations. Deep or shallow. Sizes: Shallow—22 x 13 x 7; 24 x 14 x 7; 26 x 14 x 7; 28 x 14½ x 7; 30 x 15 x 7. Deep—22 x 13 x 9; 24 x 14 x 9; 26 x 14 x 9; 28 x 14½ x 9; 30 x 15 x 9.

**EXPANDING TOP SUIT CASE.** Solid leather. Best leather round handle, leather handle chapes hand sewn and riveted. Two strong English lever locks. Watered silk lining. Straps in bottom, also across lid (these straps allow you to pack the lid independant of the case). Two strong leather straps around case. Strong steel frame stitched around top of case, also around edge of lid. Edges all strongly butted together and hand sewn. Best selected leather used on strong reinforced fibre foundations. Sizes: 26 x 16½ x 9 in. closed, 12½ in. open; 28 x 17 x 9 in. closed, 12½ in. open; 30 x 17½ x 9 in. closed, 12½ in. open.

**WE STAND BEHIND QUALITY AND WORKMANSHIP OF ALL OUR LEATHER CASES.**

HARRIS, SCARFE, LIMITED.　　　　　　　HF 97

# FITTED CASES

**DROP DOWN FRONT FITTED DRESSING CASE.** Best selected imported pig skin. Round leather handle. Two best English lever locks. Watered silk lining padded, with drawn pockets in lid and ends. All hand sewn. The Drop Down Front makes a two division case with ample room for garments. etc. Other, which is 4 in. wide, houses all fittings, including seven Cut Glass Silver Top Bottles, Chromium and Black Engraved Mirror, Brush and Comb, and Shoe Lift. Size: 22 x 15 x 8 in. overall.

Inset shows case with Drop Down Front closed for carrying.

**THESE CASES ARE MADE IN OUR OWN FACTORY. OTHERS, WITH ANY FITTINGS REQUIRED, CAN BE MADE TO ORDER.**

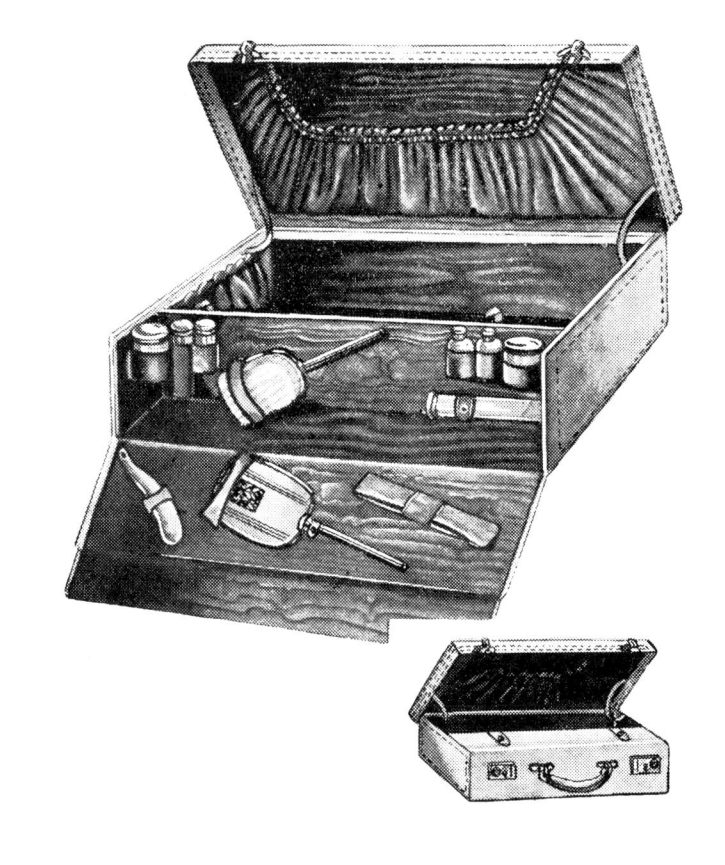

**LADIES' FITTED DRESSING CASE.** With tray. Best selected leather. Round leather handle. Two best English lever locks. Watered silk lining with drawn pocket in lid. All hand sewn. This case can either be used as a dressing case, or tray can be removed (which can be caried as a separate attache case containing all fittings), and be used as ordinary suit case. Size: 24 x 15 x 8 in. overall.

Inset shows tray removed and closed.

Fittings comprise best English Xylonite: Two Hair Brushes, one Clothes Brush, one Hat Brush, Mirror, Comb, and Shoe Lift.

**WE MAKE COVERS TO FIT ALL CLASSES OF CASES. IF COVER IS REQUIRED, WE WOULD LIKE CASE FORWARDED TO US TO ENSURE A GOOD FIT.**

HF 98            HARRIS, SCARFE, LIMITED.

# LEATHER CASES

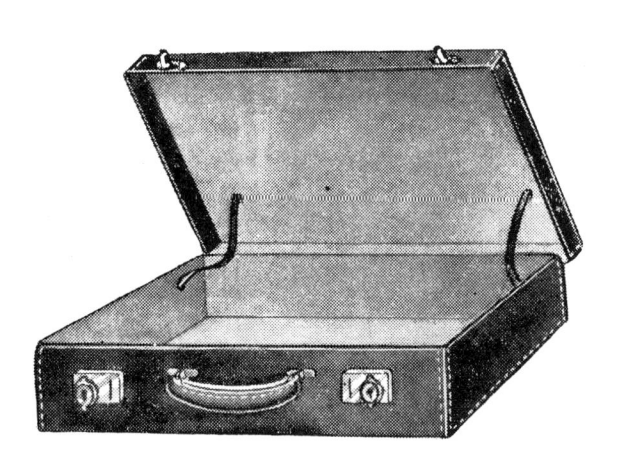

**COMMON SOLID LEATHER ATTACHE CASE.** With leather handle and stays. Two N.P. safety locks. Drill lined. Selected leather, strongly sewn. Sizes: 14 x 10½ x 4 in.; 16 x 11 x 4¼ in.; 18 x 11½ x 4½ in.; 20 x 11½ x 5 in.

**BEST METAL FRAME SOLID LEATHER ATTACHE CASE.** As above, with metal frame around edges. Round leather handle, and silk lined. Selected leather, all hand sewn. Sizes: 14 x 9¼ x 4 in.; 16 x 10¾ x 4¼ in.; 18 x 12 x 5 in.; 20 x 13 x 5¼ in.

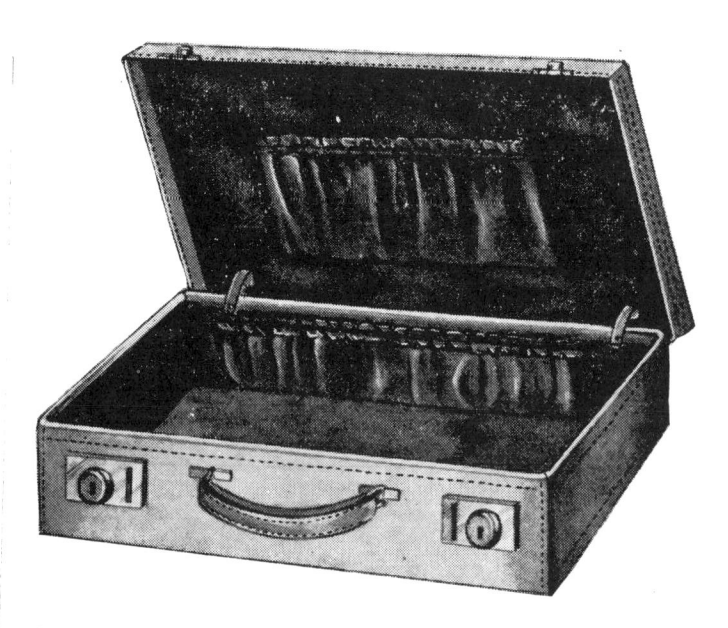

**BEST "CORO" SOLID LEATHER ATTACHE CASE.** With best quality flat leather handle. Best English lever locks. Padded top and bottom with good quality silk lining, with drawn pockets on back and lid. Strong steel frame stitched around edges. Only best selected coronation leather (light or dark) used on fibre foundation. All hand sewn. Sizes: 14 x 9¼ x 4½ in.; 16 x 10 x 4½ in.; 18 x 10½ x 4½ in.; 20 x 11 x 4½ in.

**GOVT. PATT. SOLID LEATHER ATTACHE CASE.** With round leather handle. Two N.P. safety locks. Strong steel frame stitched around top of case. Good drill lined, with elastic drawn pocket in lid. Selected leather only used. All hand sewn. Sizes: 14 x 10¾ x 5 in.; 16 x 11¼ x 5¼ in.; 18 x 11¾ x 5¼ in.; 20 x 12 x 5¼ in.

ALL LEATHER CASES MADE IN OUR OWN FACTORY. SIZES OTHER THAN ILLUSTRATED CAN BE MADE TO ORDER. CAN ALSO BE MADE IN DIFFERENT COLOURS.

**BLOUSE CASE.** Solid leather, with round leather handle. Two good quality English lever locks. Best silk lined. Drawn pockets on back and lid. Strong steel frame stitched around edges. Best selected leather. All hand sewn. A very handy case for week ends. Can also be made in coloured leather. Sizes: 18 x 12½ x 5½ in.; 20 x 12¾ x 5½ in.; 22 x 13 x 5½ in.; 24 x 14 x 5¾ in.

# LEATHER CASES AND BAGS

**TENNIS CASE. 1st QUALITY.** Solid leather, with best round leather handle. Best English locks. Drill lined, with drawn pockets and straps to hold two racquets, and pocket to hold 3 balls. Strong steel frame stitched to edges of case. Best selected coronation leather, hand sewn throughout.

**TENNIS CASE. 2nd QUALITY.** Solid leather. Particulars as 1st Quality, but cheaper material used.

**D SPECIAL KIT BAGS.** Solid leather. With side lock. Drill lined, with pockets. Sizes: 14, 16, 18, 20 in.

**No. 169. KIT BAG.** Solid leather. A stronger and bigger bodied bag than D Special. Sizes: 14, 16, 18, 20 in.

**No. 180. KIT BAG.** Solid leather. With best quality round leather handle. N.P. on brass fittings on best quality uncovered frame. Strong drill lining, with pockets. Fibre board foundation. Selected leather. Also a full bodied bag. Sizes: 14, 16, 18, 20, 22 in.

**SINGLE HINGE COVERED FRAME KIT BAG.** Solid leather. Best quality round leather handle. N.P. on brass fittings on leather covered single hinge frame. Strong drill lining, with pockets. Fibre board foundations. Best quality leather only used in this bag. Sizes, 14, 16, 18, 20, 22 in.

**DOUBLE HINGE COVERED FRAME KIT BAG.** Particulars as Single Hinge, but with Double Hinge frame. Sizes: 14, 16, 18, 20, 22 in.

**END STRAPS CAN BE FITTED TO ANY KIT BAGS.**

**BULLION BAGS.** Solid leather on strong steel leather covered frame. With slide nozzle brass lever lock. Heavy all round strap handles. Leather lined, with inside pockets. Heavy selected leather on Flaxite foundation, and heavily studded. Sizes: 14, 16, 18 in.

**BRIEF BAG.** Solid leather, with riveted frame. N.P. fittings. Sizes: 10, 12, 14, 16, 18 in.

**BULGE BRIEF BAG.** As above, but bigger bodied bag. Sizes: 10, 12, 14, 16, 18 in.

**BETTING BAGS.** A White Chrome Leather Bag, as used by bookmakers. Size, 18 in.

**WE DO REPAIRS TO ALL LEATHER GOODS AND TRAVELWARE IN OUR OWN FACTORY.**

# LEATHER BAGS

**SCHOOL BAGS. SOLID LEATHER.**

**S.A.R. PATTERN.** Best selected leather, with two rows stiching all round. Sizes: 11, 12, 13, 14 ins.

**SECOND QUALITY.** Solid leather, with single row stitching. Sizes: 11, 12, 13, 14 ins.

**LIZARD GRAIN.** Solid leather. Sizes: 10, 11, 12, 13, 14 ins.

**SPLIT LEATHER.** .. Sizes: 10, 11, 12, 13, 14 ins.

**BASIL UNBOUND.** .. Sizes: 9, 10, 11, 12, 13 ins.

**BASIL BOUND EDGES.** .. Sizes: 9, 10, 11, 12, 13 ins.

All Bags can be made with cross shoulder straps at extra cost.

No. 415. **COURIER.** Solid leather. Grained. With shoulder strap all round. Lined leather, with inside pockets divided. Also pocket outside with turn fastener. Sizes: 8, 8½, 9, 9½, 10, 11, 12 ins.

No. 416. As No. 415, without outside pocket. Sizes: as No. 815.

No. 417. As No. 416. Unlined leather divison only. Sizes: 8, 9, 10, 12 ins.

HARRIS, SCARFE, LIMITED.  HF **101**

# LEATHER CASES, ETC.

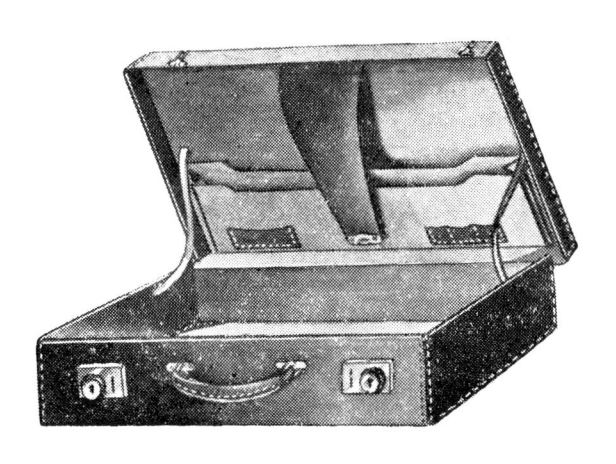

**WRITING CASE.** Solid leather. With pockets in lid for stationery, and loose pad in bottom for blotting paper. Round leather handle. Two good English locks. Rexine lined. Best selected leather. All hand sewn. Sizes: 14 x 9¾ x 4¾ ins.; 16 x 10 x 4¾ ins.; 18 x 10½ x 4¾ ins.

**MUSIC CASE.** Solid leather. With leather handle. Two English safety locks. Silk lined. Selected leather only used. All hand sewn. Size: 16 x 11 x 3 ins. Very handy for carrying to business.

**MUSIC CASE. DEEP.** .. As above. Size: 16 x 11 x 4 ins.

**MUSIC GRIP.** Made in solid leather. Size: 15 x 6½ x 2¼ gussett. With handle on top and straps and buckles.

**MUSIC ROLL.** Split or solid leather. With strap around. Size: approximately 15 x 3 ins. closed.

**SATCHEL. TRAVELLER'S.** Solid leather. Containing two divisions for stationery, pad for blotting paper. Pockets for large and small envelopes, pen and pencils, ink bottle and stamps. Fitted with leather handle. Lock in centre. Straps each side of lock and around. Very convenient to carry. Sizes, 12 x 9½ x 3 ins.; 14 x 9½ x 3 ins.

**BOWLS CASE.** Solid leather. Drill lined. With strap and buckle. Leather handle on top. For 2 or 4 bowls.

**BOWLS CASE.** Solid leather. Drill lined. With strap and buckle. Leather handle on top. For 2 or 4 bowls, and space on top for shoes.

**BOWLS. CASE.** Attache style. Solid leather, same as Govt. Patt. Attache Case. With 3-ply bottom and leather partitions, which can be folded back into corners if wanted to be used as Attache Case. Size: 16 ins. For 4 bowls and shoes.

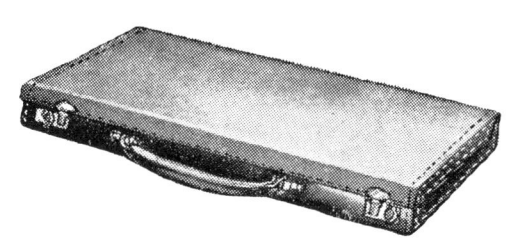

No. 3. **REGALIA CASE.** Solid leather. Leather handle. Two English safety locks. Silk lined. Selected leather, all hand sewn. Size: 17 x 8½ x 2½ ins.

No. 2. **REGALIA CASE.** As above. With best round leather handle. Two good English locks. With plush lining. Size: 17½ x 8½ x 2½ ins.

No. 1. **REGALIA CASE.** Best solid leather. With best flat leather handle. Two best English locks. Silk lined. Padded lid and bottom. Loops in lid for papers. Drawn pockets in back. Best quality selected coronation leather on wood and fibre board foundation. All hand sewn. Size: 17 x 9¾ x 3 ins.

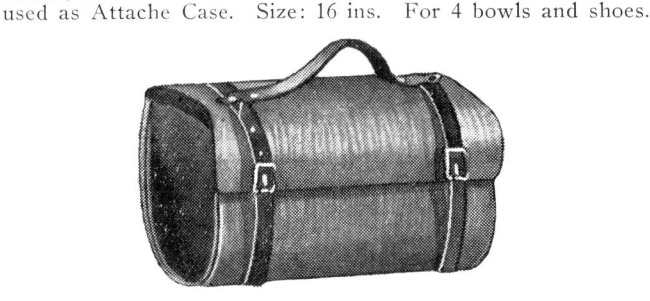

**BOWLS GRIP.** Solid leather. With ends stiffened. To carry 2 bowls only. Buckle and strap fastening.

**WE STAND BEHIND THE QUALITY AND WORKMANSHIP OF ALL OUR LEATHER GOODS.**

# LEATHER CASES, ETC.

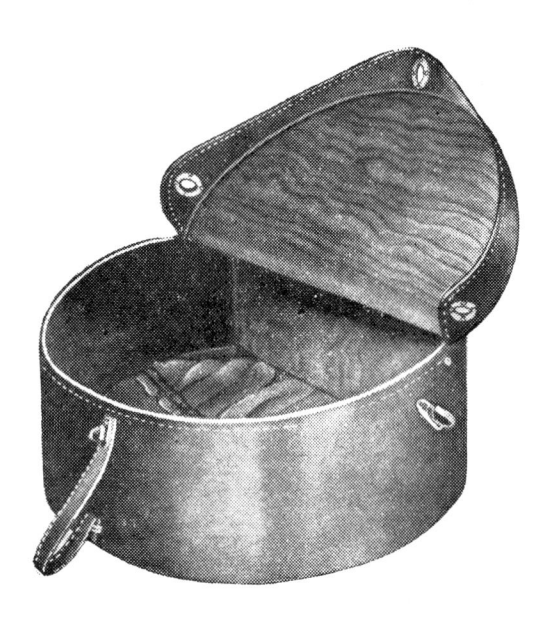

**HAT BOX.** Solid leather. Soft top. Round. Leather handle, with three turn fasteners. Watered silk lined, with drawn pocket in bottom. A very light, hard wearing hat box. In Colours: Brown, Fawn, Red, Blue, and Green. Sizes: 16 and 18 ins. Blouse Attache and Suit Cases can be made to match these Hat Boxes.

**HAT BOXES.** As above. Coloured canvas. Colours: Blue, Red, and Green. Sizes: 16 and 18 ins.

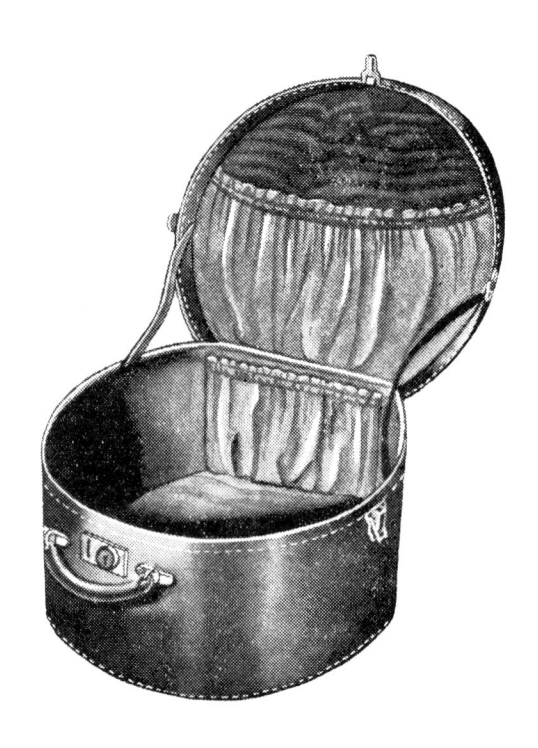

**HAT BOX.** Round. Solid leather, with best round leather handle. English lever lock. Two strong pin clips. Watered silk lining, with drawn pockets in lid and back. Best selected leather on heavy fibre board foundation. All hand sewn. Sizes: 16, 18, and 20 ins.

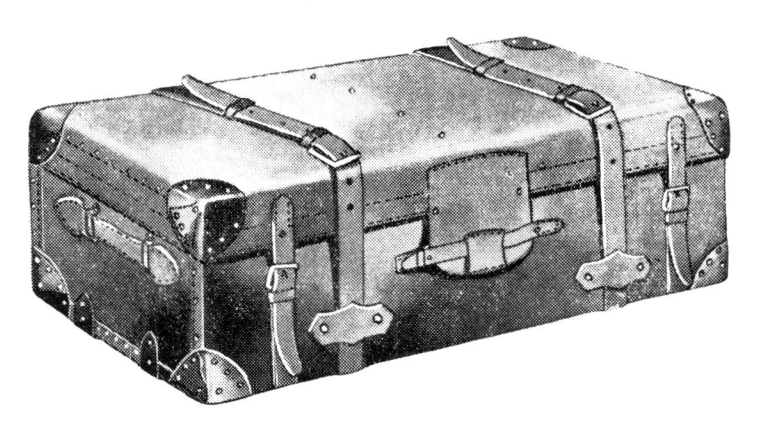

**CABIN TRUNK.** Solid leather. Turn over ends. Sewn and riveted. Eight leather capped corners. Two strong slide handles. One good English brass lever lock, with leather cover. Fastened with strap and buckles each end. Two strong straps around. Wooden battens on bottom. Strong drill lined, with tray on top. Selected leather on strong fibre foundation. Sizes: 30, 33, 36 ins. In first and second quality.
These are made to regulation sizes.

# TRAVELWARE SUNDRIES

## CANVAS HOLDALLS.

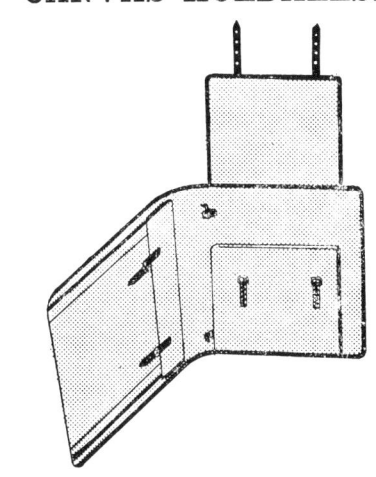

HOLDALL. Shown open.

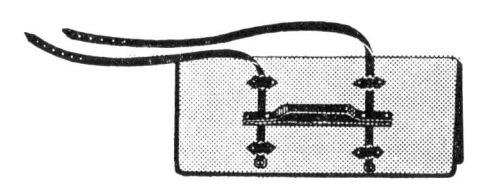

HOLDALL. Shown closed.

These Holdalls are used for carrying rugs, cushions, and various other articles. Made of strong grey or khaki waterproof canvas, bound with leather. Strong leather handle and straps. Pockets as illustrated. Sizes: 27, 30, 33, and 36 ins.

### SOILED LINEN BAGS.

Strong Waterproof Canvas Bag. Brass handle, with padlock. Used mainly for soiled linen, etc., when travelling.
Strong Waterproof Canvas Bag with kit bag frame instead of brass handle and padlock. Size: 30 x 22 ins.
Strong Waterproof Canvas with Zip fastener with attachment to lock. Size, 22 in. x 17 in. Assorted colours.

### TRAVELLING CUSHIONS.

An attractive Suede Cushion, with pockets and handle for carrying. Size: 18 x 12 ins.

### ONKAPARINGA KNEE RUGS.

**RANGE 14X.** 48 x 42 ins. A lightweight, finely woven Merino Rug.
**RANGE 14X.** As above. 68 x 54 ins.
**RANGE 13.** 42 x 42 ins. A heavier and slightly coarser weave Merino Rug.
These are used for motor travelling, or where a small size rug is required.

### TRAP RUGS.

**BLACK WATERPROOF.** With coloured back. As used by persons driving an open vehicle such as buggy, trolly, or motor lorry. Size: 60 x 48 ins.
As above. Waterproof canvas, with good quality check lining. Size: 69 x 48 ins.

### DUST RUGS.

These are a cotton fringed light rug for summer use. Size: 54 x 48 ins.

## WOOL TRAVELLING RUGS.

### ONKAPARINGA TRAVELLING RUGS.

**RENOWN.** Crossbred wool. Weight approximately 3 lb. Size: 72 x 54 ins.
**COOEE.** Crossbred wool. Weight approximately 3¼ lb. Size: 70 x 56 ins.
**RANGE 9.** Crossbred wool. Weight approximately 3½ lb. 72 x 60 ins.
**RANGE 9.** Crossbred wool. Weight approximately 3½ lb. 80 x 100 ins.
**UTILITY.** Crossbred wool. Weight approximately 3½ lb. Size: 60 x 80 ins.
**RANGE 10.** Crossbred wool. Weight approximately 4 lb. Size: 72 x 60 ins.
**RANGE 11.** Crossbred wool. Weight approximately 4¼ lb. Size: 72 x 60 ins. Fancy weave.
**ECLYSE.** Merino wool. Weight approximately 3½ lb. Size: 72 x 60 ins. Twisted weave.
**SPECIAL.** Merino wool. Weight approximately 3¼ lb. Size: 72 x 60 ins. Light weight.
**RANGE 12.** Merino wool. Weight approximately 3¾ lb. Size: 72 x 60 ins. Medium weight.
**RANGE 13.** Merino wool. Weight approximately 4 lb. Size: 72 x 60 ins. Heavy medium weight.
**RANGE 14.** Merino wool. Weight approximately 4 lb. Size: 84 x 60 ins. Fine merino yarn.
**RANGE 15.** Merino wool. Weight approximately 4 lb. Size: 84 x 60 ins. Fine merino yarn.
**RANGE 19.** Merino wool. Heavy weight. Size: 84 x 60 ins. Extra super fine. Double woven.
**TWEEDVALE.** Merino wool. Size: 80 x 60 ins. Fine merino yarn. Bright colours.

THESE RUGS CAN BE HAD IN ALL THE LATEST PATTERNS, AND A VERY GOOD ASSORTMENT OF COLOURS.

HF 104　　　　　　　　HARRIS, SCARFE, LIMITED.

# AIRWAY LUGGAGE

Made of woven-striped canvas, thoroughly waterproofed, on a dovetailed wooden body. The canvas does not scratch or stain. Leather binding protects the edges and lends distinction. Airway Cases are specially suitable for aerial travel, but are splendid for ordinary use as well.

### LADY'S CASE.

No. 305. **AIRWAY LADY'S CASE.** Is neatly finished in banded canvas on a non-warping, lightweight body. Fitted with padded leather handle, nickel mounts and locks. The rounded edges are leather bound. There are four pockets inside—one in the lid and three on the sides. Sizes: 22, 24, 26 in. and 28 in long.

### GENT'S TOUROBE.

No. 320. **AIRWAY TOUROBE.** Is built for carrying like a suit case; for use as a portable wardrobe. It has two "fall-down" hinged compartments, three hangers, and a shoe compartment at lower left. The rounded edges are reinforced, and the corners have brass guards. The locks are brass. Size: 34 in. high, 19 in. wide, 10 in. deep, closed. Colours: Black with Green Stripe (No. 151 Black); Brown with Fawn Stripe (No. 151 Brown); Brown with Dark Brown Stripe (No. 152); Brown with Light Stripe (No. 149).

No. 325. **AIRWAY WARDROBE TRUNK.** As No. 320 Tourobe, with half lift-up. Padded top. Three ordinary slide drawers. Size: 36 in. high, 20 in. wide, 12 in. deep, closed.

Can be supplied in Colours, as No. 320 Airway Tourobe.

### GENT'S WARDROBE CASE.

No. 315. **AIRWAY WARDROBE CASE.** Carries like a suit case, and is equipped with three hangers for carrying suits in the deep lid; four compartments in the body of the case. The edges are rounded, the ends leather-bound. Locks and fittings are nickel. Size: 25 in. long, 20 in. wide, 11 in. deep, closed.

No. 35401. **CABIN TRUNK.** To match. 36 in. Regulation size. With tray.

### HAT BOX.

No. 308. **HAT BOX.** This hat box has leather reinforced edges, and is fitted with four roomy pockets: one in the lid, three on the sides. The fitings are nickel. Size: 18 in. long, 16 in. wide, 10 in. deep.

# WARDROBE TRUNKS

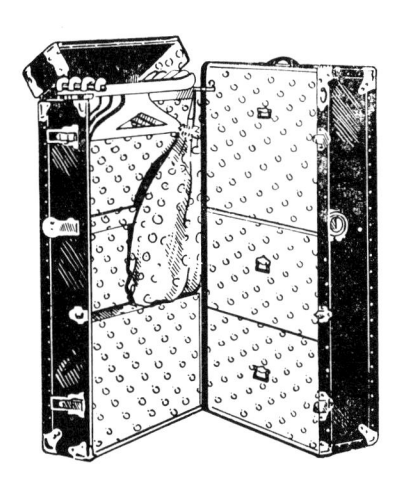

**No. W504. TAXI STEAMER WARDROBE TRUNK.** Brass plated exterior fittings. Three drawers in right side, top drawer of which is hinged. Four hangers on left side. Removable shoe box. Loose soiled linen bag. Lift-up top. Lined throughout with attractive printed lining. Size: 41 x 22 x 14 ins. Colour: Black, with black binding.

**No. W508. JUNIOR WARDROBE TRUNK.** Vulcanised fibre on plywood. Two lock bolts. Solid leather handles on top and sides. Three removable drawers. Four hangers. Shoe compartment. Lift-up cushion top. Lined with attractive two-tone lining. Size: 36 x 20 x 12 ins. Colour: Black, with grey binding.

**No. T574. PULLMAN TRAVEL CASE.** Nickel plated fittings. Two locking bolts. Solid hide handle, with nickel plated chapes. Inside removable tray, with tie tapes for packing purposes. Strong metal hinges and lid stays. Attractive floral lining. Size: 30 x 17 x 9 ins. Very easy to carry. Colours: Blue, with black binding; or light grey, with dark grey binding.

**No. W503. TAXI STEAMER WARDROBE TRUNK.** Brass plated mounts and locks. Four drawers, with locking bar, and lift-up cushion top. Removable shoe box. Exterior supporting down depth of trunk. Laundry bag lightning zip fastener. Four hangers and scarf bag. Printed cotton lining. Size: 41 x 22 x 14 ins. Stock colours: Black with black binding; Black with green binding.

**No. W501X.** As W503, but three-quarter size. 41 x 22 x 19 ins.

THESE ARE OUR STOCK LINES. OTHERS CAN BE MADE TO ORDER. GET OUR ILLUSTRATIONS.

# TRAVELWARE

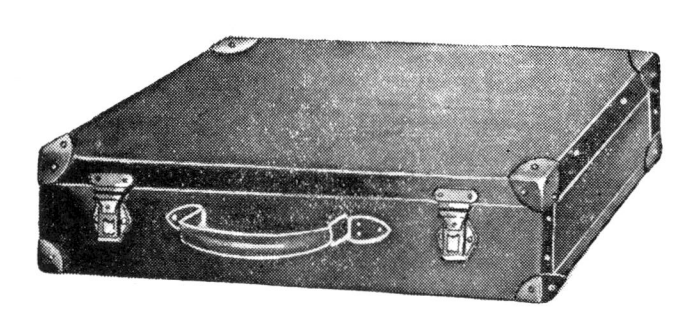

**No. 27. FIBRE SUIT CASES.** Grained fibre. Two locks. Wood frame in lid. Strong metal body frame. Steel handle. Vulcanised fibre corners. In sizes: 20 x 11½ x 6 ins.; 22 x 13½ x 7¼ ins.; 24 x 15 x 8 ins.; 26 x 17 x 8½ ins.; 28 x 18½ x 9 ins.

**No. D1. FIBRE SUIT CASE.** Grained fibre. Two strong locks. Wood frame in lid. Strong metal body frame. Steel handle. Vulcanised fibre corners. In sizes: 20 x 11½ x 6 ins.; 22 x 13½ x 7¼ ins.; 24 x 15 x 8 ins.; 26 x 17 x 8½ ins.; 28 x 18½ x 9 ins.

**No. 29B. BEATZALL FIBRE SUIT CASE.** Grained fibre. Two strong locks. Wood frame in lid. All lid and body edges metal bound. Steel handle. Embossed bands. Paper lined. Vulcanised fibre corners. In sizes: 22 x 13½ x 7¼ ins.; 24 x 15 x 8 ins.; 26 x 17 x 8½ ins.; 28 x 18½ x 9 ins.

**No. 22031. FORDITE FIBRE SUIT CASE.** Grained fibre. Two strong safety locks. Extra deep steel body frame. Lid edges metal bound. Wood frame in lid. Paper lined. Reinforced bands across lid and body. In sizes: 22 x 13 x 7 ins.; 24 x 15 x 7½ ins.; 26 x 17 x 8 ins.; 28 x 18 x 8¾ ins.

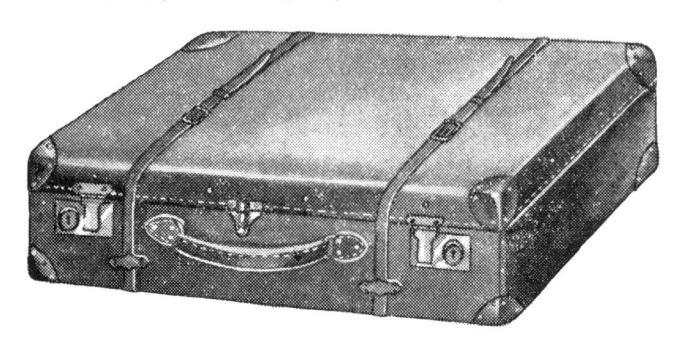

**No. 34. FIBRE SUIT CASE.** Smooth fibre. Two strong safety locks. Steel body frame. Full metal binding on lid. Wood frame in lid. Two solid leather straps encircling case. Round edges with neat fitting corners. Lid has stitching along edge. Solid leather handle and chapes. Strongly made, but light in weight. In sizes: 22 x 13 x 7 ins.; 24 x 14½ x 8 ins.; 26 x 17 x 8½ ins.; 28 x 17½ x 9½ ins.; 30 x 19½ x 10 ins.

**No. 33. FIBRE SUIT CASE.** As No. 34, with metal handle plates instead of leather chapes.

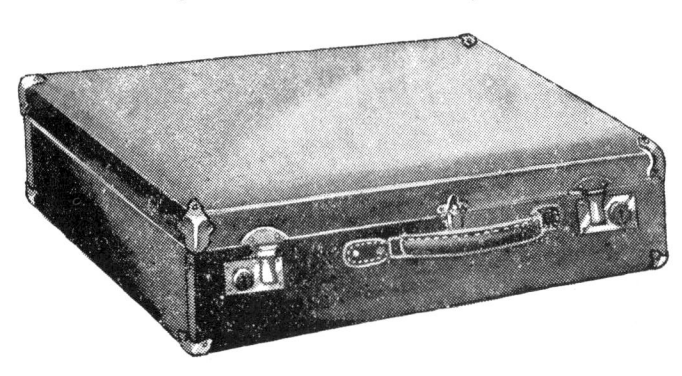

**No. 1858. GLOBITE FIBRE SUIT CASE.** Smooth fibre. Fitted with metal corners. Hand riveted hinges. Strong metal body. English lever locks. Striped cotton lining. Leather handle and chapes. With two metal lid stays. In sizes: 22 x 13½ x 7½ ins.; 24 x 15 x 8 ins.; 26 x 17½ x 8½ ins.; 28 x 19 x 9 ins.

**No. 1853. GLOBITE FIBRE SUIT CASE.** Grained fibre, with fibre corners. English slide locks. Embossed bands. Globite handle. Wood frame in lid. Paper lined. Two lid stays. Metal edging on lid. Special folded steel body frame. In sizes: 22 x 13½ x 7½ ins.; 24 x 15 x 8 ins.; 26 x 17½ x 8½ ins.; 28 x 19 x 9 ins.

# FIBRE CASES, ETC.

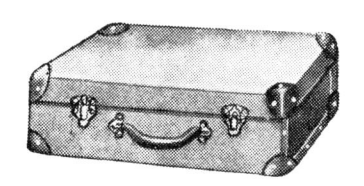

No. J54. ATTACHE CASE. Grained fibre. Two clip fasteners. Metal frame. Metal hinges and handle. Sizes: 12 x 7½ x 4¼ ins.; 14 x 8¾ x 4½ ins.; 16 x 10 x 5 ins.; 18 x 11 x 5½ ins.; 20 x 12 x 6 ins.

No. D3. "BEATZALL" ATTACHE CASE. Grained fibre. Two clip fasteners with lock in centre. Metal frame, hinges, and handle. With embossed bands around. Sizes: 12 x 8 x 5¼ ins.; 14 x 8¾ x 5½ ins.; 16 x 9½ x 6 ins.; 18 x 11 x 6¾ ins.; 20 x 12 x 7 ins.

No. D2. "BEATZALL" ATTACHE CASE. As above, with two clip fasteners only. Sizes as No. D3.

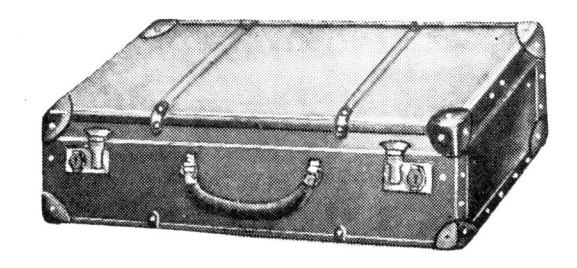

No. 22014. "FORDITE" ATTACHE CASE. Grained fibre. With two safety locks. Metal bound, with wood frame in lid. Vulcanised fibre corners and handle. With four angle metal edges to prevent wear when used as a school case. Sizes: 14 x 9 x 5 ins.; 16 x 10 x 6 ins.; 18 x 11 x 6½ ins.; 20 x 12 x 7 ins.

No. 22011. "FORDITE" ATTACHE CASE. Grained fibre. With two safety locks. Metal bound. Vulcanised corners and handle. Wooden frame in lid, and embossed bands around. Sizes: 14 x 9 x 5 ins.; 16 x 10 x 5½ ins.; 18 x 11 x 6 ins.; 20 x 12 x 6½ ins.

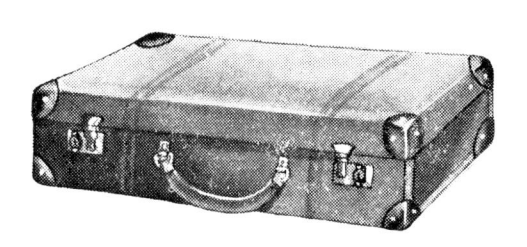

No. 1838. "GLOBITE" ATTACHE CASE. Grained, vulcanised fibre. With two safety locks. Vulcanised fibre corners and handle. Metal bound, with embossed bands. Unlined. Sizes: 14, 16, 18, 20 ins.

No. 1841. "GLOBITE" ATTACHE CASE. As No. 1840, with lining.

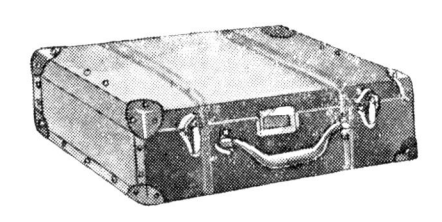

No. 3872. FITTED SCHOOL CASE. "Fordite" grained fibre. With metal hinges, pin clips, handle, and card holder for name. Metal bound pocket in lid containing ruler, pen holder, and pencil. Brown. Sizes: 14 in. and 16 in.

No. 3835. FITTED SCHOOL CASE. Grained fibre. With metal hinges and handle. With 2 safety locks. Metal bound and edged. Containing ruler, penholder, and pencil. Colours: Blue, Red, and Brown. Sizes: 14 in. and 16 in.

No. J54. FITTED SCHOOL CASE. As No. J54 Attache Case. With ruler, penholder, and pencil. Brown. Sizes: 14 in. and 16 in.

LUNCH BOXES. Grained fibre. With metal pin clip, and leather handle. Sizes: 8, 9, 10, 11, and 12 ins.

# FIBRE SUNDRIES

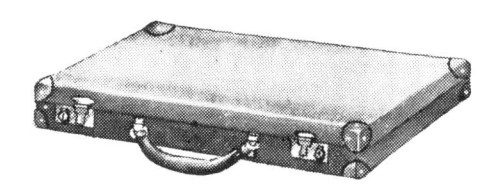

No. 4192. "GLOBITE" MUSIC CASE. Vulcanised grained fibre. With metal hinges. Two English safety locks. Globite corners and handle. Metal bound. Size: 15 x 11½ x 3 ins.

No. 4182V. "FORDITE" MUSIC CASE. Grained fibre. With metal hinges. Two English safety locks. Vulcanised fibre corners and handle. Metal bound. Size: 15 x 11½ x 3 ins.

No. J46. "BEATZALL" MUSIC CASE. Grained fibre. With metal hinges and locks. Vulcanised fibre corners. Metal handle and metal bound. Size: 15 x 11 x 3 ins.

No. H1612. MUSIC CASE. Grained fibre. With metal hinges and pin clips. Vulcanised fibre corners. Metal handle and metal bound. Size: 14½ x 10½ x 3½ ins.

No. 4195. "GLOBITE" BUSINESS CASE. As No. 4192 Globite Music Case. Size: 16 x 12 x 4 ins.

No. J61F. HAT BOX. Grained fibre. Stitched edges. Centre lock and two side pin catches. Metal handle. Paper lined. Round. Colours: Brown or Blue. Sizes: 14, 16, 18 and 20 ins.
No. J62F. HAT BOX. As No. J61F, with bound and stitched edges.

No. J35. "FORDITE" HAT BOX. Grained fibre. Edges strongly bound and stitched. With centre lock and two side pin catches. Globite fibre handle. Cloth lined, with pocket in lid. Sizes: 14, 16, and 18 ins.

No. 2056. "GLOBITE" HAT BOX. Vulcanised grained fibre. Edges of fibre turned over and strongly riveted. Centre lock and two side pin catches. Cloth lined, with pocket in lid. Sizes: 14, 16, 18, and 20 ins.

No. 1739. "GLOBITE" CABIN TRUNK. Vulcanised fibre on 3-ply. End edges of Trunk covered with vulcanised fibre angle pieces, securely riveted. Patent brass double secure English locks. Best cloth lining. Strong inside tray with tie tapes. Neat finish throughout. Brass expansion hinges. With 3 bands on 30 in. and 33 in.; 4 bands on 36 in. Sizes: 30, 33, and 36 in.

No. 1725. "FORDITE" CABIN TRUNK. Broad grain trunk weight fibre. Brass English locks. Solid leather corners. Strong lid and body frames. End handles. Cloth lined. With full length tray. 3 bands on 30 in. and 33 in.; and 4 bands on 36 in. Sizes. 30, 33, and 36 ins.

No. 1735. "GLOBITE" CABIN TRUNK. High quality fibre, otherwise as No. 1725. With Globite improvements throughout. Exceptionally light, but strong. Sizes: 30, 33, and 36 ins.

No. 1648. "FORDITE" CABIN CASE. Graned fibre, with hardwood bands. Leather corners. Two best brass English locks and centre clip. Leather handle. Strong hinges. With inside tray lined. To carry like suit case. Sizes. 24, 26, 28, and 30 ins.

No. 1885. "GLOBITE" CABIN CASE. Globite corners and handle. Two English lever locks. Round edges, with wood battens. Extra wide and deep. Strong body frame and hinges. Cloth lined. Sizes: 24, 26, 28, and 30 ins.

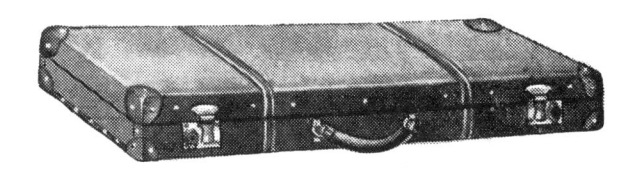

No. 3120. "GLOBITE" TENNIS CASE. Vulcanised grained fibre. With metal hinges and stay. Two English safety locks. Globite corners and handle. Embossed bands with loop and flap to hold racquet. Lined. Metal bound edges, with wood frame in lid. Size: 29 x 10½ x 4½ ins.

No. 3115. "FORDITE" TENNIS CASE. Grained fibre. Metal hinges. Leather stay. Two English locks. Vulcanised corners and handle. Metal bound edges and wood frame in lid. Embossed bands. Size: 29 x 10½ x 5 ins.

No. 42845. TENNIS CASE. Grained fibre. Metal hinges, handle, and two pin clips. Vulcanised fibre corners. Edges metal bound, with wood frame in lid. Size: 28 x 10½ x 3½ ins.

# STEEL TRUNKS

**GAWLER PATTERN TRUNK.** Corrugated body, reinforced with stamped steel corners. Stove japanned. Medium Oak. With lock and key. Sizes:

22 ins. wide x 12¼ ins. high x 12½ ins. deep.

24 ins. wide x 13½ ins. high x 14½ ins. deep.

26 ins. wide x 15 ins. high x 15¾ ins. deep.

28 ins. wide x 16 ins. high x 17½ ins. deep.

30 ins. wide x 17 ins. high x 19¼ ins. deep.


**COASTAL PATTERN TRUNK.** Strapped bottom, reinforced with stamped steel corners. Stove japanned Oak. With additional front handle. Lock and key. Sizes:

24 ins. wide x 14½ ins. deep x 11 ins. high.

27 ins. wide x 16 ins. deep x 12 ins. high.

30 ins. wide x 18¼ ins. deep x 13 ins. high.

36 ins. wide x 20½ ins. deep x 14 ins. high.


**CONTINENTAL PATTERN TRUNK.** Strapped body and cover. Reinforced with stamped steel corners. Stove japanned mahogany grained. With triple rod lock and key. Size: 36 ins. wide x 21 ins. deep x 14 ins. high.


**TRAYS CAN BE MADE FOR ABOVE TRUNKS.**

# SOLE LEATHERS AND CUT SOLES

## CUT SOLES, LEATHER.

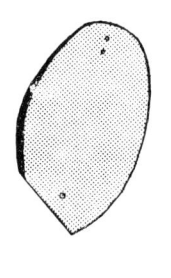

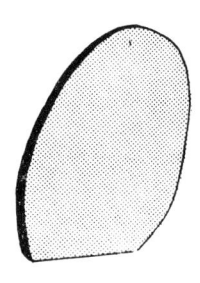

**MEN'S.** Sizes 6 to 10.
- No. 1. Best Butt. Bark tanned.
- No. 2. Second Butt. Bark tanned.
- No. 3. Shoulder. Bark tanned.
- No. 4. Chrome Shoulder.
- No. 5. Chrome Butt.

**LADIES'.** Sizes 2 to 7.
- No. 1. Best Butt. Bark tanned.
- No. 2. Second Butt. Bark tanned.
- No. 3. Shoulder. Bark tanned.
- No. 4. Chrome Shoulder.

**YOUTHS'.** Sizes 2 to 5.
- No. 1. Best Butt. Bark tanned.
- No. 2. Second Butt. Bark tanned.
- No. 3. Shoulder. Bark tanned.
- No. 4. Chrome Shoulder.

**Children's.** Sizes 10 to 1.
- No. 1. Best Butt. Bark tanned.
- No. 2. Second Butt. Bark tanned.
- No. 3. Shoulder. Bark tanned.
- No. 4. Chrome Shoulder.

## SOLES, HEELS, TACKS AND TIPS.

Special Men's. Ladies'.

## KROMHYD CUT SOLES.

| | | |
|---|---|---|
| Men's. | $\frac{3}{16}, \frac{5}{32}, \frac{1}{8}$. | Sizes 6 to 10. |
| Youths' | $\frac{3}{16}, \frac{5}{32}, \frac{1}{8}$. | Sizes 2 to 5. |
| Women's | $\frac{3}{16}, \frac{5}{32}, \frac{1}{8}$. | Sizes 2 to 7. |
| Children's | $\frac{3}{16}, \frac{5}{32}, \frac{1}{8}$. | Sizes 10 to 1. |

## HEEL, CUT.

- Men's .. Leather. Shoulder.
- Men's .. Leather. Butt.
- Ladies' .. Leather. Butt.
- Men's .. Kromhyd.
- Ladies' .. Kromhyd.

## KROMHYD OUTFITS.

In Cartons. As illustration. Containing 1 pair Kromhyd Stick-on Soles, 1 Bottle of Solution, and roughening tool. Gent's, light and heavy weight; Ladies', light weight only. As above, in envelopes. Ladies' and Men's.

## RE NU SYNTHETIC RUBBER.

For repairing tennis shoes. Also for motor tyres. Small and large.

## ESYWAY SYNTHETIC RUBBER.

As Renu. .. .. .. Large size only.

HARRIS, SCARFE, LIMITED.     HF 111

# KROMHYD SPORTS SOLES AND HEELS

### GOLF PATTERN.

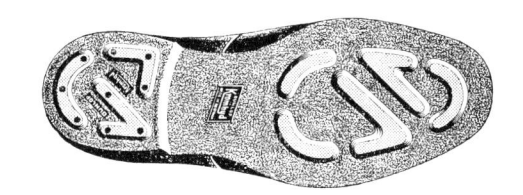

Sizes: Men's Soles    ..    ..    5–6, 7–8, 9–10.
        Men's Heels    ..    ..    5–6, 7–8, 9–10.

### STUDDED.

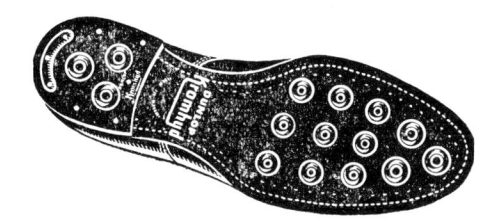

Sizes: Men's Soles    ..    ..    5–6, 7–8, 9–10.
        Women's Soles    ..    ..    2–3, 4–5, 6–7.
        Youths' Soles    ..    ..    2–3–4.
        Boys' Soles    ..    ..    9–10–11, 12–13–1.
        Men's Heels. Heavy, medium, light    5–6, 7–8, 9–10.
        Women's Heels    ..    ..    2–3, 4–5, 6–7.

### LATTICE.

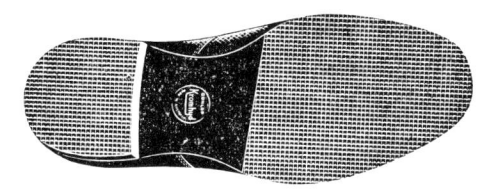

Sizes: Men's Soles    ..    ..    5–6, 7–8, 9–10.
        Women's Soles    ..    ..    2–3, 4–5, 6–7.
        Men's Heels. Heavy, medium, light    5–6, 7–8, 9–10.
        Women's Heels. Light only    ..    2–3, 4–5, 6–7.

### GRID.

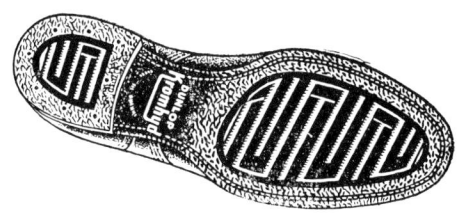

Sizes: Men's Soles    ..    ..    5–6, 7–8, 9–10.
        Women's Soles    ..    ..    2–3, 4–5, 6–7.
        Men's Heels. Light only    ..    5–6, 7–8, 9–10.
        Women's Heels    ..    ..    2–3, 4–5, 6–7.

### PYRAMID.

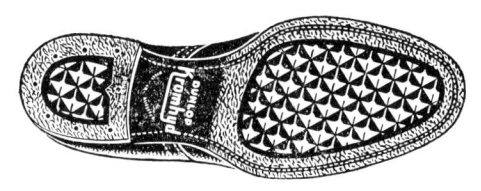

Sizes: Men's Soles    ..    ..    5–6, 7–8, 9–10.
        Women's Soles    ..    ..    2–3, 4–5, 6–7.
        Men's Heels. Light only    ..    5–6, 7–8, 9–10.
        Women's Heels    ..    ..    2–3, 4–5, 6–7.

### SPORTS PATTERN.

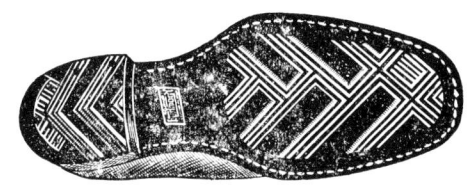

Sizes: Men's Soles    ..    ..    5–6, 7–8, 9–10.
        Women's Soles    ..    ..    2–3, 4–5, 6–7.
        Men's Heels. Medium only    5–6, 7–8, 9–10.
        Women's Heels    ..    ..    2–3, 4–5, 6–7.

### NON SKID.

Sizes: Men's Soles    ..    ..    5–6, 7–8, 9–10.
        Men's Heels. Heavy only    5–6, 7–8, 9–10.

HF 112　　　　　　　　　HARRIS, SCARFE, LIMITED.

# GRINDERY SUNDRIES

## I.R. SHAPED HEELS.

**DUNLOP OR BARNET SHAPED HEELS.** Black or Tan.

Men's. .. Sizes: 4, 5, 6, 7-8, 9-10, 10-11, 11-12. Black only.

Men's. Police. .. 5-6, 7-8, 9-10, 11-12. Black only.

Mens'. Round. .. 1¾, 2¼, 2½, 2⅜, 2½, 2¾. Black only.

Ladies' Shaped. Sizes: C, D, E, F, G, H, J, K, L. Ladies',

Ladies'. Round. .. .. 1¾, 1½, 1⅝, 1¾. Black only.

Ladies'. Louis. .. 7-0, 6-0, 5-0, 3-0, 0, 2, 4, 6. Black only.

## HEEL GRIPS.

**CARDED.** .. .. Colours: White, Black, or Brown. 1 dozen pairs on card.

**S.O.X.** Velvet, to stick in. .. Ladies' or Gent's.

**PHILLIPS' VENTILATED.** Cup shape heel grip. Ladies' and Gent's.

**BOOMERANG.** Plain cup-shaped heel grip. Ladies' or Gent's. Heel Grips fit in heel of shoe and prevent heel slipping; also adds life to stockings.

## HEEL PADS.

**SPONGE RUBBER.** .. .. Flat. ⅛ in. thick.

**SPONGE RUBBER.** .. Tapered. 5/16 and ¼ in. thick.

## INSOLES.

**CORK "HOLDFAST".** Men's sizes: 6, 7, 8, 9, and 10. Ladies' sizes: 2, 3, 4, 5, 6, and 7.

**CORK, WITH ARCH SUPPORT.** Men's sizes: 5, 6, 7, 8, 9, and 10. Ladies' sizes: 3, 4, 5, 6, and 7.

**LAMBSWOOL.** Men's sizes: 6, 7, 8, 9, and 10. Ladies' sizes: 3, 4, 5, 6, and 7.

**SPONGE RUBBER.** ⅛, ¼, and ⅜ in. thick. Small sizes, 2-3-4; medium, 5-6-7; large, 8-9-10.

---

## INSTEP SUPPORTS.

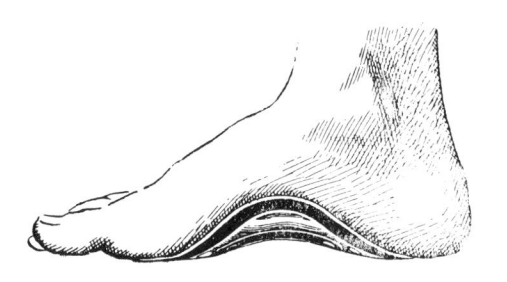

**DR. WARNER'S JOYWALKS.** Sizes: Ladies', 3 to 5 and 6 to 8; Men's, 6 to 8 and 9 to 11. A sure cure for tired and aching feet.

HARRIS, SCARFE, LIMITED.  HF 113

# SHOEMAKERS' REQUISITES

## ANVILS OR LASTS.

No. 4471. Cast iron, japanned. No. 1, small size; No. 2, large size.

**FULL FOOT.** Japanned. As above, with three full feet.

## "ADJUSTABLE" BOOT LAST.

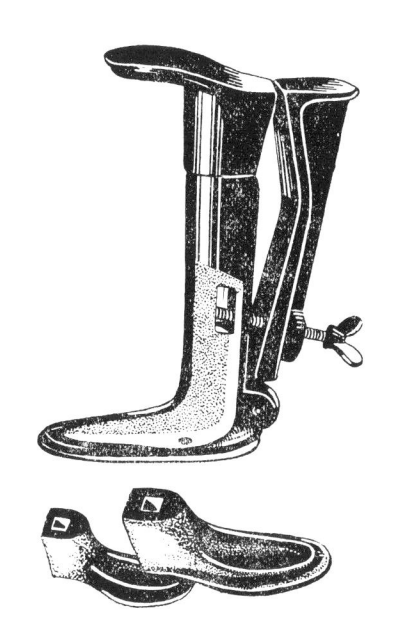

A good, solid last which can be made to fit any boot or shoe by turning wing nut on side. Also holds them firm. Complete as illustration, with three feet.

## COBBLER'S KITS.

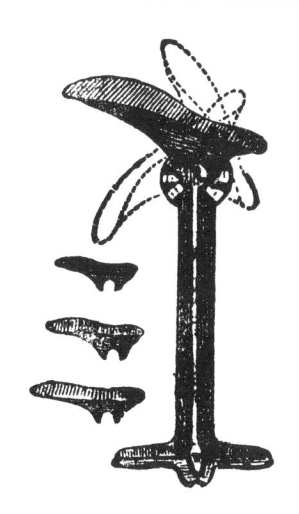

No. 4469. Cast iron Swivel lasts. Length of standard, 14 ins. Lasts, 5½, 7, 8, and 9½ ins. long. Set complete with 4 lasts.

## HAMMERS

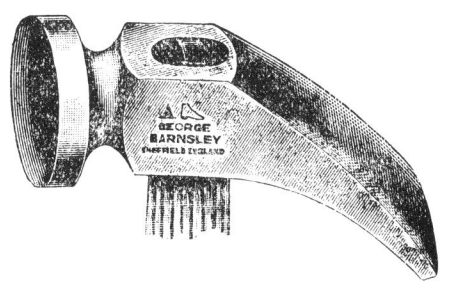

BARNSLEY'S. Black steel, with bright polished pane. Polished round ash haft. Nos. 0, 1, 2, 3, and 4.
BLECKMANN'S. .. .. As above. Nos. 1, 2, 3.
COLONIAL. .. .. As above. Nos. 1, 2, 3.

## SHOE RASPS.

BARNSLEY'S. Best quality, ¼ or ½ file. 6, 7, 8, 9, and 10 ins.

HF 114　　　　　　　　　　HARRIS, SCARFE, LIMITED.

# SHOEMAKERS' REQUISITES

## AWLS.

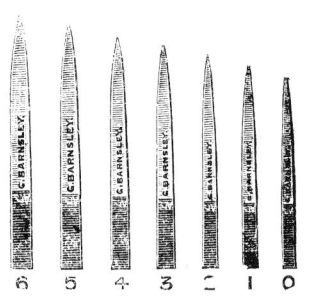

BARNSLEY'S. American Square Peg. Small and medium. Nos. 1, 2, 3, 4, 5, and 6.

BARNSLEY'S SEWING. Best quality steel. Medium bend. Assorted sizes.

THORNHILL'S SEWING. Cast steel. Medium bend. Assorted sizes.

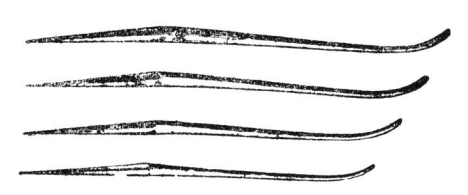

CLOSING. .. Best quality steel. Assorted sizes.

STABBING. Best quality steel. Round points. Assorted sizes.

## AWL HAFTS.

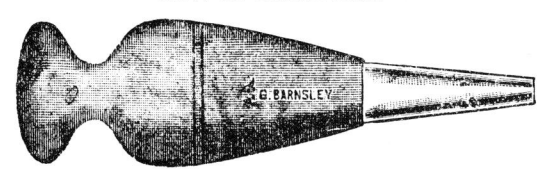

No. 01. .. Beechwood. Solid steel ferrule, polished.

## NEEDLES.

BOOTMAKER'S SEWING. Flexible, in packet of 6 pairs. Pliable, in packet of 12 pairs.

## PEG AWL HAFTS.

No. 3146½. BLECKMANN'S. Adjustable, with leather tops. Complete, packet 12 in a box.

## FORE-PART IRONS.

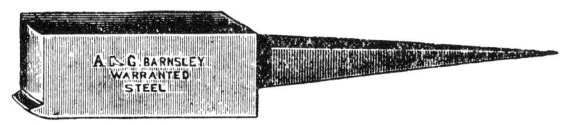

No. 1C. BARNSLEY'S. Handled. .. Cut, ready for use.
No. 48. FRENCH GLAZING IRON. Black. Round handle.

## EDGE PLANES.

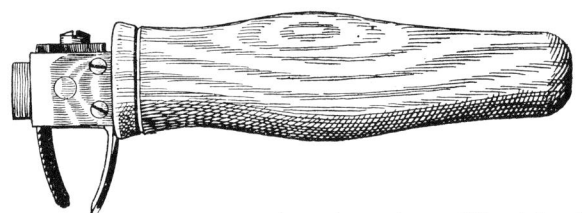

No. T325A. Best quality steel cutting edges. Wood handle.
No. 135. Edge Plain or Superseded. Best quality steel. Wood handle.

## WELT TRIMMERS.

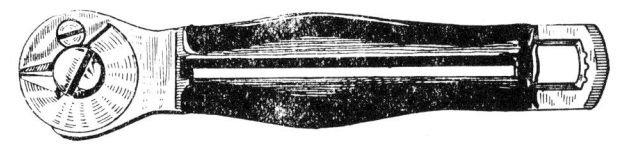

No. T323. Iron handle, concave blades. With interchangeable guards and blades.

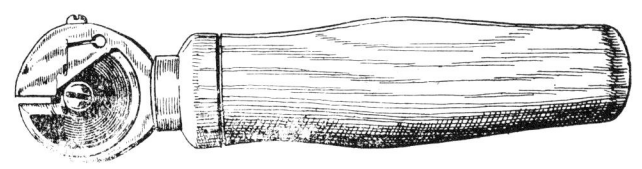

No. T324. Wood handle, concave blade. With interchangeable guards and blades.

## FUDGE WHEELS.

No. 30 x 3/16. .. .. .. For welted soles.

# SHOEMAKERS' REQUISITES

## SHOE KNIVES

No. 332. **STUTTER'S.** Beech handle, securely riveted. Blade 4 ins.

No. 333. **STUTTER'S.** Beech handle, securely riveted. Blade, 4 ins.

No. 111. **BARNSLEY'S.** Shoe. Boxwood handles. Silver steel. Scale tang riveted. Blade, 4 ins.

No. 402. **BARNSLEY'S.** Wood handles. Clip point. Damascus steel. 4½ in. blade.

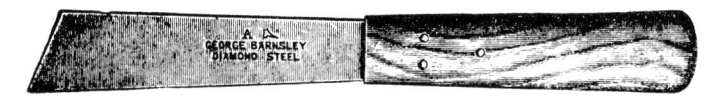

No. 707. **"WIDE AWAKE.** .. .. 4 ins., 4½ ins.

**CONTINENTAL.** .. .. .. 4 in. blade.

No. 202. **BARNSLEY'S.** Broad point. Oval rosewood handle, scale tang riveted. "Diamond" steel blade, 4, 4½, 6 ins.

## SHOE PUNCH PLIERS.

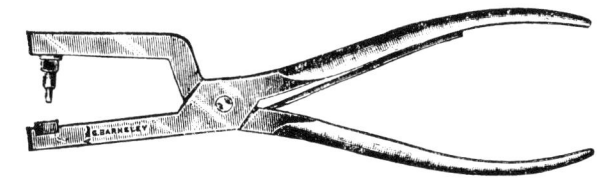

**BARNSLEY'S.** Good grade steel, bent grips. Fitted with steel punches.
Nos. 1, 3, 4, 5, 6, and 7. .. Extra steel punches stocked.

### CLICKING KNIFE.
3¼ in. blade, round handle, curved point.

## SHOE PINCERS.

Nos. **1, 2,** and **3.** Shoe Lasting. Square hammer. Bent shanks.
No. 1, 7½ ins.; No. 2, 8 ins.; No. 3, 8½ ins.

## DRAG KNIVES.

No. 52. **BARNSLEY'S.** Boxwood handle. Blades ⅝ and ¾ ins.

## HEEL SHAVES.

No. **T330.** .. Cut steel handles. Assorted blade sweeps.

## JOINT STRETCHERS.

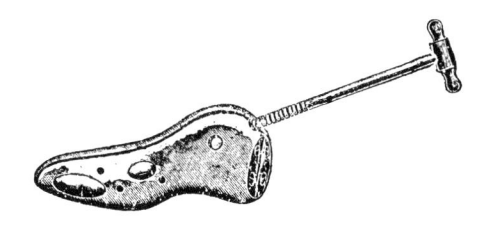

No. **T309.** Assorted sizes. Plain unpolished feet. With bunion and corn pieces. For ladies' and gent's shoes.

## EYELET HOLE PLIERS.

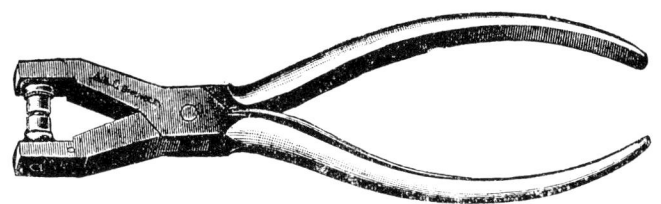

**BARNSLEY'S.** Bent grips, solid steel jaws. Nos. 1 and 2.

## BUTTONHOLE PLIERS.

For cutting buttonholes. Sizes, ½, ⅝, ¾ in.

# SHOEMAKERS' REQUISITES

## FINISHINGS, DIES, ETC.

### HOLDFAST WAX FINISHING INK.
For heels, edges, and bottoms of boots and shoes. Gives a brilliant polish if brushed when damp or dry. Black. Sizes: ½ pt., 1 pt., 1 quart, and 1-gallon tins.

### QUICK RUSSETS.
A stain for bottoms, heels, and edges of soles. ½ and 1-pt. tins. Colours: No. 320, medium tan; No. 345, dark tan; No. 61, nigger brown; No. 5232, champagne; No. 325, white. When ordering order by numbers.

### TOE STIFFENER.
"BOSTON." For making box toes. This article makes a more elastic and firmer box toe than any other preparation. In 16-oz. tins.
Size 2 = ½ pint; 3 = 1 pint; 4 = 2 pints. American measure.
elastic and firmer box toe than any other preparation.

### QUICK BLACK.
"BOSTON." A jet black finish for heels and bottoms of soles. In 16-oz. tins.
Size 2 = ½ pint; 3 = 1 pint; 4 = 2 pints. American measure.
harness leathers. Invaluable for redressing old stock.

### SIZE DRESSING.
"BOSCO." A heavy dressing suitable for split, kip, and all harness leathers. Invaluable for redressing old stock. In ½-pt. tins.
Size 2 = ½ pint; 3 = 1 pint; 4 = 2 pints. American measure.

### BURNISHING INK.
"LYNN'S." For burnishing heels, edges, and shank of shoes. Polishes easily. Will not crack or peel off. For hand or machine use. Sizes: 10 and 20-oz. bottles.

### HEEL BALL.
"BOSCO." A wax for finishing edges of heels and soles. Colours: Black and Tan. Large and small.

### CEMENT OR SOLUTION.
For sticking rubber to leather, or leather to leather.
"BEST OF ALL." Sizes: ⅛-pt., ¼-pt., ½-pt., 1-pt., and 1-gall. tins.
"SUREFAST."     ..     Sizes: 8-oz., 16-oz., and 1-gall. tins.
"GEM."     ..     ..     ..     Sizes: ½-pt., and 1-pt. tins.
"LITTLE WONDER."     ..     ..     2½-oz. tins.

HARRIS, SCARFE, LIMITED.   HF 117

# GRINDERY SUNDRIES

## BOOT PROTECTORS.

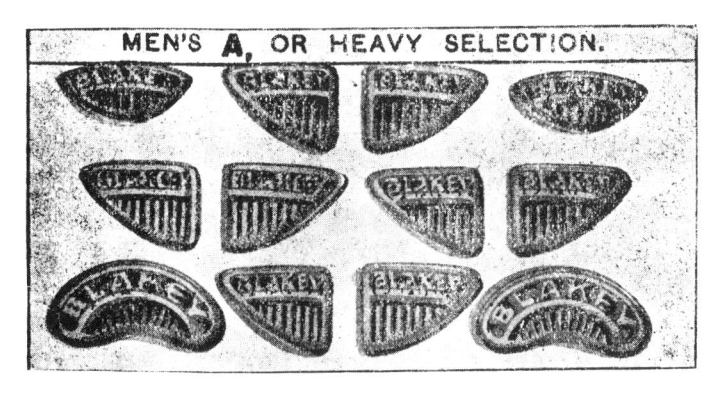

**MEN'S A, OR HEAVY SELECTION.**

BLAKEY'S. Men's A, or heavy selection. In packets comprising 12 assorted protectors.
ECLYPSE. .. In bags. Men's. 12 assorted protectors.

**BOYS' B, OR MEDIUM SELECTION.**

BLAKEY'S. Boys' B, or medium selection. In packets comprising 14 assorted protectors.
ECLYPSE. .. In bags. Boys. 14 assorted pieces.

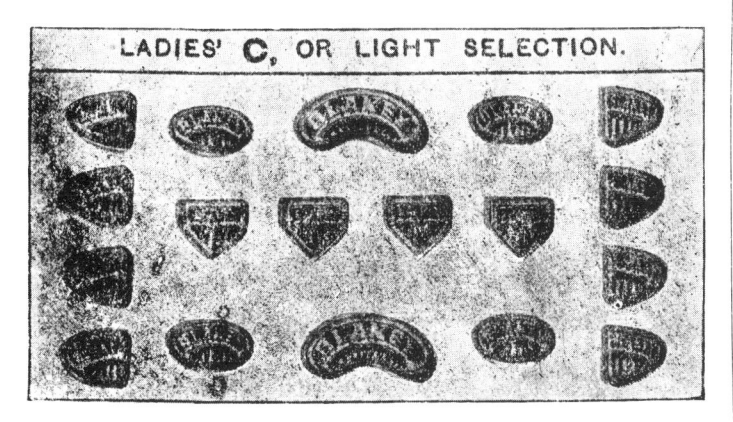

**LADIES' C, OR LIGHT SELECTION.**

BLAKEY'S. Ladies C, or light selection. In packets comprising 18 assorted protectors.
ECLYPSE. .. In bags. Ladies. 18 assorted protectors.
TEX. A round protector with three spikes. Size, $\frac{1}{2}$ in. across top. In packets or loose.

## TOE PLATES.

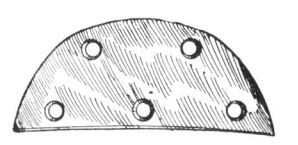

No. 10. SQUARE OR ROUND HOLE HEAVY TOE PLATES. Sizes: $2\frac{1}{2}$, $2\frac{5}{8}$, $2\frac{3}{4}$, $2\frac{7}{8}$, 3, and $3\frac{1}{4}$ ins. across.

## HEEL AND TOE PLATES.

TUFF TIPS. In packets containing 12 Tuff Tips and Special Nails; also 4 sample Disco Protectors.
NEWLEY TIPS. In packets containing 12 asorted Newley Tips, complete with nails.
REAL STEEL TIPS. In packets containing 12 assorted Tips complete with nails.
DANDY TIPS. .. .. .. See next page.
ADJUSTOE. For fixing around edge of sole at toe to prevent wear. On cards containing 12 pairs, complete with screws.

## HEEL PLATES.

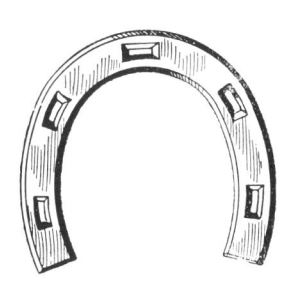

No. 21B. .. Square hole. $2\frac{1}{2}$, $2\frac{5}{8}$, $2\frac{3}{4}$, 3, and $3\frac{1}{4}$ ins.
No. 35. .. Round hole. $2\frac{1}{2}$, $2\frac{5}{8}$, $2\frac{3}{4}$, $2\frac{7}{8}$, 3, and $3\frac{1}{4}$ ins.

## QUARTER TIPS.

BLAKEY'S. .. Heavy leather plugged. Sizes: 2, 1, 0, 00.
RUBBER. Black or Tan. Sizes: Small, medium, large, and police.

## CIRCLETS.

Durable steel Circlets for around heels, to prevent wear. Shaped like a small horse shoe. Ladies' and Gent's. In packets of 1 gross circlets, and cartons of 12 packets=1 great gross.

# GRINDERY SUNDRIES

## HEEL AND TOE TIPS.

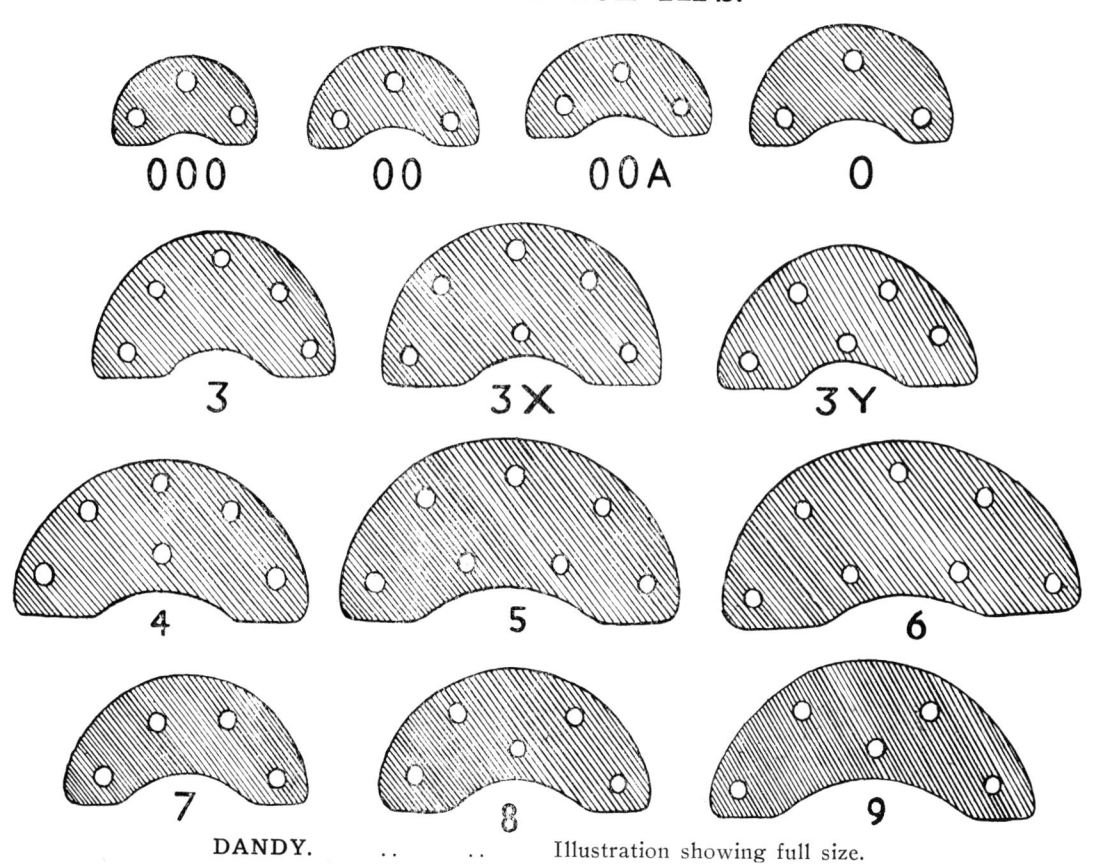

000   00   00A   0

3   3X   3Y

4   5   6

7   8   9

DANDY. .. .. Illustration showing full size.

## BOOT AND SHOE LACES.
### BOOT.

No. 9555. Flat. Black. Cotton. .. .. 36 in. long.
No. 9555. Flat. Tan. Cotton .. .. 36 in. long.
No. 9544. Round. Black. Cotton .. .. 36 in. long.
No. 9544. Round. Tan. Cotton .. .. 36 in. long.

"OLYMPIC." Round. Black, White, or Tan. Cotton. 36 in. long. Banded.

"OLYMPIC." Flat. Black or Tan. Cotton. 36 in. long. Banded.

"ROYAL SCOTS." Flat. Black or Tan. Superior Cotton. 36 in. long. Banded.

No. 353. .. .. Flat. Black Mohair. 36 in. long.

"LEATHER." Kangaroo super and ordinary. Black and tan military. 36 in. long. Per pair or ½ gross per bundle.

### SHOE.

No. 9555. .. Flat. Black or Tan. Cotton. 24 in. long.
No. 9544. Round. Black, Tan or Nigger Brown. Cotton. 24 ins. long.

"OLYMPIC." Round. Black, White, and Tan. Cotton. 24 ins. long. Banded.

"OLYMPIC." Flat. Black or Tan. Cotton. 24 in. long. Banded.

HARRIS, SCARFE, LIMITED.     HF 119

# GINDERY SUNDRIES

### HUNGARIAN NAILS.

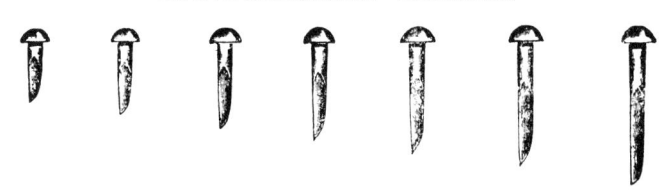

**13 GAUGE.** Round head. $\frac{3}{8}$, $\frac{7}{16}$, 6, $\frac{9}{16}$, $\frac{5}{8}$ ins. In 1-lb. packets.
**12 GAUGE.** .. Round head. $\frac{3}{8}$, $\frac{1}{2}$, and $\frac{3}{4}$ ins. In 1-lb. packets.
**CUT TIP NAILS.** $\frac{3}{4}$ and 1 in. In 1-lb. packets. For round or square hole heel and toe plate. When ordering state whether round or square.

### BOOT RIVETS.

**7 GAUGE.** Brass or brassed iron. Large or small head. $\frac{3}{8}$, $\frac{7}{16}$, $\frac{1}{2}$, $\frac{9}{16}$, $\frac{5}{8}$, $\frac{3}{4}$, $\frac{7}{8}$, and 1 in.
**17 GAUGE.** Iron. .. $\frac{3}{8}$, $\frac{7}{16}$, $\frac{1}{2}$, $\frac{9}{16}$, $\frac{5}{8}$, and $\frac{3}{4}$ in.

### SHOE TACKS OR TINGLES.

**FLATHEAD.** In 1-lb. packets. $\frac{1}{4}$ in. or $\frac{3}{4}$ oz.; $\frac{5}{16}$ in. or 1 oz.; $\frac{3}{8}$ in. or $1\frac{3}{4}$ oz.; $\frac{7}{16}$ in. or 2 oz.; $\frac{1}{2}$ in. or $2\frac{1}{2}$ oz.; $\frac{5}{8}$ in. or 3 oz

### HUNGARIAN OR HOB NAILS.
Sizes: $\frac{3}{8}$, $\frac{1}{2}$, and $\frac{5}{8}$ in. x 12 gauge.    ..    ..    In 1-lb. packets.

### BOOT PEGS.
**BARNSLEY'S.** Wood.    ..    $\frac{1}{2}$, $\frac{5}{8}$, and $\frac{3}{4}$ in. x 10. Loose.

### STEEL POINTS.
A cast pont. Tapered.    ..    ..    $\frac{3}{4}$ in. long. Loose.

### CUT BILLS.
Sizes: $\frac{3}{8}$, $\frac{1}{2}$, and $\frac{5}{8}$ in. x 12 and 14 gauge.    ..    Loose.

### STUBBS.
Sizes: $\frac{3}{8}$ in. x 14 gauge; $\frac{1}{2}$ in. x 12 and 14 gauge.    ..    Loose.

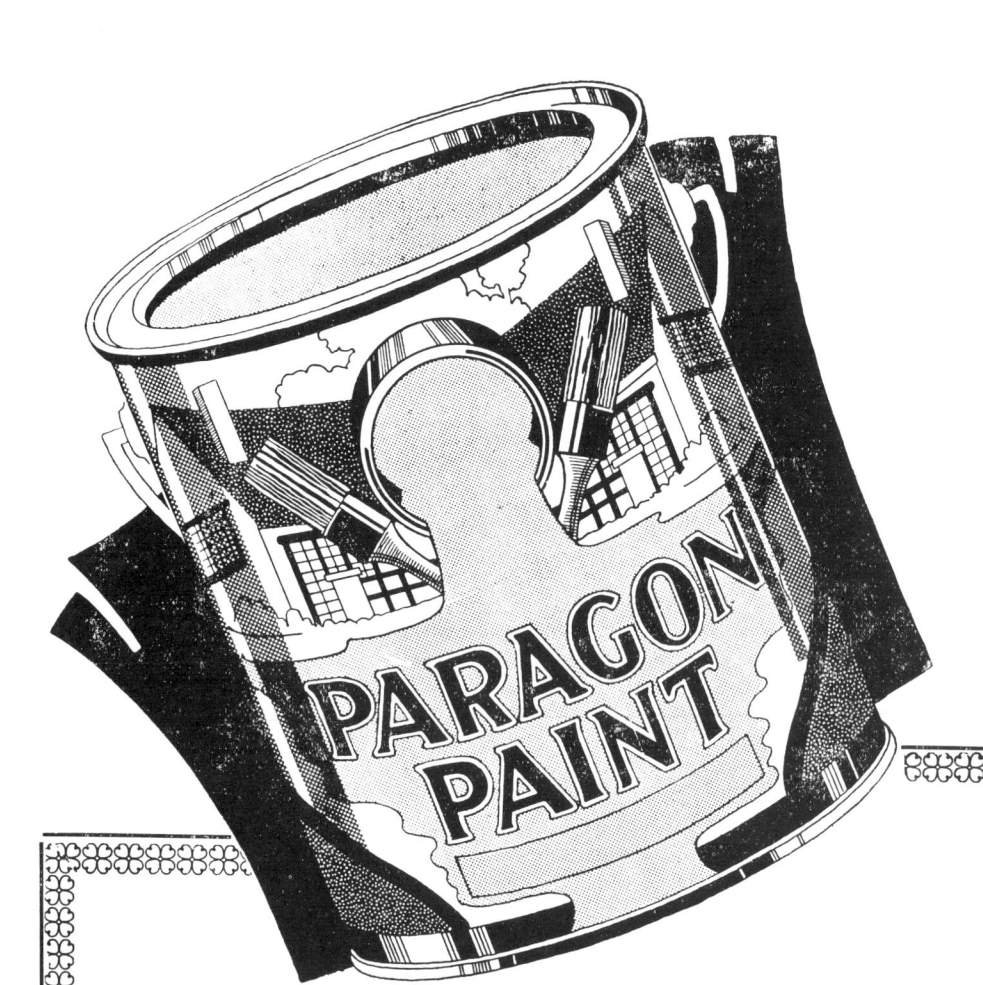

## *You'll do it better with*
# PARAGON PAINT

For all exterior or interior work, you can't beat Paragon---the QUALITY Paint!

Paragon Paint at the reduced price costs less today than ever before, and you can't do better than Paragon---it has such remarkable body and obliterative powers, brushes out so easily under the brush, and dries with a hard, durable, glossy finish in from 10 to 15 hours. There is a full range of all the popular colors, also Black and White from which to choose.

### There's a Paragon Product for every Painting Purpose

Whatever your need may be, Lacquer, Varnish, Stain, Kalsomine, even a Brush you'll find it in the "Paragon" range.